Lewis & Clark

4

DEAF CHILDREN AT HOME AND AT SCHOOL

Dr D. M. C. Dale is Senior
Lecturer in Education of the
Deaf, Department of Child
Development, University of
London Institute of Education.

Deaf children should be made independent as early as possible (p. 36)

Deaf Children at Home and at School

D. M. C. DALE

UNIVERSITY OF LONDON PRESS LTD

SBN 340 06526 5

First published 1967
Text and photographs copyright © 1967 D. M. C. Dale
Illustrations copyright © 1967 University of London Press Ltd
Second impression 1968

University of London Press Ltd
St Paul's House, Warwick Lane, London EC4

Printed and bound in Great Britain by
Cox and Wyman Ltd, London, Fakenham and Reading

Contents

Acknowledgments

The author and publishers thank the following for permission to reprint copyright material: *Volta Review* for extracts from 'Clarifying Speech Problems for the Deaf', by Bessie Pugh, and 'Individual Instructional Seatwork', by Sister Mary Walter; *Language and Speech* for the extract from 'The Effect of Time Distortions on the Intelligibility of Deaf Children's Speech', by J. E. J. John and J. N. Howarth; *Talk* for the extract from the article on induction loops; *The Teacher of the Deaf* for extracts from the article on 'Suggestions for Lipreading Classes for Deaf Adults', by M. Galliat; Blackwell Scientific Publications for the extract from 'A Study of Causes of Deafness amongst 2,355 Children in Special Schools', by G. R. Fraser in *Research in Deafness in Children*; Porter Sargent and L. Elstad for the extract from *Special Education for the Exceptional* Volume II; and the Garrard Press of Champaign, Illinois, for the Dolch 220 Words Basic Sight Vocabulary by E. W. Dolch.

The diagram on page 95 is reproduced from *Community Services for the Mentally Handicapped*; J. Tizard, Oxford University Press.

Foreword

For more than two hundred years, small numbers of scientists and educators have been interested in the diagnosis and treatment of deafness and in the educational and social problems presented by children with impaired hearing. It is only quite recently, however, that any society has begun to consider seriously the planning of services to deal with the whole of its deaf population: and in no country can provision as yet be regarded as satisfactory. A Department of Education and Science survey carried out in one area of England and Wales in 1962, for example, showed that of 276 profoundly deaf children aged over fourteen years who were being educated in schools for deaf children, only thirty-eight had reasonably adequate speech (56).

In the United States, *Education of the Deaf*, a report made in 1965 to the Secretary of Health, Education and Welfare by his Advisory Committee on the Education of the Deaf opens with the following paragraphs:

The American people have no reason to be satisfied with their limited success in educating deaf children and preparing them for full participation in our society.

Less than half of the deaf children needing specialized pre-school instruction are receiving it.

Seniors at Gallaudet College, the nation's only college for the deaf, rank close to the bottom on performance on the Graduate Record Examination.

Five-sixths of our deaf adults work in manual jobs, as contrasted to only one-half of our hearing population.

It is evident that in spite of many advances, many problems remain unsolved, and the majority of deaf children could still leave school much better equipped for life in the ordinary community than they now do.

A matter of particular concern to parents and educators is how best to provide the language training for deaf children which is essential for their participation in society, while at the same time meeting their ordinary needs as children. Of course every good teacher of the deaf realizes that education is much more than schooling; and opportunities are created in nearly all special schools for pupils to have a wide range of experience 'outside'. Today, however, people are asking whether this is really enough. Is it *ever* possible to give handicapped children who spend most of their young lives in special schools, where they mix mainly with children who have similar handicaps, the range of experience which will enable them, both as children and later as adults, to live satisfying lives in the ordinary world? Or, to put the question the other way: is it possible to provide in ordinary schools the specialized services that handicapped children require while at the same time ensuring that the handicapped mix socially and in school with the ordinary children from their neighbourhood?

This is one of the questions which Dr Dale discusses in this book. He is exceptionally well qualified to do so, both academically and by long experience as a teacher of the deaf and as headmaster of the Kelston School for Deaf Children in Auckland. Before he took up his present post as Senior Lecturer in the Education of the Deaf in the Department of Child Development, University of London Institute of Education, Dr Dale pioneered over a period of years a policy of integrating deaf and partially hearing children in units attached to ordinary schools. He has, moreover, made a close study of developments on somewhat similar lines which have been occurring in this country, the United States and elsewhere; and he approaches this particular issue with a refreshing openness of mind and an understanding of its complexity which do not prevent him from expressing firm opinions.

This book is not, however, just about education for children with defective hearing. It is also about education itself. Dr Dale writes throughout of deaf children – but most of what he says is relevant to the whole field of special education and indeed to education and educational psychology generally. The student of educational psychology will therefore learn much from this book. Developmental psychologists who are interested in psycholinguistics will also gain from it an idea of the *educational* problems of language and communication.

JACK TIZARD
Professor of Child Development
University of London Institute of Education

Preface

This book is written as an introductory text for people who care for children with defective hearing.

In recent years, increasing interest has developed in this field. Progressive teachers of deaf children are, more actively than ever, adapting their specialized methods to meet the psychological, social and emotional needs of all children. Research work is becoming focused more and more on the practical everyday problems of parents and teachers. Teacher training courses are being revised. The more accurate diagnosis of the various causes of language disorders and the implications of this for better educational and social treatment are being recognized. Work on the preventive side of medicine is also making very significant progress. Some of the most interesting advances have been made in, and in the next few years may come from, electronic instruments: modifications to hearing aids, to visible speech translators and to electroencephalographic instruments could make a really significant breakthrough in the near future in helping deaf children and adults to understand speech better and to speak more intelligibly.

An attempt has been made to discuss – albeit very briefly – most of the factors which have been found to be helpful in the educational and social treatment of deafness in childhood. Numerous references are made to literature where more detailed information may be found. I have not considered finger spelling or conventional sign languages, because at the present time I know so little about them. Much more research by really competent workers is required in the whole field of education of deaf children. Different methods of teaching them at home and at school, for example, could then be evaluated much more objectively than is often the case at present. An analysis of the various factors which contribute to the children's speech intelligibility could be extremely useful to teachers. A study of both the content and the amount of language used by parents and teachers when speaking to the children could, again, be most revealing, and make a positive contribution to our present practice. It is hoped that this book may suggest a number of lines of research.

A second major purpose of the book is to try to ensure that the closest possible liaison exists between parents and teachers. In my work as principal of Kelston School for Deaf and Partially Hearing Children in Auckland, New Zealand, who was also responsible for supervising a number of classes for deaf children in ordinary schools, and of some two hundred children who wore hearing aids and attended ordinary schools by themselves, I continually saw the tremendous contribution which parents and teachers could make when they worked closely together. If each knows something of the other's work then they can cooperate more easily and effectively. What a child does out of school hours has an important bearing on what we teach him in class. What he does in class should be reinforced at home or in the hostel if he is boarding. Teamwork is so very important. One doesn't want a deaf child to be like the snail getting out of the well who climbed up two feet each day and slipped back one foot each night.

Considerable emphasis has been placed on the value – to children, to teachers and to parents – of most deaf and partially hearing children being taught in very close association with those who hear normally. A review of some of the current practice in this very important field is reported. A short section on deafness in adulthood is included, largely to assist teachers and parents to establish realistic gaols and to profit from the experience of a number of adult deaf people.

Many people have contributed to this book (both wittingly and unwittingly) and I am grateful to them all. I should like particularly to thank Miss A. D. Burns, ex-Headmistress of Farrar Oral Day School for Deaf Children in Sydney, Australia, Mrs V. Thielman of John Tracy Clinic, Los Angeles, Mrs Beatrice O. Hart, Lexington School for Deaf Children, New York, and the staffs at Kelston School and here in the Department of Child Development. Mr A. C. Miller, F.R.C.S., has given invaluable help with the medical sections of the text. Finally, Mrs Helen Fullerton and Miss Helen Sausman are thanked very sincerely for typing the manuscript.

D. M. C. DALE

1 Some Basic Information about Deafness

The ear is usually described as consisting of three parts: the outer ear, the middle ear and the inner ear.

The outer ear consists of the *auricle* (which we call 'the ear') and a tubular canal (the *meatus*) leading into the temporal bone of the skull and closed completely at its inner end by a delicate membrane, the ear drum (or *tympanic* membrane).

The middle ear is a tiny air-filled space shaped roughly like a narrow room. The ear drum forms the outer wall of the room, the ceiling is part of the base of the skull, on which the brain rests, and in the front wall is the opening of the *eustachian tube*, which opens at its other end into the back of the nose, near the *adenoids*. It is through this tube that the air pressure on each side of the drum is kept equal and it is along this tube that any infection of the middle ear passes from the back of the nose. The back wall of the middle ear leads into the *mastoid*, which consists of tiny air spaces in the bone.

The internal wall separates the middle from the inner ear. It has two openings, or windows, an *oval window* and a *round window*. The latter is closed by a membrane like the drum and the former is closed by the foot-plate of the *stapes* (stirrup), one of the three small bones which stretch across the middle ear from the drum to the oval window. The other small bones (or *ossicles*) are the *malleus* (hammer) and *incus* (anvil).

The inner ear is part of a complex fluid-filled space still deeper in the temporal bone. This space is called the *labyrinth* and consists of the snail-shaped *cochlea*, or inner ear, in front and the balancing mechanism, or *semi-circular canals*, behind.

Inside the bony cochlea floats the delicate membranous cochlea which contains the *organ of Corti*, the end organ of hearing. From this comes

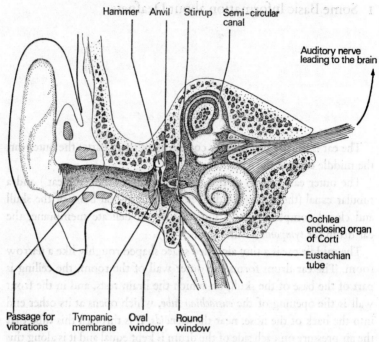

Hammer Anvil Stirrup Semi-circular canal

Auditory nerve leading to the brain

Cochlea enclosing organ of Corti

Eustachian tube

Passage for vibrations Tympanic membrane Oval window Round window

Figure 1 Ear in normal state

the nerve of hearing which carries the coded sound messages to the brain.

The sound vibrating in the air causes the drum to vibrate and thus moves the chain of ossicles, which act like levers, concentrating the sound energy at the oval window as the stapes moves in and out with the vibration. These movements produce waves in the fluid of the cochlea and special 'hair cells' in the organ of Corti respond to these waves by producing coded electrical impulses in the nerve of hearing which carries them up to the brain where they are decoded and interpreted.

There are two kinds of deafness: *conductive*, where there is some mechanical block in the hearing path, and *perceptive*, or nerve deafness, where there is damage or failure of development in the tissues of the organ of Corti, or the nerve of hearing.

Conductive deafness may be caused by wax in the ear canal, catarrhal fluid in the middle ear, inflammation or abscess in the middle ear (*otitis media*) perforation of the ear drum, scarring or adhesions round the ossicles or round window, or new bone formation round the oval window, fixing the stapes so that it cannot move in or out (*otosclerosis*).

Perceptive deafness may be caused by the failure of development of the organ of Corti or auditory nerve due to hereditary causes, damage to the organ of Corti from the virus of German measles (rubella) contracted by the mother in the first three months of pregnancy, or damage to the auditory nerve or organ of Corti by meningitis (inflammation of the coverings of the brain.)

In conductive deafness the mechanical block can be removed by treatment or an operation in which a special microscope is used, but in perceptive deafness there is no treatment which will help the damaged tissues.

In practically all cases of congenital deafness, the deafness is perceptive in type, but there are rare cases in which the deafness is conductive and can be helped by an operation.

Total deafness is very rare, as there is usually some hearing left – *residual hearing* as it is called. It is most important that this residual hearing should be preserved. The loss of any further hearing through common childhood illnesses has to be guarded against as far as possible, and regular examinations by an ear specialist are necessary.

PREVALENCE OF DEAFNESS

Very slight deafness is far more common than it was previously thought to be. In the county of Surrey during 1963, routine audiometric screening tests of hearing were administered to 18,353 children. Of these children 1,563 failed the test, and in only 245 of these cases was no further action recommended by school medical officers (although on the day that children were seen by them, 467 were considered not to have a significant hearing loss). It is likely, therefore, that in the Surrey schools for normally hearing children, one child in twelve or thirteen at this time had a significant hearing loss.

In nine health districts in New Zealand during 1963, 56,722 eight-year-old children were tested and 2,987 were found to have some significant deafness in one or both ears. On the average then, approximately one child in every twenty in New Zealand is likely to be affected. It is interesting that, in country areas, the hearing of the children was significantly better than those living in the cities. In the Canterbury district, for example, one child in forty in the country failed the screening test, but one child in twenty-five failed in the city. In some Auckland city areas, the incidence was as high as one in fourteen. This is possibly due to the increased noise levels and the greater opportunity for infection to spread in the cities.

In the Republic of China, where screening tests are administered annually to every schoolchild, a very significant increase in the prevalence of screening-test failures occurs in both hearing and sight during the last year at primary school. At this time, children are working extremely hard in order to win a place at high school. Professor L. Wang at Taiwan Normal University considers that this high failure rate is due to mental and physical exhaustion and that this factor also should not be overlooked when reasons for screening-test failure are being considered.

Most of the deafness discovered by these tests is of the *conductive type* which responds readily to medical treatment. Even without treatment, much of it seems to clear up by itself fairly adequately. The fact that the deafness is of a temporary nature, however, does not make it any less significant to the child at the time. Quite severe upsets may occur when a child is bewildered by not being able to understand instructions and 'ignores' the teacher or other children when spoken to. Sometimes marked fluctuations can occur within a very short time. Hearing may deteriorate by as much as forty decibels within only a matter of twenty-four hours and may clear up again in perhaps two or three days. It may, however, take several weeks or even months before it returns to normal. Teachers and parents should be on the alert for signs of deafness among their children.

Severe and profound deafness in children is much less common than the slight deafness referred to above. The figure often quoted for most European countries is one in a thousand profoundly deaf and another one in a thousand partially hearing. 'Partially hearing' means sufficiently deaf to need a hearing aid but capable of developing almost normal speech and language. In Britain in 1963 approximately one child in every 438 had been issued with a hearing aid. In New Zealand (with a school population of 400,000) there were over 300 children attending schools and classes for deaf children and just under 400 less severely handicapped wearing hearing aids but attending ordinary schools.

CAUSES OF DEAFNESS

One of the most comprehensive studies of causes of deafness in severely deaf children was conducted by Fraser (1). A total of 2,355 children attending special schools in Britain and Ireland were seen, and from his preliminary analysis of 1,412 perceptively deafened cases, the following groups have been abstracted:

Non-genetic causes		Genetic causes	
Unspecified meningitis	235	With goitre	133
Maternal rubella	133		
Tuberculous meningitis	106	Waardenburg's syndrome	56
Haemolytic disease (*Rh* factor)	62		
Streptomycin (other than for meningitis)	35	With retinitis pigmentosa	28
Jaundice of prematurity	26	With abnormal electrocardiogram	14
Pneumococcal meningitis	25		
Birth injury	24	Sex linked (recessive and dominant)	13
Meningococcal meningitis	19		
Influenzal meningitis	8		
Accident	8		
Maternal syphilis	6	Causes not clear	456
Measles	2		
Whooping cough	1		
Maternal toxoplasmosis	1		
Post-natal causes not clear	21		
	712		700

The balance of the initial total seen contained one group of some 222 cases where the parents' reason for their child's deafness was not acceptable to the investigator. Measles and whooping cough were the main reasons given, but Fraser points out that these are conditions through which the majority of infants pass. Another group of 103 children, included in the balance of children seen, weighed less than five and a half pounds at birth, 'suggesting that apart from the risk of jaundice, birth injury and streptomycin, prematurity is associated with subsequent deafness in some non-specific manner.'

Dr Fraser concluded:

Prevention of deafness must be preceded by a thorough study and understanding of causation and it is encouraging that this preliminary analysis reveals that only in 15 per cent or so of the children does the cause of deafness remain an enigma.

In at least half the children the cause of the deafness is the sequel of illness or prematurity or their treatment. In the past, many such children would have died. In the future, as medical treatment improves, it may be expected that they will recover completely without untoward sequelae such as deafness. The virtual eradication of otitis media as a cause of profound deafness in children is a case in point. Prevention of genetically determined deafness, on the other hand, is an altogether different proposition which must be tackled on a very long-term basis.

Arthur(2) has described in detail a number of the groups of hereditary symptoms which include deafness. He has also provided perhaps the best bibliography on hereditary deafness so far compiled. Parents and students interested in this subject could profitably make this article and that of Fraser their initial study. Two other extremely useful references are those of Rainer(3) and Kallman(4). The former briefly reviews the literature on this subject and then gives details of an investigation conducted into the genetic aspects of early profound deafness in the total New York State population. Dr Kallman describes basic principles and procedures in counselling families about genetic problems.

Everyone, of course, looks forward impatiently to the day when some brilliant research team will finally enable a profoundly deaf person to hear normally. It must be said, however, that at the present time the prospect seems fairly remote. Occasionally work is reported where some nerve-deafened patient obtains a slight improvement in hearing, but other or subsequent research seems largely to discredit it.

Dr Hallowell Davis, Director of Research at Central Institute for the Deaf in St Louis, Missouri, and recognized as a world authority on the physiology of hearing, said recently that before any duplication of auditory mechanisms could be considered, it was necessary to understand more completely the *composition* and the *function* of the hearing organ. In consequence, he was concentrating on this aspect.

The problem does not seem primarily to be one of finance. In the U.S.A., for example, the Government is tremendously generous in allocating funds to worthwhile research projects. It does stand to reason, however, that if for example ten research scientists are working on a particular problem, the solution might be found more rapidly if another ten or twenty were employed. The Deafness Research Foundation, largely through the initial efforts of Mrs Collette Ramsay in New York, is now assisting research into deafness in some twenty-five American universities where none was in progress ten years ago.

TESTING THE HEARING OF CHILDREN

Pre-school children

During World War II, the Ewings tested the hearing of babies in a London hospital by using drums, whistles and pitch pipes for stimulus sounds. One baby did not respond to these sounds at all although Dr Irene Ewing was sure the child heard them. When she took a spoon and stirred it round the rim of a cup the baby licked his lips. This apparently simple little experiment was really very significant: little children had been shown to respond to meaningful sound but to ignore sounds which meant nothing to them. It was found, for example, that infants would turn and locate immediately the source of sound made by crinkling tissue paper or by shaking a rattle when the sound was of minimal intensity, but the same children would ignore an aircraft which flew overhead creating noise levels of a very much higher order. From these beginnings the Ewings developed a series of

B

sound stimuli suitable for testing the hearing of babies. The main ones were the spoon and cup, tissue paper, high- and low-pitched rattles, saying 's-s-s' very softly, and quietly calling the child's name. Other sounds, like the noise made when a liquid is shaken in a bottle and chime bars and xylophones played very quietly, can also be used. These tests are extremely useful and quick for screening the hearing of babies from about seven months of age. It is often possible to test children by these means as early as four months, but after seven months the results can usually be guaranteed.

Professor Suzuki and Dr Sato(5) at Shinshu University in Japan have reported an experiment in testing the hearing of many young children using tape-recorded sounds of cows mooing, a rooster crowing and a cuckoo singing. These sounds were fed through four loud-speakers which had been placed in a six-foot square above the child. The authors concluded that children from three months of age did respond at an intensity level very closely approximating their actual thresholds when tested by means of this *free field startle response audiometry*. Professor Di Carlo(6) at Syracuse University, using a somewhat similar test situation, except that the loud-speakers were at ear level rather than above the children, concluded that the most reliable stimulus sound was music.

Waldon(7), adopting the Ewings' theory that the test sounds must be meaningful, has found that the sound of a baby crying evokes a response in even new-born babies. At the present time he is studying the effect of narrow band-pass filters on the recorded crying sounds. If the babies respond to only one octave of this stimulus sound, then a much more accurate diagnostic test will, of course, be possible.

More recent developments in the testing of infants have been the *pure-tone waking-level tests*(8) which can be administered to babies during the first few hours of life. In Scandinavia, the U.S.A., Japan and Australia most interesting exploratory work is being done.

Electroencephalography (EEG), measuring the brain waves or, more correctly, measuring the changes in the electrical impulses given off by the brain each time an audible sound is produced, is another technique which could eventually become an effective means of testing very young children and other difficult cases. Such tests would be particularly useful because the person tested is not required to make any conscious response at all. Even with EEG tests, however, it has been shown that a cat may give clear and regular responses to sound until a mouse is brought into its range of vision and the responses then cease. An even more involuntary test seems to be required.

The great advantage of early testing is, of course, that where deafness is discovered, loud sound can then be presented to the child through hearing aids from a very early age and the results which some workers claim to have obtained are really quite remarkable. It is likely that, within the next few years, hearing aids will be fitted as a routine during the first few weeks of life, where children's auditory acuity proves not to be within normal limits and a reasonably accurate threshold has been established.

Older children

There are two main types of hearing test used for children from about the age of three and a half to four years. These are *audiometric* and *speech* tests.

Audiometric tests

Very approximately an *audiometer* is an instrument which produces clear whistling sounds of different pitch and loudness. The person being tested listens, to begin with, to one tone at a fairly high level. If he indicates that he hears the sound the tester decreases the loudness to a lower level and tests once more. This goes on until the patient fails to respond and the loudness is then increased until he responds again. The *threshold* of hearing for that particular tone is the lowest level at which the patient responds accurately.

The process is repeated with a sound of slightly higher pitch. Gradually thresholds are obtained, showing the degree of deafness present at several different pitches (or *frequencies*). These are plotted for both ears on a graph called an *audiogram*.

Loudness is measured in units called *decibels*. The level of loudness of the test tone is shown on the vertical lines of the audiogram, from minus 10 decibels right down to 120 decibels. Zero on this line is a sound

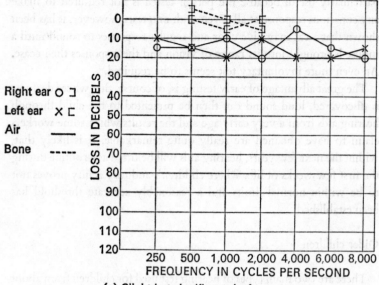

Right ear O ⊐
Left ear X ⊏
Air ——
Bone - - - -

LOSS IN DECIBELS

FREQUENCY IN CYCLES PER SECOND

(a) Slight but significant deafness

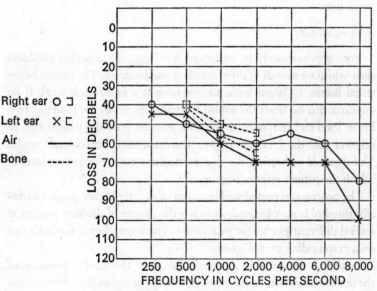

Right ear O ⊐
Left ear X ⊏
Air ——
Bone - - - -

LOSS IN DECIBELS

FREQUENCY IN CYCLES PER SECOND

(b) Partial—severe deafness

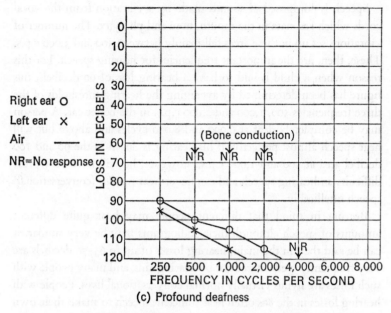

Figure 2   Audiograms illustrating degrees of deafness

which can just be heard by the normal ear. Quiet conversational speech is at a level of 60–70 decibels; shouting is round about 90 decibels and a level of 120 decibels is quite unpleasant to most of us. The International Standards Organization decided on a calibration for pure-tone audiometers in 1964. Audiometric figures given in this text refer to the I.S.O. standard except where the earlier American scale is referred to, it being some ten decibels lower.

On the horizontal scale of the audiogram *pitch* is shown in *cycles per second*. If a violin string is plucked and vibrates backwards and forwards 250 times in one second, the sound which is produced is called 250 cycles per second (c.p.s.). If the string is pulled tighter and vibrates more rapidly, say 500 times in a second, then, of course, the sound is known as 500 c.p.s. and is heard by us as roughly an octave higher than the first note. Middle C on the piano is about 256 c.p.s. and every octave above this contains almost double the number of vibrations, i.e. 512, 1,048, etc.

Speech is composed of sounds made by a vibration from the vocal cords which resonate in the mouth, nose and pharynx. The number of vibrations set up in these areas fall mainly between 300 and 3,000 c.p.s. These, then, are the important frequencies for hearing speech. For this reason when a child is said to have a hearing loss of 60 decibels, this figure has been determined by averaging the hearing thresholds of the three frequencies 500, 1,000 and 2,000 c.p.s. in the better ear. A person may be completely deaf at 6,000 and 8,000 cycles and above but will hear speech almost perfectly. If his hearing is down in the 90 and 100 decibel area at 500 and 1,000 c.p.s., however, he will have very great difficulty in hearing speech and can never hear *running* (conversational) speech intelligibly.

Bearing in mind that different people may hear quite different amounts of speech although their audiograms may be very similar, it can be said that, in the main, hearing losses of up to 65–70 decibels are very frequently well catered for by hearing aids, and many people with such losses are living virtually normal conversational lives. People with hearing losses in the 80s often hear sufficient speech to make their own speech lively and intelligible although one can usually pick out quite definite speech difficulties especially with the consonant sounds. At more than 90 decibels of deafness, it may be said that really intelligible speech reception is never possible. People with this loss may hear a speaker's voice, sometimes fairly clearly, but the different vowel sounds are often hard to distinguish from one another and consonant sounds, if perceived at all, can be heard only as dull unintelligible noise, something like a person clearing his throat.

In nearly every case, hearing aids are of use to people whose audiograms show hearing losses as severe as this. Although they are unable to distinguish between words very well, they do know when voice is present and this can be very important. When a profoundly deaf child does not wear a hearing aid and his mother says to him: 'Come and have your tea now', the only sensation he has is seeing his mother's face with her lips moving. It is as though he is sitting in a glass case observing the world about him. If, on the other hand, he wears a powerful hearing aid and, when his mother says: 'It's time for tea now', as well as seeing the movement of her lips and her expression, he does hear a trace of sound – say, part of four of the vowel sounds – sounding rather like a muffled 'oo', it seems likely that he then feels part of his environment and experiences a sense of belonging, which must be of tremendous significance psychologically.

Speech tests

Audiograms alone are not sufficient to tell us everything about a child's hearing. It is necessary to administer speech tests as well as these pure-tone ones.

One child with an average hearing loss of 60 decibels may hear 75 per cent of a list of words correctly when they are delivered at a high level, while another child with an identical audiogram and the same list read at the same level might hear only 40 per cent correctly. There are a number of possible reasons for this difference – age, intelligence, familiarity with the words read and the cause of deafness all seem to contribute. There is some evidence to suggest, for example, that children whose deafness is caused as a result of measles hear rather better with amplification than do children who are deaf as a result of cerebral palsy(9). There is certainly a very big difference in the ability to hear between children with *conductive* and those with *nerve type* deafness. The former usually hear perfectly when the speech is made sufficiently loud, but the nerve deafness group rarely, if ever, achieve 100 per cent comprehension by listening alone.

Speech tests are then the proof of the pudding. They are very valuable for telling us which hearing aid and receiver are the most suitable for a person, which ear should be fitted with a hearing aid, and whether a hearing aid is of any benefit at all. There are some people who do not hear better when speech is amplified. Fortunately, most children do hear better, but a condition of adults called Menière's disease is one which prevents people from benefiting from the using of a hearing aid. Speech tests also tell one the degree of loudness which is most suitable for each person, that is, on what number the volume control of his hearing aid should be set for achieving his best listening level.

For pre-school children who have some language, short lists of ten or twelve words have been compiled(10). All the words in these lists are represented by little objects. The tester begins by taking out from a box one object after another and asks the child to name each one as he does so. He then places the box beside the child and says: 'Now would you put the knife in the box', 'Put the fish in the box', 'Put the house in the box', etc. Properly administered, these speech tests tie up very well with audiogram data and are most useful for small children although, of course, not as accurate as the longer word lists used for older children and adults. For older children lists such as those shown in Appendix 6 are used and for adolescents and adults similar lists using a more sophisticated vocabulary e.g. 'splash, lunge, cleanse, nook'(10).

Reed(11) has constructed a very useful speech test for *screening* the hearing of school-age children suspected of having some deafness. The much wider use of speech tests by general practitioners, educational psychologists and speech therapists is recommended.

Neither the pure-tone audiometric tests nor the speech tests of hearing are really sufficient alone, although either test is very handy at times when proper clinical facilities are not available. Used together, they are excellent, and, as Professor Raymond Carhart(12) has said, 'pure-tone and speech tests of hearing form the basis of clinical audiometry'.

INTELLIGENCE

A number of studies have shown that despite a much reduced vocabulary the distribution of intelligence among deaf children, when non-verbal tests are used, approximates the normal(13, 14, 15). That is to say, a few are brilliant, a few are extremely dull, and the majority are of average intelligence. In the Auckland School for Deaf and Partially Hearing Children, the performance sub-tests of the Wechsler Intelligence Scale for Children were administered to the eldest ninety-three children in 1964, and the mean I.Q. obtained was 90·1. This would appear to be a reasonable figure since some of the conditions which cause deafness, e.g. German measles in the mother during the early weeks of pregnancy, and cerebral palsy, sometimes also cause other handicaps which include mental retardation. In addition, partially hearing children who are slow learning often require full-time special educational treatment, while bright ones can cope in an ordinary school.

Many deaf children who attain mental ages of, say, fifteen years, have reading vocabulary ages of only eight or nine and their oral English is frequently not as syntactically correct as is that of many three-year-old children who have normal hearing. This would seem to confirm Furth's (15) finding 'that intellectual development does proceed independently of the acquisition of language'. The experience of virtually all teachers of deaf children would seem to provide additional confirmation of this. The children are able to cope with new concepts quite adequately, provided they are taught skilfully. It often does, of course, take much longer to establish the language form or concept than is the case with less deaf children.

SOCIAL ADJUSTMENT

There is evidence that children with defective hearing do not mature socially quite as rapidly as do normally hearing children. For example, Myklebust(16) using the Vineland Social Maturity Scale found that 150 deaf children in a residential school scored approximately 15 per cent below normally hearing children in social development. It is significant that the younger children (under fifteen years) were less than 8 per cent below, but that the gap between deaf and non-deaf scores widened with age until the nineteen- and twenty-year-old deaf group were 25 per cent below the average for normally hearing people. Streng and Kirk(17) found the mean social maturity rating of a similar group (six- to eighteen-year-olds) in a day school to be considerably higher (96·2) although different methods of scoring were employed so that the results are not directly comparable. The writers also found that there was 'a slight decrease in social maturity scores with increase in life age'.

Myklebust concludes that the primary task in social maturity confronting the child under the age of fifteen years is the attainment of ability in self-help, with beginnings of achievement in self-direction.

'The implication is that deaf children are not inferior in achieving self-help, but as higher levels of social competence become necessary because of increased age, they find attainment more difficult.'

It has been observed, however, that starting work, mixing mainly with men and women rather than other children, doing their own budgeting, having regular contact with normally hearing people, and experiencing greater freedom during leisure hours, all have a rapidly maturing effect on young deaf people. It seems likely, therefore, that Myklebust's older groups might have achieved significantly higher scores had they not attended a residential school for the deaf until the age of twenty-one years.

Myklebust(16) made a very significant contribution to present knowledge regarding the personality and social adjustment of people handicapped by deafness when he studied a group of 127 hard-of-hearing adults who were in attendance at a Hearing Society. These were adventitiously deafened people (average age of onset 22·21 years) and in many cases, the hearing loss was not too severe (mean 67 db. American scale). Their communication problem was thus much less serious than that of those who are born severely or profoundly deaf – i.e. they have only a 'one-way' problem since their speech is usually quite intelligible. Despite this, Myklebust found that 'very few held the same friendships they had prior to the onset of the deafness. The social isolation resulting from impaired hearing was markedly apparent . . . Almost all found it necessary to develop a basic identification with others who had impaired hearing.'

There are, of course, far more adventitiously deafened people who are *not* members of Hearing Societies than there are who *are* members so that generalizations from these data would not be valid. In New Zealand, for example, although there are over twenty branches of the League for the Hard of Hearing throughout the country, the number of hearing aid users who belong to them is less than 10 per cent of the total. Myklebust's findings, however, represent a realistic appraisal of the needs of a substantial group of people with impaired hearing.

2 The Young Child and his Family

Parents are usually in a unique position to educate their deaf child. They spend more hours each day with him than does anyone else; in many cases much of this time is with the child alone; excellent opportunities for learning and teaching are occurring in the home each day; and the attitude of the parent to the child is likely to be one of very deep affection and respect, which is an ideal one for a teacher to have for his pupil. Some parents do not realize that they have this opportunity to help, or they realize it too late, and then valuable time is lost.

Both parents must accept the child's handicap. This is not easy, but it is generally agreed that the parents' acceptance of the fact that their child has a hearing loss is the first step towards correct treatment and a number of factors have been found helpful to parents in making this initial adjustment. First, they must know as much as possible about the handicap in general and its severity in their own child's case. They know then what they are facing. Profound deafness, for example, is a very different problem from partial deafness, children with additional handicaps, e.g. dullness, partial sight, cerebral palsy, etc., have different problems from those who are simply deaf; and brilliant deaf children have some different problems again from those of average intelligence or below.

Some parents are able to accept a handicapped child during infancy, although their feelings may sometimes become ambivalent when the effects of the handicap become more obvious in later life. Helping the parents understand the handicap at all stages and be aware of whether the child is achieving reasonable results for the extent of his handicap, is of very great importance.

A parent should make sure that the grief he feels over the child's deafness is not very largely self-pity. When parents help each child in the family to realize his or her potential, whatever that potential may be, the children are usually well adjusted and happy. Parents sometimes have a feeling of personal failure if their child has a handicap. For most people this feeling may be very intense for a time, but for 'perfectionists' it is especially painful. They feel that all their hopes for the child are dashed. But of course not *all* the hopes are – only *some* things will not be possible – and hard work can make a child's deafness a great deal less of a handicap than it would otherwise be.

Fear often makes it very hard for parents to speak freely to anyone. Professor I. G. Taylor, at Manchester University, is one of many workers who have found that the parents' discussion of common problems in a group brings about a very considerable release of emotional tension. No one understands the feelings of parents of deaf children quite as well as other parents of deaf children. Parents find, after a time, that they can begin to look at the education of their child as an absorbing adventure from which they themselves can emerge as more interesting and worthwhile people. One mother of a deaf child said to a visiting teacher recently: 'It seems awful to say this, but I'm sure my husband and I have had a much more interesting life since we discovered Peter was deaf. We've met many wonderful people, read more than we ever did, and somehow little things don't seem to worry us as they used to.'

No feeling of guilt should distress parents. They are very seldom responsible for their child's deafness and therefore have no reason for guilt, but they *have* a responsibility to help educate their young child so that he may minimize his handicap.

Although much of the deaf child's early training will be undertaken by the mother, it is good when fathers realize just how important they can be in helping their child. If a deaf child's father is prepared to spend some time every day with him, it is one of the finest assets the child can have. A father who says: 'When he is old enough to come to football with me, I'll show an interest in him' may find that it is then too late. A part of each day should be set aside as early in the child's life as possible for his father to talk and play with him.

It is a very great help for the mother of a deaf child if her husband can lend a hand when he gets home, remembering that she has been under the strain of looking after the child all day long. It is equally helpful and encouraging if the father listens carefully to what she has to say about the child and discusses him with her. He should take an equal interest in parents' meetings and the books and notes which are available, taking time off work occasionally to see the child in school, and should see that there are plenty of family outings so that the child has interesting things to think and talk about and his mother has a change from the household routine. Mothers of handicapped children need this change and if a mother can have one full day off, perhaps once a month, away from the child but knowing that he is well looked after, it is very good for the whole family.

Because the father of a deaf child can spend so much less time with him than his mother can, this time becomes precious to the child and the things his father says are very important. Father has not been with the child all day and it is easier for him to be patient. He is an exciting person who comes home each night with exciting things to talk about and, too, he is an excellent person for the mother to talk about to the child: 'Daddy forgot to take his coat', 'Daddy is bringing a new watering-can home tonight', and so on. The child can join in, too, when his mother tells his father what has happened during the day: 'This afternoon we made some gingerbread boys. Mrs Jones gave us a cabbage', etc.

There is usually a chance at week-ends for a deaf child to be with his father doing interesting things: the child may be hammering tins or painting boxes in the yard while his father is painting the shed or working in the garden. Of course the father cannot keep interrupting his work to talk to the child but, if he has spoken to him once during a Saturday morning, it is much better than not speaking at all and if he has spoken to his deaf child five times in the course of the morning, he has done a great deal for him.

Good health

Because he is continually trying to understand what is going on around him all day, even normal life can be a strain for a deaf child and good health is of special importance to him. Parents should see that he gets plenty of rest, exercise, fresh air and sunshine and has a sensible diet to ensure that he is able to face up to each new day and take advantage of each new learning situation as it comes along. Sickness and especially going into hospital can be bewildering to a young child and to a deaf one even more so. Despite this, parents often comment that their deaf children accept being confined to bed when they are ill much better than do children with normal hearing.

If a child is taught to stand correctly he is best able to breathe freely and naturally and this can be important in making his speech intelligible. Although they should not, of course, 'coddle' him, parents should see that a deaf child does not suffer from colds too frequently. Correct posture allows the muscles to develop properly, the child will be more attractive as a result and, if he can move quietly and gracefully, he will be more acceptable socially.

In certain cases cosmetic surgery may be called for; modern surgery and orthodontics can be of very great assistance to children of unattractive physical appearance. In the few cases where a child's ears protrude markedly or the upper and lower jaws are seriously maloccluded, for example, specialist advice should be sought. Deafness is sufficient handicap to social acceptability and sound emotional adjustment without remediable physical abnormalities being added.

HOME ACTIVITIES

Deaf children should be doing things as often as possible: experimenting, pushing, pulling, watching, learning, lifting, thinking, carrying, fitting, shaping, measuring, 'talking', laughing and rarely sitting idle without something interesting or stimulating in front of them. All children need activity, but since the deaf ones receive less stimulation from the hundreds of sounds about them, they need this experience more than hearing children.

Generally speaking, the interests of a deaf child are those of a hearing child of the same age. Making the most of the way in which the child spends his time means that parents must think really hard about it. They should ask themselves: 'Is our house as good as it can be for a child to play in and keep busy without upsetting everything? Is there any way to make it better? Are the facilities all they might be?' People who live in the country are usually luckier than town-dwellers in this respect. Perhaps a corner of the garden could be screened off to make a place for the child to play in without having to worry about making a mess – although some parents may complain that their whole garden has quickly turned into that sort of place! Things for the child to play with need not be expensive – boxes, basins, blocks of wood, old pots and pans, sand and water are the sort of things called for.

Parents of deaf children have found that the usual nursery school activities are enjoyed during the pre-school period – playing with sand, water and dough, playing with dolls, blowing bubbles, finger-painting, cutting out, making houses, trains, etc., from boxes and odds and ends, and radio and television programmes like 'Listen with Mother'.

Deaf children, like hearing ones, enjoy games involving other people and ball games and other action games like 'Nuts in May', 'Ring a Ring o' Roses', 'Pat-a-Cake', and acting nursery rhymes are usually well received. Other games such as 'Hunt the Thimble', dominoes, jigsaws and simple card games like Snap, Happy Families and Pelmanism do not involve hearing and so give the deaf child a chance to do just as well as, or better than, his companions.

JOHN TRACY CLINIC CORRESPONDENCE COURSE

When Mrs Spencer Tracy had helped her deaf son through childhood and adolescence, she decided to devote most of her life to helping other mothers of deaf children. John Tracy Clinic was established in Los Angeles twenty years ago. For those who were unable to come to the clinic, the John Tracy Correspondence Course, for parents of pre-school deaf and hard-of-hearing children, was begun.

To date, over 20,000 families have been enrolled in John Tracy Clinic's programme. The course covers approximately one year's work depending on the age and ability of the child. It is sent free of charge to parents of deaf children all over the world. The Clinic staff have no illusions that a correspondence course can be as effective as face-to-face contact with experienced teachers of pre-school deaf children, but the information offered can help the parents tremendously to be more understanding and helpful to the child, regardless of his age or level of schooling. When regular specialist help is not available, the John Tracy Clinic course and the personal letters to the parents have brought help and comfort to countless families. (In Holland teachers supervise the parents' use of the Tracy course, and this is done in a number of cases in New Zealand.)

The course consists of twelve lessons that cover such topics as language training, lesson plans, teaching materials and so forth. Each instalment is accompanied by a personal letter that gives suggestions and ideas for the individual child. At the end of each instalment there is a list of questions that parents are asked to complete and return before the next is sent. This questionnaire has a place on it for parents to say how their child is progressing with the lessons. It also provides a space for questions or problems that come up during the course of that instalment.

Parents may enrol by writing to John Tracy Clinic, 806 West Adams Boulevard, Los Angeles, California, 90007, U.S.A. The course is designed for children between the ages of two and six years, although there is special material for the parents of even younger children.

CONTROL OF DEAF CHILDREN

No one likes an unruly child and a disobedient one can also get himself into a great deal of bother, especially in traffic. For these reasons alone parents must be able to control their children. If a child is deaf, however, there is a third very important reason why they must be particularly careful about this; there are so many more things they need to teach him.

If a deaf child is biddable, this can be a pleasure but, if he is not, it is extremely difficult to teach him anything. All too often one meets parents who are not firm enough with their little deaf children, who may come to school at four or five years of age without any words and with no idea of watching the lips for speech. Often the reason for this is that parents have not learned to expect obedience from their deaf children.

Parents must be sensible about this. The control should not come about through fear, but through a genuine affection and respect on the child's part because of the parents' interest in and love for him. The first task, then is to get 'on side' with the child so that he does what his parents ask gladly because he wants to please them.

Parents must be sure the child understands what he is expected to do. It is no good getting concerned because he has not taken off his coat when asked to do so unless he knows the word 'coat'. There are times, though, when a parent may be quite sure he understands, but chooses to do something else. For example, he may be asked not to touch things in a china cabinet and yet he tries again to do so. Then it is a case of the parent's will against his, and in such situations the parent *should not give way*; there should be no ranting or raving, but quiet, purposeful action. The child may have to be taken bodily and made to do something else. If parents are consistent and always insist on obedience, the child will realize that what is said is meant – every single time. If he is continually 'let off' he will do as he likes whenever it suits him. There are, however, a number of slight 'naughtinesses' which it is better to disregard than to draw attention to; mild disapproval, too, is more effective than punishment.

A child needs to be reassured quite often that both his parents love him and they must remember to praise him and show pleasure in what he does whenever possible. All children like smiles, but *a smile means more to a deaf child than anyone else on earth*. Parents should smile at him when he has done something good but at other times too – for no particular reason. It would not interrupt the conversation with a neighbour too much to give the child a smile and a nod as he goes past on some errand – and then relationships with him may be much easier that evening. Getting the child to do one or two kind little things each day for his parents can forge a bond of affection so that discipline is much easier to maintain at other times.

c

Just because the child is deaf, parents must not be tempted to say 'poor little thing'. They are being unkind to the child if they let him grow up selfish and disobedient.

Parents must remember that what applies to the training of their hearing children applies equally to the upbringing of their deaf child. A great deal can be taught by parents' example – tidiness, patience, unselfishness and so on.

As with hearing children, many of the little upsets and temper tantrums are merely signs that the child is weary. Age is an important consideration, also. Two-year-olds, for example, are notoriously difficult to manage and the expression 'the terrible twos' has not come into existence by chance. Children of this age are often very active and boisterous, with only short spans of being attentive and, as one exasperated mother has said, 'no conscience at all!' At three years the same children are often much easier to control and communicate with.

Some parents can train their children successfully without ever having to smack them. If parents are continually smacking a child, it is certain that the fault lies with them rather than with him.

An intelligent supervisor, who herself wore a hearing aid, noticed that a little deaf boy in her play group was becoming something of a bully. When one day he hit another boy in the eye with a cardboard pellet from a catapult, many people would have been tempted to smack the culprit with the explanation: 'You hurt Peter, so I'll hurt you; don't do it again.' This particular supervisor, however, took a different line: 'Hemi, look at Peter's eyelid. It's red because it's sore. If the cardboard had gone down a bit, it might have gone in his eye. Then he would be deaf and only able to see out of one eye.' Hemi afterwards behaved much better.

Hemi was seven years old and by that age it is possible to make such appeals to reason. Although with two-year-olds it is much more difficult to explain why certain behaviour is not acceptable one should try whenever possible to give some sort of true explanation.

A research into the problems of disciplining deaf children was undertaken by the Volta Bureau in Washington and the results published in the June number of the *Volta Review* in 1960. These were the general conclusions reached:

Discipline of the deaf child need not differ from that of the hearing child, provided that it is timely and the child understands the reason for disciplinary action. It is meaningless to punish a deaf child tomorrow for something he has done today. The most effective discipline is firm, timely and consistent and is tempered with a thorough understanding of the child's problem. If anything, discipline should be stricter than for hearing children in the earlier years because a deaf child's limited vocabulary prevents a parent from reasoning with him. He must learn to obey if he is to fit in socially.

If there are hearing children in the family, they too should receive special help and attention when they need it and they should then understand that if the deaf child needs more time and patience, it is simply because he cannot hear. A deaf child's world is a little like television without sound.

When a deaf child misbehaves, parents must make sure that he understood what was expected of him. He may be feeling 'left out' and wanting attention or he may be bored, without enough to occupy his time and interest.

With deaf children, the level of social behaviour is likely to be the same as for hearing children in the early years, and later they may be expected to follow the pattern of hearing children, although more slowly. The more deaf children can associate with hearing children of the same age in normal happy play, the more they will keep pace with them.

One of the most difficult things to teach a young deaf child is to *wait* for a deferred activity; John Tracy Clinic Correspondence Course has a whole section on teaching a deaf child to understand 'wait'. It is helpful to arrange things so that there is a minimum of waiting or to divert his attention to some other interest if waiting is unavoidable. The desire to 'do it now' is natural but patience will develop as the child begins to mature through education. He must learn what 'after a while' or 'in a minute' mean and he can be shown *when* things are going to happen on a calendar or a watch.

Good manners

In order that he may attain his greatest possible success in life (the deaf child) must be a little better than his hearing fellows. He needs to be more courteous, more considerate of others, more energetic, more ambitious and more efficient. He must be willing to work harder, to take more pains to do his work well, to be more alert in recognizing needs and opportunities. (*John Tracy Clinic Correspondence Course*)

The deaf child should be encouraged to be neat and clean always and having really nice manners is an easy way for him to get 'on side' with the people he meets. Parents should wait for the child to say 'please' before they pass him anything and should insist on his saying 'thank you'. He should be taught to say (or try to say) 'Hello', 'Goodbye', and to wait his turn.

When he is old enough to understand, he should be trained to be quiet when he moves chairs, when he is eating or washing or in the toilet. Deaf people do not *have* to be noisy; they can be just as quiet as those who hear normally.

Manners are learnt most easily by example, so parents, brothers and sisters should all try to set a high standard. If a deaf child has good manners, he is far less conspicuous than if he is inconsiderate and unruly.

Independence

Deaf children should be made independent as early as possible; there is nothing worse for a young deaf child than to have everything done for him. He should be encouraged to dress himself, tidy his clothes, set the table, feed the chickens and generally make himself useful.

As the child gets older, he can take little messages or do errands for his mother. If he is to fetch some plums from a neighbour's house, the neighbour might be warned in advance that he is coming and so keep a look out for him. The child can be given a basket and shown a picture of some plums before being taken outside and shown the house where he is to go. He may be reluctant to go at first and his mother may have to go part of the way with him, but if he does finally complete the errand, he will be thrilled with himself and have taken an important step towards being independent.

Facing up to little problems is what everyone has to do each day and if a deaf child has plenty of these opportunities early on, the experience will stand him in good stead always.

Deaf children must have only reasonable protection; they must be self-reliant, not continually interfered with by their parents. If parents have confidence in their deaf children, the children will have confidence in themselves.

HEARING BROTHERS AND SISTERS

If there are several children in the family and their ages are fairly close together, mothers may worry that they themselves are so busy looking after them all that there is not enough time to give the deaf child the special help he needs. Also, when the deaf child is given special help, the others sometimes become jealous. One hears of the others really disliking their deaf brother or sister if in games or in household chores they have continually to 'give in' to the deaf one. Provided deaf children take their share of tasks along with the rest of the family and are not allowed to shirk their responsibilities because they are deaf, such problems need not be serious and in the long run brothers and sisters are a wonderful thing for deaf children.

Other children can be the deaf child's best teachers of 'give and take' and excellent teachers also of lipreading and language. It must be made clear to the rest of the family that deaf children need a great deal of help if they are going to learn to lipread and speak well and that everyone must work as a team with him; all are then able to share in the inevitable ups and downs of his progress.

There is a real incentive for a deaf child to try to be like his brothers and sisters, to succeed in things and to learn their games. They will bring interesting friends home to play with and talk to and when the children are out as a group or have brought others to the house, the brothers and sisters can often help by interpreting words that the deaf child does not say clearly and by making sure that other children speak clearly to him.

While it is good for a normally hearing child to learn a little tolerance through having a deaf brother or sister, the deaf child himself can be helped in being responsible and thoughtful if he has younger brothers or sisters and has to learn to take care of them and speak clearly to them.

Although too much responsibility should not, of course, be laid on hearing children, there are dozens of occasions when the parents are too busy to look after their deaf child and hearing brothers and sisters can provide both companionship and language experience for him. A happy family life is the best foundation a deaf child can have.

OTHER HEARING CHILDREN AND ADULTS

We are realizing more and more the value that mixing with hearing people *can* be to deaf children and if possible the deaf child should be with hearing children and adults both in and out of school. This value, however, may be very great or it may be negligible depending on the amount of assistance that hearing people give. Everyone who comes into contact with the deaf child should know a few basic principles: the importance of talking to him often, the need to wait to speak until he is looking, facing him and speaking carefully, expecting him to speak in complete phrases and sentences and so on. People who call at the house, like the postman or other tradesmen, can be told something about this. As the child grows older he should be encouraged to join social groups like Scouts, Brownies, Sunday school and other church clubs, tennis and swimming clubs, etc. The help of people in charge of such groups must be enlisted, however, and they should be given some information about deafness in children.

If he mixes with hearing children regularly, the deaf child often loses much of his self-consciousness, he learns to share, speech comes more naturally to him and the use of signs and gestures becomes less and less necessary.

Parents should make their homes attractive places for other children to come and play and invitations for the deaf child to visit the homes of hearing people should always be welcomed.

The deaf child should be included in everything, so that he often has new and interesting experiences, which will help to keep him alert and interesting to other people. If he mixes continually with hearing people from the time he is a baby, he will learn to adjust his way of living to that of the hearing world.

NURSERY SCHOOL

Should a child go to an ordinary nursery school or a day or residential school for deaf children? Given normal circumstances, and if a choice is available, probably the ideal placement for a pre-school child who wears a hearing aid is in an ordinary nursery school of about twenty-five or fewer normally hearing children to which, say, five deaf children and a competent teacher of the deaf has been attached. If a school for the deaf is handy, so that the teacher does not feel too isolated, and an additional opinion can be obtained regarding the deaf children's progress, so much the better.

The advantages of this are that the deaf children mix freely with normally hearing children while living in their own homes, and specialist help is available to them and to their parents.

If this is not possible for one reason or another, then day nursery schools for deaf children, either on their own or attached to schools for the deaf, can be extremely good.

Bearing in mind that generalizations about deaf children can be dangerous it can be said that residential care of pre-school deaf children should be treated with extreme caution. Living in well-run 'cottage homes', where every child goes home for the week-end, can be beneficial to both child and parents in some cases, but full-time residential care of deaf children before they have attained a mental age of five years has in my experience frequently done more harm than good. The relationship between the children and their parents is often affected, and the general psychological development of the child can be retarded.

If a deaf child reaches the age of three and a half or four years and has shown no signs of speaking, however, parents naturally become distressed. If it is not possible for them to move their home near enough to a pre-school group, they are tempted to consider sending him to a residential school. Alternatives should, however, be considered: regular help from experienced visiting teachers of the deaf who can both guide and encourage the parents; enrolment in a local nursery school or play centre so that the child learns to play with other children and the mother is able to get a welcome break from managing the child; individual tutoring from an ex-teacher of deaf children or a speech therapist or even a capable teacher of young children. Many housewives who have been teachers or therapists are pleased to do a little part-time work of this nature. If the education authority is unable to employ them, frequently local Rotary Clubs or women's organizations have been found very willing to assist with the necessary financial help.

A nursery school teacher, even if she is not a qualified teacher of the deaf, can give a great deal of help both to the deaf child and his parents. If there are other handicapped children in her group, it may be possible for her to introduce their mothers to each other so that troubles may be shared and new friendships started. Some mothers of handicapped children are lonely during the pre-school years, believing that their neighbours are unwilling to accept their child's disability and they shrink from being snubbed.

If the deaf child wears a hearing aid, the teacher should have a general idea of how it works and should see that the child always wears it. She should also see that the deaf child sits near the front in group periods and should always show pleasure at any attempt at speech the child may make. As far as the other children are concerned, she should not make a point of telling them that Mary is deaf but should mention the fact as occasion arises. She should *not* make the hearing children always 'give in' to the deaf one.

It depends largely on her attitude how the hearing children will react to the deaf one's disability: hearing aids, for example, are very interesting to inquisitive four-year-olds and in some cases can even lend the owner prestige when, say, everyone wants a turn at listening to the feedback!

Nursery school offers so many advantages to deaf children that most parents are happy to accept them. There are some, however, who are reluctant to do so, having protected their child from all contact outside the home through fear of ridicule. Such parents need time to gain confidence through preliminary visits to the nursery school and personal contact with the teacher. Once they are convinced that their deaf child can be kept busy and happy among other children, they are usually eager for him to begin nursery school.

Usually deaf children gain a great deal from contact with hearing ones, are soon accepted as equals and join in group play very well. This is mentally stimulating for them and they become independent in a way which is impossible if they are always over-protected by their parents at home. Occasionally, however, they are left out of some game because of their handicap and this can cause some frustration which they have to learn to cope with themselves; there is not always time for the teacher to sort things out for them and this, too, helps them towards independence. By the time they leave nursery school, deaf children are beginning to accept that there are some situations in which they cannot join.

On their side, too, hearing children gain something important from the deaf ones if they learn to accept, without staring or cruel comment, that some children are different and need help and kindness. If pre-school children begin to learn patience and tolerance at this early stage, it will stand them in good stead later in life.

But it must be emphasized that if a child is severely or profoundly deaf, some form of individual specialist help is necessary from about three years onwards in addition to attending a nursery school. (See Ch. 5.)

The following account by the mother of an intelligent deaf man (hearing loss 95 decibels) shows how much intelligent thoughtful parents can do in helping their deaf children to lead normal lives. Not all deaf children can achieve as much as this but parents of all deaf children should learn something helpful from the mother's attitude and approach.

My son is twenty-four years old. He is working on a farm – at the moment in the midst of lambing – aided by two dogs he has trained himself. He has a small car, and spends most week-ends visiting friends in the district – playing tennis in the summer and golf in the winter. He leads an interesting life, reading the daily papers and a wide variety of books, and his general knowledge is considerable. He became engaged to a normally hearing girl four months ago.

John is profoundly deaf as a result of my having had German measles in early pregnancy. I first suspected deafness at two months and was certain at five months, but it was not confirmed by a specialist until John was a year old.

At three John went to nursery school for normally hearing children. He stayed there for two years and was very happy – joining in all the activities and being treated just as any other child. The head teacher remarked that John had complete faith in adults.

An article in a weekly magazine about the Spencer Tracys and their deaf son led to our embarking on the Tracy Correspondence Course, then in its very early stages. I had been feeling my way rather uncertainly without much knowledge, and the relief and stimulation of having definite lines to work on was wonderful. We carried out the programme set out by the course fairly thoroughly – even when nursery school began – but the biggest help seemed to be in directing my thinking.

We kept a diary in these early years; a simple affair at first – mostly pictures or rough drawings illustrating our daily activities, with a sentence or two beneath. Gradually the drawings became smaller and less frequent, while the sentences grew longer and more complicated, until by the time John was nine or ten there were very few illustrations. I would write and draw in these diaries every evening – usually while John watched – then we would read the day's doings together after he was in bed. It was a wonderful way of getting reading practice in simple straightforward language about everyday things. *We kept these diaries for nine years.*

When John was just five he began attending a small school for deaf children. Soon after he started I realized how wrong I was in thinking that school – any school – could solve all problems, or indeed completely educate any deaf child. Though it was not necessary for me to continue the daily formal lessons of the last four years, there was still much to be done.

I often wish I could start again – there have been big advances in the education of deaf children, and I myself could have been of much more use to my son. Yet I still believe the fundamental things stressed by the Tracy Clinic to be as vital now as I did when John was little. *Parents are the most important people in a deaf child's education, but the encouraging thing is that any ordinary parent can do the job and do it well.*

Suggestions for further reading by parents

Bloom, F. (1963) *Our Deaf Children* Heinemann

Dale, D. M. C. (1967) *Applied Audiology for Children* (Chapters 1, 6, 7 and 8) Charles C. Thomas, Springfield, Illinois (second edition)

Davis H., and Silverman, S. R. (1960) *Hearing and Deafness – A Guide for Laymen* Holt, Rinehart and Winston, New York

Ewing, E. C., and Ewing, A. W. G. (1964) *Teaching Deaf Children to Talk* Manchester University Press

Ewing, I. R., and Ewing, A. W. G. (1958) *New Opportunities for Deaf Children* University of London Press Ltd

Gardner, D. E. M. (1956) *The Education of Young Children* Methuen

Groht, M. A. (1958) *Natural Language for Deaf Children* Volta Bureau, Washington, D.C.

Illingworth, R. S., and C. M. (1954) *Babies and Young Children* Churchill

Spock, B. (1957) *Baby and Child Care* Pocket Books, New York

Spock, B. (1961) *On Being a Parent of a Handicapped Child* National Society for Crippled Children and Adults Inc, 22–23 West Ogden Avenue, Chicago 12, Illinois

Streng, A. *et al* (1958) *Hearing Therapy for Children* Grune and Stratton, New York

Reports to the Carnegie United Kingdom Trust (1964) *Handicapped Children and Their Families* Dunfermline, Scotland

Illinois Annual School for Mothers of Deaf Children (1950) *If You Have A Deaf Child* University of Illinois Press

(Most of these books are obtainable from the Librarian, Royal National Institute for the Deaf, 105 Gower Street, London, W.C.1, or from the Alexander Graham Bell Association, 1,537, 35th Street, New York.)

3 Language Development in the Young Child

People still talk about the 'deaf and dumb'. This is probably because a long time ago many deaf people were unable to speak at all and partly, too, because, when children are born profoundly deaf, it is impossible for them to develop absolutely normal speech. It is very rare these days, however, for a child not to learn to say some words, if not to develop a really extensive vocabulary. It is unfortunate but true that many people still think that deaf people suffer from another complaint called 'dumbness'. Dumbness, however, is a *result* of deafness in nearly all cases. We speak as we hear; if a person is born in Italy, he hears Italian all round him so that, when he is old enough to talk, Italian words are produced. If he was born in Scotland, his speech would have the typical Scottish accent. If he was born profoundly deaf, he would hear no speech at all and as a result would speak very little until specially taught to do so. If he was born with partial hearing his speech would show the typical speech defects of the partially hearing, i.e. defective consonants like 's' 'sh', 't', and 'k'.

There is, of course, nothing the matter with the organs required in speaking, the tongue, the lips, the larynx and the lungs of deaf children but, because they have not heard speech, they are unable to reproduce it. When the speech develops it is usually slow, laboured and difficult to follow unless one is familiar with the child's attempts to speak.

Something which deaf people have to learn is how to control their breath, as they tend to use far more breath in speaking than a hearing person does. Helpful exercises in breath control for little deaf children which can also be fun are blowing bubbles, dandelion clocks or plastic ducks or boats in the bath to make them move over the water. Blowing simple musical instruments helps too – tin whistles, mouth organs, comb-and-paper as well as blowing up balloons and paper bags, playing blow football (on a table with a table tennis ball) and races where a pea must be carried on the end of a straw by the player sucking air through the straw held in his mouth. Parents will think of plenty of similar 'breath control' games.

LIPREADING

When parents have realized that their child is deaf, they must begin as soon as possible to help him live in a world of hearing people by encouraging him to lipread and so understand what is said to him and then to speak so that he himself may be understood. At the same time children must be encouraged to use whatever residual hearing they may have.

There are three main steps in learning to lipread:

1 The child must learn to look at the speaker's face. These looks will be brief glances at first, but if something interesting is said each time and attention paid to the points listed below, the child will learn to look at faces for longer periods.

2 He must understand what is said in a situation when the objects being talked about are present, e.g. 'Push the boat to Mummy.'

3 He must understand what is said without clues being given; when he is asked the questions 'Where are your gloves?' he should lipread the word 'gloves' and fetch them from his bedroom without any further prompting. It is a wonderful day when this first happens but parents must not be impatient – if a child is very deaf, it is often about six months after they begin working that such real lipreading is achieved. Sometimes it is very much longer.

The first thing parents have to learn is to watch the child's eyes. Words have to be linked with thoughts and actions. Whenever the child glances at his mother's or father's mouth, they should say the word they believe he is thinking. For example, if he is at the door and beginning to push it, looking over his shoulder at his mother, she should say: 'Shall I *open* the *door*?' or 'Mummy will let you *out*.'

The child must have a good clear pattern to lipread; some people are easy to lipread and others are not. If a person is difficult to lipread, it may be that he does not move his lips enough – or perhaps he moves them too much. Practising with a mirror will help parents to check this, and which words are difficult to lipread. It is most important to give good lipreading patterns as otherwise parents are making it unnecessarily hard for their child and themselves.

All the family and friends must learn to speak carefully – this is extremely important. They should speak a little more slowly than usual, emphasizing important words. There should always be light on the speaker's face; if he stands with his back to the window, the child cannot see his lips clearly. One must beware, too, of a 'dead pan' face. The speaker's eyes and face as a whole should be full of interest and expression. He should not be too close to the child – about four to six feet is the best distance, and at about his level when talking to him. There is no need to pull at the child; a touch will attract his attention as easily as a sharp tug. Visual distractions behind the speaker, like acoustic tiles or spotted wallpaper, should be avoided as far as possible.

Sentences should be kept short but they should be complete. Many people make the mistake of using single words or a kind of jerky 'shorthand', e.g. 'John – Daddy – car' instead of 'John, come with Daddy in the car.'

When teaching very young deaf children to lipread, parents must be sure to do the *talking* before the *giving* of a toy or food. This is important as, once the child has the object, he is more interested in it than in looking at the person talking about it.

When the parent is sure that the child knows a few words and expressions, they should be used as often as possible and new phrases gradually introduced. These will generally be linked with the child's interests which give scope for lipreading and vocabulary development.

The relationship between parent and child becomes much easier as he begins to understand through lipreading.

LANGUAGE DEVELOPMENT

To begin with, deaf children do not realize that words exist. They see all sorts of things about them and have all sorts of experiences, but words play no part in these. Gradually, however, they become aware that the movements of mother's or father's lips do mean certain things. So words and phrases like 'bath time', 'soap', 'Where are your shoes?', 'Come to Daddy' can be lipread and heard with whatever hearing the child has.

The very most should be made of the *daily routines* of washing, dressing, and feeding, as these are the most valuable times in the day for parents. A mother said recently: 'There were twelve times a day when I made a point of talking to my daughter – when she was getting dressed and going to bed, at meal times, at bath time, when the postman came, at 'potty' time, when she washed before lunch, when she was going out to play and coming in again, and finally when Daddy was coming home.'

These everyday happenings make it easy to revise words every day. Parents *have* to be with the child at these times, so the most should be made of them. It must be remembered, of course, that listening and lipreading demand concentration and there will be times when the child is tired or not very well when he will not feel like having any practice. On these occasions parents will be wise to leave the child alone. Six times as much will be accomplished on another occasion when he is ready and wants to communicate.

When practising language, it may be helpful to bear the following points in mind:

1 The parent should always get the child's *full attention* before speaking.

2 It should *never* be taken for granted that the command has been understood, although sometimes it seems incredible that the child has not understood a simple thing like 'wash your hands', especially if it is obvious that the hands are very dirty.

3 The sentence should not be repeated and repeated in a loud voice, even if it appears that the child is being 'just naughty'.

4 If there is no immediate response, the parent should try again quickly, finishing with a glance at the hands and perhaps the bathroom.

5 If there is still a puzzled expression, it may be possible to demonstrate what is to be done – 'Look, Mummy will wash her hands; now you wash your hands too.'

6 Now is the time to repeat. The phrase should be repeated as soon as possible after the action is completed and again later in the day and every other day until it is certain that the words are understood. It may be necessary to demonstrate many times.

John Tracy Clinic recommends that, in addition to the intensive language work during the daily routines, parents should concentrate on one particular word: one that is fairly easy to lipread – 'shoes' for example, would be better than 'socks' – and one in which the child has shown some interest. One parent used the word 'open' twenty-four times when making a sandwich. It has been found, not surprisingly, that the word concentrated on like this is the first one that the child lipreads. When three definite responses have been given to a word, the parents introduce a second one, and so on.

Some weeks after the child has learned to understand a few words, he will try to say a word himself and, as one parent has said: 'It's worth all the tears and trouble when words begin to come.'

The more interests a deaf child has, the more there is for him to talk about and the greater his incentive to learn new words. To assist his language development at home, parents should see that the child has plenty of *meaningful activity*, as only language based on real experience is of value.

Making a model house

One excellent kind of 'meaningful activity' is the making of a model house or, in fact, models of any kind. This gives him an opportunity to use the names of everyday household things, and to practise sense training – colour, number, touch, etc. The activity should be fun and should take place at a pleasant, relaxed time of day, e.g. in the evening.

The plan can be adapted to suit the age of the deaf child: the house and garden must be very simple and even rough and ready for the two-to three-year-old, but may be endlessly improved and made more elaborate to interest an older child. The important thing is that the deaf child should help with the building, and his real efforts should be accepted and praised.

Cardboard boxes, paper of all kinds and colours, paint and scraps of cloth can all be used as building material. It should not be necessary to buy anything except, perhaps, adhesive tape or paste.

All members of the family can and should join in this – perhaps not all at once, but mother one day, father another and so on. A short time spent each day on the house is best, then it may be put away 'until tomorrow'.

Playing shop

Another good game to assist language development is 'playing shop' as soon as the little deaf child is familiar with shopping. (He should, of course, go with his mother to the shops, helping to carry some of the parcels and talking about things before, after and during the visit.) At home there will, at first, be only a few obvious articles like fruit or bread 'for sale' on a table, packing-case or anything handy. The child should be shopkeeper and customer in turn.

This is a game to be played often. Gradually the shop can be made more elaborate, and the number of articles for sale will increase. These may be real food, or empty packets and cartons. There need be no complications about money to begin with; the child can pretend to hand over money. Later on real or cardboard money may be used.

This is a wonderful chance to use simple language forms like 'please', 'thank you' and 'good-bye' as well as names of everyday foods. The names of simple things will become more complicated later: 'bread' will be 'white bread' or 'brown bread', 'biscuits' will be 'chocolate biscuits' and so on.

Question forms are difficult for deaf children and here is a good opportunity for using expressions like 'have you . . .?' – 'how much?' – 'how many?' – 'what kind?' – 'do you want?' If the game is fun and the child enjoys it, he will soon learn.

Pictures and photographs

A really good assortment of pictures is one of the most valuable assets that parents of deaf children can have. Even though some pictures may not be used for quite a time, a collection of pictures and photographs may be begun early on in the child's life.

It should be stressed, however, that learning begins with real experiences, not pictures, and the most useful pictures will be those of objects that the child has already seen. Pictures of baby animals, toys, friends and members of the family are especially suitable.

One way to begin is to show the child a large picture book. 'Single impact' pictures, with a minimum of detail, are best. If the child will pay attention to the pictures as the pages are turned, his mother might tell him a story, holding the open book near her face but not obscuring her lips, turning the pages as the story goes on. One or two sentences per page should be enough, as in: 'This is a little rabbit. His name is Peter. Peter has pink eyes. Peter went hop, hop, hop. He ate some lettuce. Peter was very fat. He lay down and went to sleep.'

A little deaf child, of course, is not going to understand all of this story – indeed, he may not understand any of it at first. But he will make some associations, especially if the story is repeated quite often. Children love repetition.

As early as possible, the child should be helped to act out the story and its vocabulary. Children love to mimic and pretend they are the characters in a story. Show the child how the rabbit hopped in the story and then let him hop himself.

Real life stories, of the child's own experiences or his family's, can be developed by pictures or photographs pasted into a scrap-book.

Of course, speech and auditory training should go along with the pictures and word and story exercises. The mother can say the word in his ear or near the microphone of his hearing aid as he points to a picture. For the child who hears very little, 'feeling' the word from his mother's lips as it is spoken provides some form of association. Since, with the young child, it is often difficult to obtain an exact measure of his hearing, every means must be used to reach him. He may be shown the pictures and allowed to see (or feel) the word or sentence.

Commands given by pictures are often fun. Pictures to suggest daily activities that really need to be carried out are preferable. 'Go out to play' – 'It's bedtime' – 'Wash your hands' are commands easily given in pictures. They should, of course, be relied on less and less as the child's ability in lipreading develops.

Scrap-books and collections

Deaf children can make scrap-books with all kinds of pictures that interest them: boys may have pictures of cars, trains or aeroplanes; girls may prefer animals, babies or pretty clothes but the important thing, from the language point of view, is that they should *talk* about them.

Parents might help in the making of a scrap-book with a page, or pages, for each room in the house. They might go through magazines and catalogues with the child, choosing beds, tables, television sets and cutting out and pasting the pictures on the appropriate pages. There could be pages for a garden, too – with flowers, lawn, motor-mower, etc. Parents and children should talk about them.

Scrap-books can also be used to teach colour; the child might see how many different shades of red or blue he can find from magazines to paste into his scrap-book.

Other excellent language topics are collections – of shells, pretty stones, pressed flowers, matchboxes, postcards. The child may need and appreciate help in making these collections – and he should be encouraged to talk about them.

Animals and plants

If a deaf child's family can keep a pet or, better still, several pets – puppies, kittens, budgerigars – the child can be shown how to feed and look after them and, when he is old enough, encouraged to be responsible for his pets.

Apart from pets, forms of animal life interesting to children are silkworms, which can be kept in a cardboard box with holes in the lid and fed on mulberry leaves or lettuce, or caterpillars kept in a glass jar. The deaf child can be shown how they develop into chrysalises and, later, into moths and butterflies – all excellent talking points.

Goldfish can be kept in a glass jar or a pond in the garden and if frogspawn can be obtained in the spring, it too can be kept in water in the house or garden and watched while the tadpoles develop and later begin to turn into frogs. If tadpoles or goldfish are kept in a glass bowl, the deaf child can be taught how to keep the bowl clean, how to feed its inmates, and how to release the tadpoles in a suitable pond when they are ready.

One of the best ways of interesting children in plants is to grow some quickly developing bulbs – hyacinths, say – in water in a jar showing their roots. The deaf child can watch them develop and flower – and talk about them.

A bird table in the garden (high enough to keep the cats away) and putting out bread will attract different kinds of birds so that the deaf child can learn their names. It may be helpful, too, to find pictures of birds which come to the table.

When a deaf child really knows a new word, his parents should write it in a notebook with a picture or drawing to illustrate it. They should praise him and explain that they will put each new word he learns in the book until it is full. *The words should be used continually.*

SIGNS AND GESTURES

Before a deaf child has any words, he has to point and gesture if he is to communicate at all. In a young deaf child lots of gestures are good, as they show that he has an active mind and wants very much to communicate his thoughts. Although a little child's gestures should not be repressed, he should be encouraged to try to speak rather than make signs, and, as soon as he knows a word, he should say it every time.

Parents should at all times resist the temptation to point to things; that is, they should put as little emphasis as possible on the use of the hands. Looking will often do as well as pointing. If, for example, a child is told: 'Look what Daddy has' by his mother, he may keep on looking at his mother's mouth, not having understood. She should then repeat the phrase and *look* over at the father, so that the child's eyes follow hers.

When it is not possible to indicate to a child what is required simply by looking, it is better to *show* him rather than gesture. For example, if, after being told 'Bring your coat; we're going out', the child does not understand, his mother may say: 'Let's get your coat' and *go with* the child to get it. She should not give a mime of putting on a coat. It is much easier, of course, to sign than to bring the coat but it does the child no good and the extra effort is well worth while in the long run.

The Ewings have said that gestures are the greatest threat to the child's future mental life. If he uses gestures for all his needs and ideas, he is using a poor sort of shorthand which not only leaves out words but puts them in the wrong order. A child who signs 'Bed – me – there' instead of saying: 'My bed is in there' is leaving out two important words 'is' and 'in', is confusing 'me' with 'my' and puts 'bed' first instead of second. This jumbled way of thinking becomes so ingrained that if he persists with signs, he will have great difficulty in both reading and writing. He must learn, as soon as possible, to *say* complete phrases and sentences.

The 'oral' method of teaching deaf children is based on lipreading, hearing and speaking. It does not use finger spelling. In many oral schools signs and gestures *are* used for about 5 per cent of the children who have great difficulty in lipreading, but this, of course, is in addition to reading. Signs restrict the number of people with whom the deaf child can communicate. If parents build up a good set of pictures to help their child to learn to lipread, there is often little need to resort to gestures.

One word of warning: in the parents' desire to do away with signs and gestures, they should never be so strict that the child will not communicate for fear of being scolded for not talking. Indeed, with very young children, 'finger plays' with rhymes and jingles of the type 'Here is the church and here is the steeple' and 'Two little birdies sat on a wall' may be of the greatest help in encouraging the child to form words with his lips. Nor should parents insist on making the child lipread against his will; it is possible to make him dislike the very idea by forcing him to look when he is tired or interested in something else. Lipreading can be made into a kind of game with hearing brothers and sisters joining in and everyone saying short sentences. If the sound is turned off the television, the whole family is on the same footing and has to try to lipread what the characters are saying.

HEARING AIDS AND THEIR MAINTENANCE

Although hearing aids are of benefit to nearly all deaf children, it must be realized that they help some more than others. For children who have partial hearing, these aids can make all the difference to their speech and language development. Many partially hearing children can attend normal schools who, if there were no hearing aids, would have to go to special schools and classes. Most children with hearing aids rely on lipreading as well as listening.

For profoundly deaf children, making the sounds of speech louder still does not make them clear enough to be understood. Nearly all can hear some sound of voice but all the vowels are muffled – something like 'oo' in 'room'. Hearing the sound of *his own voice*, however, stimulates a deaf child to speak even though what he hears is distorted. In addition hearing aids enable these very deaf children to hear such sounds as laughter, crying, the low notes of music, cupboard doors shutting, dogs barking, the noise of a spoon on a plate and a host of others. For such children these meaningful sounds, although not of great assistance in their speech development, give a sense of belonging – of being more a part of their environment. One profoundly deaf girl said, when she took off her hearing aid: 'Now I am alone again.'

Hearing aids should be worn full time. For the first few weeks, of course, the aid may be put on the child for short periods each day – half an hour after breakfast, after his afternoon rest and just before going to bed at night. Quite soon, though, aids should be worn as many people wear glasses and taken off only when the child is in bed or having a bath. The aid may be switched off – not *taken* off – if the child makes a long journey by train or car.

Hearing aids operate best when one speaks close to the microphone – about six inches away. One should *never* shout into the aid. The deaf child should be encouraged to listen to the sound of his own voice.

There are several ways in which parents can help their deaf children to obtain full benefit from their aids. *They must see that it is worn correctly and is as comfortable as possible.* Much time and money may be wasted in replacing parts for an aid damaged by being carelessly worn. For very small children, a harness is usually best. In the u.s.a. parents can usually purchase harnesses ready-made from the hearing aid companies and in Britain the Royal National Institute for the Deaf, 105 Gower Street, London, W.C.1, provides them at a nominal cost.

The style of the harness may vary but it should be made of strong material to prevent it from quickly rumpling into a string, it should be adjustable so that it can be kept firm, no matter what clothing is worn, and it should be easy to put on and take off. The harness should also have a pocket which should be just large enough to hold the hearing aid with a button-over flap to stop the aid falling out and with a hole in the front to leave the microphone grille clear. A piece of stiff card, placed behind the aid in the pocket and extending about a third of an inch above it, is often useful to protect the delicate little controls on the top.

The aid should be worn fairly high on the chest so that it is not damaged when the child rolls on the floor or uses climbing apparatus. For older children, a pocket can be sewn into a blouse or shirt. This is quite successful provided the garment is not too loose. The aid should be kept firm to the body so as not to bump about when the child runs.

It is important that the cord of the aid is threaded through a button-hole and up under the collar to the earpiece. This keeps the cord out of the way so that it is comfortable and does not get caught when the child is playing. Little children will chew the cord if it is not kept out of their way.

Daily testing and maintenance

The aid should be tested at least once during the day to see that it is working. If the volume is switched to maximum and the earpiece held about ten inches from the microphone of the aid, there should be a strong whistling noise (*acoustic feedback*). The aid can, of course, also be checked by putting the receiver to the parent's own ear.

If the aid is not working, the following points should be checked in this order:

1 See that the controls are in their proper position.

2 Replace the battery with a new one.

3 The silver contacts of the battery terminals should be shiny and should touch the batteries. They may be rubbed with a nail-file or fine emery paper to clean them.

4 The cord should be examined for breaks, especially near the plugs. Check it by replacing, if necessary.

5 Clean any wax out of the canal of the ear mould. (Wax here can also cause acoustic feedback when the aid is being worn.)

6 Check the receiver by replacing.

If the aid does not work when all these points have been checked, the fault will be an internal one and the aid should be sent for servicing.

There are dozens of different types of hearing aid. Tiny ones are advertised – some in brooches, others to fit into spectacles and ear-rings. Most of these are probably no use to a deaf child. While many of them are quite good little aids, they have insufficient power to be of real use to most severely deaf children. They are also expensive to buy and run and are easily lost.

A specialist teacher or audiologist will advise on whether a large table model hearing aid should be used. If the child has a good individual aid which is working well, the expense of a table model aid is frequently unwarranted.

Binaural aids

Although fitting two hearing aids to each child is becoming increasingly common – particularly in Britain where the Government Medresco aids are produced so cheaply – it is difficult to prove that listening with two aids, i.e. with both ears, enables people to hear speech any more clearly than when listening with only one. For this reason, binaural aids have never been universally recommended, although there is considerable subjective evidence that two aids seem preferable in a number of cases.

Neurologists maintain that stimulating both ears seems preferable to stimulating only one. Like so many other aspects of work in this field, however, more carefully planned and controlled research is required before a definite statement on this point can be made.

The use of one aid connected to two receivers by what is called a 'Y' cord is probably beneficial to children whose hearing losses are not too severe and are almost identical in both ears. In this way the cost and care of a second hearing aid is obviated. This is not, of course, true binaural listening, because the use of only one microphone does not allow any focusing of the hearing which enables the source of sounds to be located.

Loop systems

The 'loop' (or 'induction loop') system enables sound to enter an individual hearing aid by means of electro-magnetic waves. In this way, speech and music reach the hearing aid wearer in a much less distorted condition than when the sound travels in the normal way, since room noise and reverberation interfere with the sound waves in transit. Most of the better makes of commercial hearing aids and the Government Medresco hearing aid in the United Kingdom (see page 193) incorporate an induction or telephone coil.

The loop is a coil of wire placed round the room. For maximum benefit the wire should be about three feet above the floor but it usually works quite effectively round the skirting board. For the sake of appearance it can be taken round doors and window-frames. Any thickness of wire will do but insulated aerial wire or lighting flex is recommended.

If the radio or television set has a pair of sockets marked 'extension loudspeaker' or 'L.S.', the mains plug should first be removed, the two ends of the loop fitted with appropriate plugs and fitted into the sockets. Most sets, however, will not have this facility and an isolating transformer will be needed.

Battery-transistorized sets, apart from car radios, are usually not sufficiently powerful to drive the loop. The loop takes some power from the loud-speaker when in normal use but this can be compensated by the volume control. A switch can be fitted to silence the internal loud-speaker so the programme can be heard through the hearing aid only. Turn the volume full on with the switch in the loop position. Slowly turn up the volume of the set until the required level is obtained at the aid receiver. It may be necessary to adjust the two controls until best results are achieved.

Should parents have an induction loop fitted in their house? It is probably worth experimenting with a loop of wire round the room attached to the radio, or, better still, the television set. A local radio dealer would install this at very little cost. Buying a microphone and amplifier as well is probably unjustified.

Low frequency aids

Hearing aids giving great emphasis to the low frequencies have been found beneficial(18, 19). For children who are profoundly deaf, an aid similar to the Danish *Audium 1820* which gives a gain of 53 decibels at 50 c.p.s., might well be extremely helpful.

AUDITORY TRAINING

This training does *not* mean that a severely or profoundly deaf child will hear normally, but it does mean that the child can be helped to make the most of what hearing he has and to get pleasure from listening.

The best thing is to direct his listening – he can be encouraged to hold his hearing aid near the source of a sound: a running tap, the squeaking and banging of a door, an egg beater, a car engine or music on the radio. Parents should not persist with one particular sound if the child does not seem interested; it may be that he cannot hear that sound at all well.

Tape recorders should be particularly useful in auditory training. Experiments are being made in Japan with everyday phrases recorded on a continuous magnetic tape. The deaf child listens to these after he is in bed and the tape is left playing for some time even after he has gone to sleep. The mother of one two-and-a-half-year-old boy reported that her child seemed to like the experience, as, if the earpiece fell out, he would grope about and replace it without completely waking up. It is too early yet to make a definite statement about this technique but the increased use of tape recorders both at school and pre-school age seems very likely.

Suggestions for further reading

Lowell, E. L., and Stoner, M. (1960) *Play It by Ear* John Tracy Clinic

Ewing, E. C., and Ewing, A. W. G. (1964) *Teaching Deaf Children to Talk* Manchester University Press

4 Cooperation between Home and School

Parents should try to develop a really close relationship with the school their child attends. The head teacher should know the family as one which is genuinely concerned about the deaf child's welfare and that all members are working hard to provide the best possible opportunities for the child to learn. The class teacher needs to know such things as the names and ages of the brothers and sisters of the deaf child, names of pets in the home, the make of the car if one is owned, how the deaf child spends most of his time at home, how he behaves at home as compared with how he behaves at school, and so forth. The best way for the teacher to get this information, of course, is by visits between home and school, but where home visits are not practicable letters and snapshots can do a great deal.

Every deaf child should carry a little notebook to school and back each day. If well kept, these little *home/school notebooks* (Figure 3) are a wonderful help to teachers, parents, supervisors and children. In them the parent writes down a sentence or two about some happening that has interested the child the previous night or that morning before going to school. The teacher has a little news session and the children come out in turn and tell the rest of the class their news. Without the book and with poor language and speech development, as many of the children have, the teacher and the other children are at a loss to know what the child is trying to say. I remember one little five-year-old coming to school one day and gesticulating very excitedly about something. I could not tell what she was getting at until she rushed to her school bag and took out her notebook and showed me. Her mother had written that a visitor had called the previous night and inadvertently put her plastic handbag on a hot element on top of the kitchen range. We were able to talk about this for quite a time and found pictures of electric ranges, fires and so on in magazines – all of which would not have been possible had she not brought the notebook. Similarly, when the children go home at night, parents often have difficulty in knowing exactly what they are telling them. The teacher, one day, might write: 'Mary has learnt to say 'the blue car' very well today.' The parents can then ask her to repeat it and she may show it off to visitors.

This repetition of successes achieved at school is very important for consolidating the language work done. Parents should try always to write the most vital and interesting thing that has happened to the child while he was at home. Entries such as 'I played football', or 'I watched television' may be all right for young children but to write the same thing day after day is certainly not worth while. A statement like 'Peter tackled me at football and I hurt my shoulder' or 'I was excited when Robin Hood fought Little John over the stream' would be much more suitable.

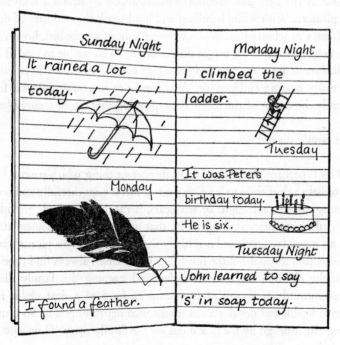

Figure 3 Home/school notebook for a young child

As the children become better at writing, they could begin making their own entries in their home/school notebooks. These original efforts can be discussed and corrected with the teacher and then re-written by the children. It is better for them to make mistakes and have them corrected than never to attempt original work. As one teacher put it: 'It's better to let them "go down for the third time" than it is to spoon-feed them everything.' This is because, when they do get a sentence correct unassisted, the language form will stay with them longer than that which has merely been *told* to them – even though it has been told a hundred times.

READING

One of the best aids to children handicapped by deafness is to read for pleasure. With skilful handling and hard work the majority of deaf children can achieve this. When wrong methods are applied, however, it is not uncommon for bright deaf children to be unable to read at all well. *Parents are in a unique position to help a deaf child to read.* Even with normally hearing children 'the determinant of success or failure is frequently the extent of the parental cooperation that can be secured'(20).

The family diary

This is perhaps the best and most important thing which parents can do to help a deaf child to learn to read. If this is kept carefully and con-scientiously for, say, eight or ten years, it can be promised, provided the child is not very dull mentally, that he will read quite adequately for his everyday needs and it is likely that he will read for pleasure and information throughout the rest of his life. Parents always find time to give the children three meals a day and keeping this family diary conscientiously is almost as important as food to a deaf child. His mental health and development might well depend upon it. So something else must go by the board but *not* the family diary. Time *must* be made for it.

For little children a big book is best so that pictures and photographs can be stuck into it and sketches and printing can be of a reasonable size. When the child is older, say, seven years, a smaller stiff-covered notebook seems most satisfactory. Plenty of pictures and illustrations should be used to begin with, but gradually these are less and less necessary and the diary can use words entirely.

It is helpful if parents can use the same style of printing as is being used by teachers in the classroom. In New Zealand we have adopted the letter forms shown below, largely because they lead naturally into cursive writing at a later date. Some parents use block capitals when printing and this can be confusing for little children.

abcdefghijklm
nopqrstuvwxyz

Into the family diary go all the little interesting things that happen not only to the deaf child but to all the family, to relatives and friends. Generally it will be written by the mother or the father, but sometimes a close relative or an older brother or sister can do it. It is important, however, that it is not turned over to the deaf child to write – if he wants to keep a diary he should keep a separate one for himself. What goes into the family diary should be in good English with correct spelling and punctuation.

This is possibly the best form of reading the child can get. An important principle in language work that *the experience should precede the language* is adhered to naturally and meaningfully. The child has had a certain experience and within an hour or two he sees it written down in conventional English sentences and phrases. One good example which comes to mind was a statement in a family diary which said: 'John went to get his hair cut after school, but there were too many people waiting, so he came home.' One could imagine this little boy going to the hairdresser's, looking in and seeing a crowd of waiting customers and deciding to himself that he would be better to go on another day. On arriving home his mother would say to him: 'You were supposed to get your hair cut today, weren't you?' In his way, the child would perhaps say: 'Many people' and pull a face. That night when he gets into bed, he is able to read exactly what happened. The awkward little words like 'but' and 'so', which are included in the sentence, occur so naturally and easily in this way. Frequent repetition in meaningful situations fixes many of the language forms in the child's mind.

Reading books

It is a good idea for deaf children to become members of a children's library so that a wide selection of books can be obtained. They are too expensive for most people to buy and of course there is no guarantee that the book selected will be acceptable to the child. Parents should be advised by the teacher regarding suitable books for their child. In the beginning the books are best used as a basis for story-telling. A parent can sit on the child's bed at night and work through the book talking about everything – especially those parts the child shows most interest in. If it is a new book then one should make the most of it from a lipreading point of view before the child is allowed to see it all. It's like giving him an ice-cream – the talking should be done before the giving.

As the child gets older mothers and fathers can make this story technique more interesting by *anticipating*. They must, of course, have read through the book quickly themselves beforehand to do this. They can work along through the story a little way and then say to the child: 'What do you think will happen?' It is possible gradually to work them up to the stage where even some very deaf children of eight and nine years can be asked: 'What do you think he might have done if he hadn't done that?' Not all children are capable of this but it is well worth trying and their vocabularies and interests can be extended in this way.

While they are small, the pictures are the only interest but gradually they start to pay attention to the printed word. They can be shown the words – especially the adjectives and verbs and not only the nouns, i.e. words like blue, yellow, white, red, beautiful, happy, running, scratching, catching, pulling, pushing, fighting and flying. One should not just point at the dog, the cat, the boy, the girl, etc., but rather say: 'Look at the girl; she is swimming' or 'She is running' or 'Oh dear, the boy has fallen over'. Later on parents can say to the child: 'Can you show me the boy falling over?' 'Can you show me the bird sitting on its nest?' 'Where are the blue balloons?' 'Where are the red ones?' As he progresses away from pictures to the written words, similar exercises can be given, always remembering to keep it a game rather than a formal lesson. Whenever possible, it should be made into a listening game as well as a watching one: the activity can first be given when the child is both looking and listening and then repeated when he is listening only. If the deaf child is ten years old and parents have never done this sort of thing, it is not too late to begin now; for example: 'Show me on the page "the boy fell down the hill".'

Every child should have two or three good books beside his bed and should do some reading every night of the week, even if it is only for five minutes to begin with.

Books are a very worthwhile gift at Christmas and for birthdays. A good dictionary, for example, which may be fairly expensive but which can be a constant source of joy even to quite small deaf children, is a first-rate gift. There are a number of very good dictionaries available today. Children should be encouraged to work out meanings of words from their place in the sentence, before looking the word up.

Seeing his mother and father read often stimulates the child's interest in reading. If parents have got out of the habit of reading they might consider going back to it for the child's sake and, of course, for their own pleasure.

Comics

All deaf children seem to love to look at comics, and should be permitted to do so. For those who are slow at reading the use of carefully selected comics is often very useful. Comics can be cut up and pasted on card and phrases written under each picture in words that should mostly be within the child's reading vocabulary.

STORY-TELLING AND STORY-READING FOR YOUNG DEAF CHILDREN

The following advice, from an experienced teacher of the deaf, may be helpful to parents:

Story-telling is an excellent way to arouse an interest in reading and in books and stories generally. The benefits of story-telling are numerous and include pleasure, play for the imagination, a limitless source of knowledge of people, places, things and customs, social and spiritual training and the development of word power. Some of these are available to the hearing child from other sources, such as conversations with others, the radio, television and films. Without stories, both told and read, the deaf child will miss much pleasure and enjoyment, will be ill-informed, will have little scope for imaginative development, and will go through life with an extremely limited language power.

1 Remember always that the chief aim of the story is to bring joy to the listener. This will only be achieved if the teller also enjoys the story. All the other beneficial factors will develop if care is taken not to rob the child of the pleasure of enjoying it. Do not feel shy or childish about entering into the stories. Enjoy them with the child.

2 It is important to have interesting stories; but on the whole it is the manner of telling the story which makes it interesting. A variety of stories of different kinds is a good idea, some about animals, some about people, some true and some fairy stories.

3 It is essential that you know your story thoroughly before telling it. If you have to break the spell while you refer to the book, or to make up something which differs from the last telling, you will not be so successful.

4 Children love repetition. Do not think you will save time or avoid boredom by leaving out the repetition. That time will come soon enough. Meantime, repetition satisfies a rhythmic need, helps in the acquisition of language and fact and, for deaf children, greatly aids lipreading. So tell your story with plenty of repetition in the early stages.

5 Simple, natural language is best. Avoid the common error of long words and involved sentences. On the whole keep your sentences short and choose simple words whether your audience is deaf or not. Do not, however, feel that you must keep only to words which your deaf child knows. It is not necessary for him either to have previous knowledge of, or to understand, every word.

6 Keep the story sequence in mind; a story should not wander aimlessly about. It moves from point to point. This sequence is essential to stories. Remember how eagerly you yourself wanted to know 'what happened next' and how a well-told story still makes you eager for the completion of the story sequence.

7 As each new phase of the story is reached, show the child the pictures or draw a sketch. Failing either of these, or in addition to them, act little pieces as you go to make them quite clear. At first you may be self-conscious, but the real enjoyment to both yourself and the child should banish this self-consciousness soon. Do not be afraid someone will see you!

8 Introduce the characters by pictures. It is much easier for the child to follow the story if he knows all the characters. He will quickly match the lipread name with the pictures.

9 At the end, do not expect the child to reproduce the story. It is for his enjoyment. But encourage and help him to dramatize it, mostly in pantomime at first but adding more words and phrases with each repetition. Here the whole family or class can take part. Let your imagination and the child's have full play. There is no need for a stage and a full set of properties. The variety of uses to which ordinary household furniture and fittings can be put is amazing. In any case, a symbol will suffice; in fact, it will be better than a too elaborate stage setting. Dressing up can be very simple and most enjoyable. One or two items of clothing or accessories can be filled out with imaginative pieces and can be fun for everybody.

10 Make story-time a pleasure, not a duty. Much can be achieved by your own pleasurable anticipation. Say with real meaning: 'Shall we have a story?' or 'I will tell you just one story before bedtime.' Soon you will be able to teach your little deaf son or daughter to say: 'Please tell me a story' — an achievement of which to be proud.

11 Continue with older children; read and tell whole books, e.g. one period weekly.

Reading stories follows naturally after story-telling. At times in the beginning it is helpful to underline the phrases and sentences which are essential to the story sequence. Details should not be worried about at first.

Another way is for the parent and the child to look at the pictures and discover the interesting points together. There will be much that is not understood at first, but at each reading more will be added. One should not be afraid of skipping. As the child's ability to read develops, so will he have to leave out less and less. *Stories with plenty of action should be chosen.* Pictures which tell the whole story with the minimum of printed matter are best for beginners. As the story sense is being developed, the power to read stories will develop too, but more slowly. Remember that the more they are able to read books with pleasure and profit, the nearer to normal will they be in ideas and knowledge and the better able to continue their own education.

LANGUAGE DEVELOPMENT

Apart from the *family diary* mentioned earlier, perhaps the best thing that parents can do to help their school-aged child develop good language is to give him something to talk about. They should see that he has those interesting experiences that make him want to tell them things. As with younger children, outings and visits, people coming to the home, keeping pets, having adequate and interesting things to play with all help in this direction. If this stimulating environment is provided, it is a matter very largely of talking often to him in clear phrases and sentences and encouraging him to use phrases and sentences himself. I remember once seeing a teacher in a school for the deaf whose seven- and eight-year-old children were talking better than most I had seen. One little boy came up to her and said: 'Paste, please?' She replied: 'You ask me properly.' He then said: 'May I paste, please, Miss Brown?' She said: 'May I *have* the paste, please, Miss Brown?' He then repeated it correctly. He knew where the paste was but she caught hold of him, to make sure he did not go straight away, and said: 'Yes. The paste is in the corner of the cupboard.' In this way she put into words the thought that was in his mind and nine times out of ten she would ask him to repeat that second sentence as well: 'The paste is in the corner of the cupboard.' Parents should not overdo it so that the child becomes sickened with saying sentences but they should keep at it in a pleasant, helpful way.

Another way for parents to help in language work is to take particular note of things written in the home/school notebook and try to create as many opportunities as possible to have the child recall them. The book may say, for example: 'Today we have been learning "it doesn't matter" as a phrase.' Parents and brothers and sisters should watch for opportunities to bring this phrase in, particularly on the same day and as often as possible thereafter. It is best to concentrate on two or three phrases at a time for, say, a week or more and 'do them to death'. By glancing back through the home/school notebook and the family diary, one can, from time to time, revise much of the material worked on. One should not keep on and on for weeks with any particular phrase or sentence; the child should be given time to forget and should be expected to forget and then, as interestingly as possible, reminded again of it. In this way, the language forms gradually become fixed in his thinking.

Grammar dictionary

Some parents have helped their children a great deal to develop good grammatical phrases by writing out sentences on a blackboard often kept in the kitchen, or in a notebook kept for the purpose. It is often best to start off with the little blackboard in the kitchen, and, as the child gets older, to begin a notebook. Some families keep jotter pads in every room in the house so that words and phrases can be written down quickly for the deaf child. The notebook can be made into a sort of dictionary. One child used to come in each night and say to her mother: 'Tea – what?' Her mother grew tired of correcting her and the grammar book was introduced. Under a heading *Meals* appeared the phrase 'What's for tea tonight?' The next night when the child said: 'Tea – what?', the mother was able to say: 'Go and look in your notebook and come and ask me again.' A game should be made of it – all these activities should be made as much fun as possible. Other headings in this dictionary might be *Films and Entertainment, School, Hospital and Sickness, Games, Manners,* etc. The following are extracts from one parent's grammar dictionary. The parts in italics are those which the deaf ten-year-old boy omitted to say when he was speaking.

Questions

Did you work with another man?
Did you work by yourself?
Have you *any* new comics?
What *did* you buy?
What time *is* father com*ing* home from work?

Conversations

Ron Brown*'s* father told me the motor-bike *and* the car crash*ed*.
Mr Johnson told me *there would be* football practice tomorrow.
The lady *at the* shop *said*: 'Where have you been? I haven't see*n* you for *a* long time.'

School news

The horse *belongs to* another boy.
I forgot my blazer. *It's* at school.
In the test Sheryl *was* first, Patricia second, *and* I *was* third.
Marion *is* not very well. *She has a* sore throat.

It is interesting to notice that the pieces left out are often words or parts of words that are difficult to lipread or words which do not alter the sense of the statement or question very much, or both. For example, 'what you buy' is clear enough as it stands.

The following is an account of how one mother, a teacher of ordinary children before her marriage, helped her bright, profoundly deaf boy in language, reading and social adjustment after he started at school:

At five and a half Peter had made a good start with lipreading, could print a few words, count and do simple number combinations. We wanted him to live at home so I travelled many miles daily delivering and collecting him, continuing this for the two and a half years he spent at the school for the deaf.

When we moved to our own farm we brought Peter with us and with much trepidation started him at the tiny local school. For his first year the school had only one teacher. I offered to battle along with the three Rs relying on the school for the social side of education, but this was not really necessary. Although much help at home was needed, to our great joy he fitted in naturally as an ordinary pupil. The adjustment was easier and quicker than we dared hope. He immediately established his prestige by being very good at arithmetic, and punching one of the big boys!

Anticipating that the children would be critical of a deaf child entering their midst, we made sure that Peter's school clothes, while quite ordinary, were immaculate – at least when he entered the playground. And knowing that some of the big boys shared his lunch, he took a large one, always containing something attractive. It was good for Peter to share even if it might have been bribery on my part.

Our blackboard in the kitchen continued to hold pride of place and I'm sure never a day passed that it wasn't used. A question about something not understood during the day often led to quite a little lesson – not thought of as such though. *He wanted to know because he wanted so much to be the same as the other children.*

Apparently Peter had quite a good memory and spelling was no trouble to him, but the meanings and use of the words! I realized the tremendous drain on his nervous energy compared with his hearing classmates. It was vital for him to get sufficient rest as overtiredness always seemed to court the 'current bug' which he managed to get bigger and better than most.

Reading was extremely difficult. Peter could recognize individual words and read quite well – but without comprehending. My method of attack was to exploit his natural curiosity. When he arrived home from school I would recount anything of interest in the day's happenings and soon his afternoon greeting became a ritual: 'Hello, Mum, any news?' Often I would write a sentence or two on the blackboard serving as a reminder for myself and a reading test for Peter. He eagerly awaited the thrice-weekly delivery of mail and newspapers. When discussing items of interest from these, I would tell him the news and then always show it to him in print. The most powerful driving force behind his reading, however, was his great love of football and interest in all games. Any major football games which were broadcast I 'relayed' to Peter and he would then await the arrival of the newspaper report of the game and unconsciously give himself a wonderful reading lesson.

SPEECH

Parents often say: 'If only Mary or John could speak more clearly!' (Teachers of the deaf frequently say this too.) Parents should appreciate that teaching speech to deaf children is a fascinating but very slow process, i.e. one should not expect quick results. They should also remember that, as suggested earlier, good speaking is something like good piano playing; the more one practises, the better one becomes. With these two facts well in mind, there is quite a lot they can do to help.

The biggest and most important contribution is in their whole approach to the question of clear speaking. They should always be *positive*. Encouragement is much better than continually criticizing things that are wrong. An occasional 'sally-up' often does some good, but continual nagging is not only embarrassing and depressing for the child, but can have the opposite effect of making him not want to speak at all. Years ago a landlady said to me: 'By Jove! you are neat when you do your washing. The student I had before you came used to have the floor of the laundry awash every Saturday morning.' This landlady, whether she knew it or not, was a good psychologist. There-after I took particular care that there was never a drop of water on the floor. It seems to be just the same with deaf children's speech. If one day, out of the blue, father says with obvious pleasure on his face: 'That was lovely. You said "school" beautifully. I heard you say "school" and it sounded just the same as if Mummy said it. That was lovely speech' (he might also go and write it in the home/school notebook), it is likely that the child will go off happily thinking to himself: 'I can say "school". Daddy says I say it beautifully – school, school, school.' Aunts and uncles who know the child well or a friend can all help in this way.

Another good thing to encourage is *nice voice*. Often the children speak with a fairly wooden quality or a very tight constricted type of speech. Occasionally the same children, perhaps when they are laughing or crying and sometimes without thinking, will say a word or sentence with perfect or almost perfect quality. Be quick to say to them on these occasions: 'That was a lovely voice' so that they will try to repeat it on other occasions.

Parents should be careful to practise any material written in the home/school notebook about speech. Teachers should only write things in this book that the child is able to say really well. The teacher should be informed, too, of course, of any successes in speaking which children have at home.

The little period of reading aloud to a parent at night is good for speech development. As the child gets older the parents can say to him: 'Read a sentence from that page and I shall find it for you.' This is a good way to make him speak as carefully as he possibly can. Card games like 'Happy Families' are also very good for this. Bingo is a game which helps deaf children to learn to say numbers clearly. Talking to Daddy on the telephone can be another good little game. Mother could make up a list of phrases and Father could write them down and bring them home with him. This could be played with a neighbour of course just as well.

Mixing with children and adults who hear normally is one of the best ways of improving a deaf child's speech. The family gets used to his speech and when he says perhaps: '*ayvee – ar*' they know that he is saying: 'David – car.' A stranger of course does not know this and the child must concentrate to say the words as clearly as he can.

Finally, a great help to the child's speech is to make use of whatever hearing he has. Hearing aids should be worn full time and parents should encourage the child to *listen* to them when they speak and give him practice in trying to identify words and sentences without watching. The listening-reading-speaking method described in Chapter 7 can be most helpful.

Speech therapy

Is there any point in parents sending their children to a speech therapist after school two or three afternoons a week? This depends on several things. Is there a good speech therapist available? Does the class teacher or the school approve of speech therapists taking deaf children like this? (Some teachers prefer not to have any outsiders handling the child.) It is always a good idea for the teacher of the deaf and the speech therapist to get together and discuss the child's problems, and work out a common policy if it is decided to give extra help. Sometimes the best person to do this work is a retired teacher of the deaf who has been a successful teacher of speech throughout his or her career. Again, parents should be sure that what they are doing is not cutting across what the teachers are doing at school. They should be sure, too, that transporting the child to and fro is not making him so tired that it is affecting the rest of his work. Quite a good idea is to take the child to speech therapy for a short period, perhaps three times a week if possible for six weeks. (Incidentally, this is quite a good idea for adult deaf people too.) It is then in the nature of a sort of refresher course, a 'booster' which can make the child interested again in good speech, can make the parents' and teacher's task easier, and does not go on year in year out as though there is no end to it. It is short and intensive and often does a lot of good. It is only under exceptional circumstances that a child should be taken from a class for deaf children to be given speech therapy and if the child is attending an ordinary school on his own one should think twice about having him go to speech therapy during school time. Other school subjects should not be jeopardized by having the child miss periods two or three times during the week unless it is arranged when the work missed does not matter very much.

PERSONAL AND SOCIAL DEVELOPMENT

Parents should try to make sure that their child has a chance to join clubs and church and social groups. The more things he can do with normally hearing children of his own age, the better it will be for him throughout his life. If he is going to join the local Scout group the parent should go down and see the scoutmaster first and talk over the case with him. When the boy first attends, one parent should go with him and if possible have a word with the other children there. They might say something like this to them: 'I want to thank Mr So-and-So (the scoutmaster) for letting me enrol my boy with you. John is deaf so unless he is looking at you he can't tell that you are talking. Because he is deaf, his speech isn't as clear as yours either, but you can help him a lot if you will talk to him carefully and try to make him talk carefully to you. I'll show you how I talk to John and that will give you an idea of how you can talk to him too.' The parent may then proceed to have a little conversation with the child which has already been rehearsed with him at home: 'John, would you tell the boys how old you are? How do you go to school in the mornings?' and 'Do you want to be a Cub or Scout?'

Religious education

When people are in situations where they feel they are unable to cope, they frequently resort to prayer. There are going to be numerous occasions when a deaf person's inability to understand what people are saying to him, or his difficulty in making himself understood, or his difficulty in establishing close friendships with normally hearing people, will cause him to become discouraged. Even for this reason alone, parents and teachers have a responsibility to let deaf children know that many very intelligent people do go to church regularly and pray at least once each day and that they feel it helps them very much.

The basic principles of teaching that one must proceed from known material to unknown, from the concrete situation to the abstract, and that the experience must precede the language, all apply in full measure to religious instruction. The sensible thing seems to be to tell the children the Bible stories as interestingly and graphically as possible, using plenty of apparatus, flannelgraphs, pictures, and perhaps some elementary costuming so that the stories can be acted out, and then to apply the point being made to happenings within the children's everyday lives. After giving the children an example or two, they should be encouraged to suggest others. In this way, it is hoped they will absorb the full meaning of the parable or story and then will perhaps try to live their lives accordingly.

Sex education

Giving sex instruction to deaf boys and girls is not really any more difficult than giving it to normally hearing children. One should not avoid it and, in fact, there is a great deal to be said for parents and teachers bringing up the subject, when the right occasions occur. It should be remembered that the more matter-of-fact one is in one's own attitude, the more matter-of-fact the child will be in his or hers. In some respects, deaf children often seem to be better adjusted and to have a more wholesome attitude to the question of sex than a number of normally hearing children. The latter group's introduction to the subject, for example, may have been in some whispered, giggling sessions of 'smutty' talk and 'secrets'. Deaf children are usually spared this.

With little children the observations of pets and animals is often a good introduction to the topic of reproduction. Seeing a chicken peck his way out of an egg is a fascinating sight for any child. Seeing a cat just before she has a litter of kittens can also provide an excellent talking point: 'See the cat's fat tummy. Soon she will have babies called kittens. The kittens are inside.'

Many children from farms seem to have a very simple and uncomplicated acceptance of the subject of reproduction in animals and, in consequence, in humans as well.

The subject of a teenager's approach to sex is not, however, so simple. Certainly, just showing them films on human reproduction is not enough. They require help about dating, petting and boy-girl relationships. For example, they may be told that, generally, hugging and kissing are acceptable, but further experimentation is not advised. Masturbation should be discussed and they should be told that in moderation it is nothing to worry about. It is very important to make these facts clear to the children and they then seem to accept them quite cheerfully.

All the other factors, such as plenty of physical exercise, a variety of hobbies and interests, apply in full measure when helping deaf children at this time.

There is no doubt that much more could and should be done in all countries to give more assistance to young deaf people in marriage guidance, genetic counselling and so on. Like so many aspects of work in the field of deafness, there is a tremendous amount still to do.

DISCIPLINE AT HOME AND IN THE HOSTEL

Many of the points mentioned in Chapter 2 for controlling pre-school deaf children apply equally to older ones. Perhaps the most important single factor is the degree of understanding which exists between the parent or supervisor and the child. As suggested earlier, if one likes a person, one also likes to please him rather than cause him distress.

Where little *rapport* exists some of the following suggestions might be considered to improve the relationship.

In the case of supervisors who have just taken up work in a school or hostel, especially where there have previously been numerous changes of staff, a certain amount of antagonism can be expected on the part of the children. There is a tendency for children to 'rag' a new member of staff or a new child in most schools – it possibly stems from a feeling of insecurity while the children get to know the new-comer. It seems a fairly natural reaction on their part, and one must just try to be patient, prepare one's work carefully, present as cheerful an appearance as possible, and have faith that things will right themselves in a week or two. A warm introduction to the group and continued tactful assistance from senior staff can be invaluable during this initial period. Getting to know one or two of the less deaf children in the group and the leaders, as quickly as possible, can be a great help also.

Parents or supervisors who are having control problems should first of all look to themselves to ensure that they are not doing something which irritates or in some way causes the children to be apprehensive or antagonistic. Am I firm but gentle in my management of the child or children? Am I able to do some of the things that children enjoy, e.g. catch a ball (this one skill, for example, can be a tremendous help), take an interest in sport of all kinds, and in hobbies? Do I cater for the children's interests although not necessarily taking part in them? e.g. help them get started to make a house in a tree; put up a swing for them; move the car so that they can roller skate or play hopscotch in the garage on a wet day, etc.? Am I generally cheerful and ready to have a laugh over things? Am I neat and attractive in my appearance? Do I praise the child sufficiently when praise is due? Do I tease the child a little but not too much? (Teenagers particularly do not like too much teasing.) In short, do I observe the child's interests while he or she is with me and think about him often when he is not present?

For educational, developmental, economic and social reasons, as well as disciplinary ones, deaf children should be kept busy. Many of the 'misdemeanours' of these children are simply an indication of ennui. Keeping the child informed of what one is speaking about to other normally hearing people is another way of educating them, as well as keeping them from feeling left out, and therefore doing something which will attract attention and thus appearing 'naughty'. It does not have to be a lengthy explanation – a phrase or two at a time is usually sufficient.

If all the above factors are reasonably well provided, then one should consider the child himself. Is he receiving adequate rest and exercise, and a wholesome diet? What playmates has he? Is their influence for good or otherwise? Occasionally a strong and wayward group leader can cause an otherwise well adjusted child temporarily to behave in a manner which appears quite foreign to him.

Emotional outbursts (or 'temper tantrums'), usually of short duration, occur in most children from time to time. In normally hearing children, these usually disappear after the fourth year, but they can persist until the child is much older. Some children have many more than others and, when they are frequent and violent, this can be very distressing to all concerned. Good management can reduce their incidence markedly. There seems to be no one 'formula' for treating these upsets, but the following suggestions have been found helpful with deaf children in a number of cases. After the initial outburst it is usually advisable to move in quickly and restrain the child. They sometimes can frighten themselves if allowed to 'flail' about with arms and legs for any length of time and a minor tantrum can then become a major one. Removal from the room (or street or bus stop!) as soon as possible is usually wise. It is important that one's disapproval of that type of behaviour be registered with the child at the time, but that an attempt to reason with him should *not* be made until a later date. When he is quiet and relaxed, perhaps the following afternoon, one can say to him: 'Do you remember yesterday when you behaved like a baby? Well, what was the matter?' Sometimes the child will look sheepish and might say: 'I bad' or 'I silly' but at other times they may not wish to communicate at all. Sometimes there is a really valid reason for their behaviour but children, of course, do find that sometimes a tantrum, or even the threat of one, enables them to do fairly much as they please. If there appears to be a genuine reason for the child not wanting to do something, e.g. not go to a neighbour's house because the children there teased him last time, one must try to find out what the reason was. One can then, of course, sympathize with him for not doing as he was asked, but it must also be made clear that the way to express his distaste for your suggestion is not to have a tantrum. One can say to him that all that screaming and fighting is for two-and three-year-olds, that eight-year-olds *talk* and tell people what is the matter. One could give examples of other occasions when the child has given way to outbursts of temper and tell him: 'Next time you behave like that (show him if he is not a good lipreader), you will not be allowed to watch television' or 'You will miss your weekly comic' or some other little privilege. Say: 'This time it is all right and it is finished with, but *next* time you will have no television, etc., because you must learn to grow up.' It is absolutely vital of course, that one does deprive him of the privilege after the next upset. It is important that when the tantrum has subsided, it does not mean that all is well and that one is 'back to normal'. It is necessary that some reference should be made to it and some thought given to it when the child is in a more receptive mental state.

A good way of avoiding difficulties, is to *anticipate* them. For example, a supervisor might say to his or her group, when going out: 'When you are in the bus you must keep your feet off the seats, and not put your hands out of the window. When we get to the beach I want you all to stay together until we have had lunch. After lunch we can go for a long walk and the boys can fish.' Supervisors should try to select three or four of the most important things which might cause difficulty, and mention them – along with some of the nice things that are going to happen as well, of course. This tends to quieten the children down and they show more restraint than if they are allowed to go on without any forewarning of things that might happen.

Parents, too, should anticipate difficulties. 'When we get to Auntie Betty's, don't you go racing round the garden and jumping over the rose bushes as you did last time. (Draw the scene if necessary.) You can do this and that, etc. – but *no* jumping over those roses.' It has been found that when such precautions are taken, children do behave better when they are out.

Supervisors, too, can frequently keep better control of a group of children by the judicious use of pencil and paper. The children are told before they go out that good behaviour is expected and that if anyone is silly, his or her name will be written on the piece of paper. (The written word seems to impress deaf children rather more than does the spoken.) When the group returns home, it is important that any whose names were written down should again be deprived of some privilege.

Sending children to bed early is often quite effective, but it usually needs only to be five minutes earlier than usual to have the desired effect. When children are sent to bed half an hour early in the hostel, it can, of course, lead to further misbehaviour if they are unsupervised.

Teenaged deaf children require different management from younger ones, and many of their difficulties result from faulty handling by parents or supervisors who do not realize this. Generally, it seems that they should be treated as far as possible as adults – although, of course, there are frequently times when their behaviour reverts to that of little children again. Gradually these lapses become less frequent. They are usually very sensitive emotionally at this time and can, in consequence, be delightful to talk with on moral and ethical subjects such as kindness, loyalty, patience, love and hate, altruism, justice, jealousy, and so on. This emotional condition also makes them behave in fairly irrational ways at times, however, and sudden displays of temper as well as outbursts of laughing and crying are not uncommon. To help maintain the child in a state of 'equilibrium', the following techniques have been found effective:

The satisfying discussions mentioned above frequently seem to have a beneficial effect on the child's over-all behaviour.

Despite appearing self-possessed and confident, adolescents are often quite insecure and require plenty of praise and admiration. Such

Plate 1 Simple card games give the deaf child a chance to do well (p. 31)

Plate 2 Set aside a part of each day for his father to play with him (p. 28)

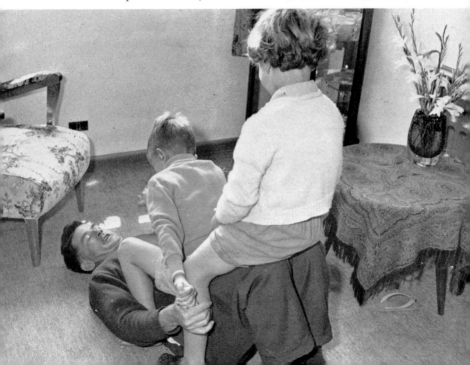

Plate 3 Flowers help in
language development (p. 52)

Plate 4 Learning to lip read (and read) in the kitchen (p. 46)

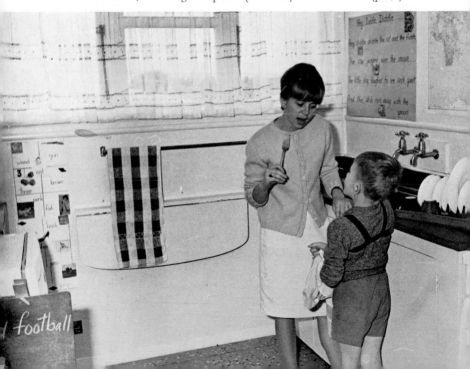

commendation should be sincerely meant, however. There is no place for flattery, but instead of just *thinking* the little praiseworthy things, one should make a point of saying them. For example, an adolescent boy can be told how tall he is growing or how strong, how thoughtful he was for doing this or that, how smart his clothes are, how good he is at some aspect of sport or a hobby or some subject at school. Girls can be complimented on their dress, their hair, their speech, their choice of colours, their taste in art or decorating – in fact, all the little feminine things about which they are particularly concerned at this age.

But, of course, the children are not always good. What can be done when they revert to some childish behaviour which could do some mischief to themselves or to some other person's property? For example, boys wrestling in the drawing-room obviously must be stopped, but often stopping them is sufficient punishment. They feel rather stupid for their behaviour and just to frown or to say (more in sorrow than in anger!): 'Don't do that sort of thing, boys' is quite enough at the time.

For other types of misdemeanour, a different technique is required. Suppose a water fight has developed in the bathroom and, on the arrival of the housemaster, the floor is awash, a wash basin cracked and emotions running high. It is well to act quickly and firmly – telling them that this is silly behaviour (which they already are beginning to appreciate) and that they must clean the whole place up and that the housemaster will be back in half an hour when every spot of water must be mopped up, etc., and that he will speak to them about it in the morning. With these words, one is better to leave adolescent children to themselves. Standing over them while they tidy up, which is often necessary with younger children, can be very embarrassing to these elder ones and can create more difficulties than it solves.

One of the major causes of friction between deaf adolescents and those who are responsible for their care is that the adult 'nags' or continually draws attention to minor misdeeds. This can be irksome to anyone, child or adult, but is particularly so for the hypersensitive adolescent. It seems much better to ignore trivial things completely, but to note the more serious lapses and then, after four or five have

F

occurred, to say to him privately: 'Look, John, I think it is about time you grew up a bit. Last week you pushed those two little boys in the swimming-pool, on Saturday you went out without letting me know where you had gone or when you would be back. On Sunday you spoilt the lawn broadsiding your bike all over it and didn't stop when you were told and now . . .' Often the child will accept this and say he is sorry, but he may even still appear resentful. In this case, it is better to walk away and leave him. He will probably feel rebellious for a time, but usually the message will have been received and understood and he will later make an effort to improve. These children often feel that they have 'lost face' if they appear to accept criticism meekly, no matter how justified the criticism may be. For this reason, it is particularly unwise to correct adolescents in front of other people.

Suggested dictionaries for children

A First Dictionary (1951) Nisbet
Thorndike First Dictionary (1964)   ⎫ University of London
Thorndike Junior Illustrated Dictionary (1959) ⎭   Press Ltd

Suggestions for further reading

Religious education:
Lee, R. S. (1965) *Your Growing Child and Religion* Penguin

Sex education
Baines, K. C. (1958) *He and She* Darwen Finlayson
Bibby, C. (1946) *Sex Education* Macmillan
Church Information Office (1964) Sex Education in Schools
Heron, A. ed. (1964) *Towards a Quaker View of Sex* Friends' House, Euston Road, London, W.C.1
Richards, M. (1963) *Design for Living – Girls, Design for Living – Boys,* Blackwell
The following titles are suitable for use with younger children:
Griffith, E. F. (1948) *The Truth About the Stork* H. K. Lewis
Hegelen, S. (1957) *Peter and Caroline* Tavistock Publications
Spock, B. (1957) *Baby and Child Care* Pocket Books, New York
Tame, H. W. (1960) *Peter and Pamela Grow Up* Darwen Finlayson

When doctors and otologists require an accurate assessment of a child's hearing, they should have access to an audiology clinic or centre. Such clinics are often under the control of the Department of Health and have an otologist as the director. This is the case in most parts of Britain, in New Zealand and Japan, and in some clinics in the U.S.A. Throughout Australia and elsewhere in the United States, however, an audiologist (i.e. an experienced educational psychologist with additional post-graduate training in audiology) is placed in charge of the clinic and otologists come in on two or three days each week to examine children.

Irrespective of who directs these centres, the following workers should be available as required: an audiologist, an otologist, a paedo-neurologist, a specialist teacher of the deaf, a speech therapist, two audio-metricians, a hearing aid technician and the school medical officer.

Audiology clinics should really be the focal point for hearing assessment in an area. The administration of screening tests to pre-school children and of pure-tone audiometric screening tests to school-aged children becomes their responsibility. So, too, do short training courses for, and supervision of, audiometricians and hearing aid clinic technicians. Again, the central training officer should be the educational psychologist with post-graduate qualifications in audiology – who probably has a background in teaching anyway.

Although a teacher of the deaf is a very important member of the audiology clinic team, it is not generally desirable for such clinics to be attached to schools for deaf children, since only a handful of the cases seen there will require education in the deaf school. Anxieties can be set up unnecessarily in parents of children with minimal hearing losses who are referred to an audiology centre which is located at a school for deaf children.

EDUCATIONAL FACILITIES

In most countries where the education of deaf children is being tackled seriously, two services are developing in addition to the schools for deaf children. One is the establishment of classes in ordinary schools for both deaf and partially hearing children and the other is the specialist visiting (or 'peripatetic') teacher service which helps parents of pre-school deaf children and those children who wear hearing aids but are able to attend ordinary schools without daily specialist help. Where the three services operate independently of one another, it is very easy for difficulties to occur within and between them. These are some of the problems which may be observed in most areas where such diffused administration of services exist:

More and more severely deaf children are attending classes for the so-called 'partially hearing' in ordinary schools. This fact reduces the enrolments of the schools for the deaf. In some cases the salaries of the head teachers have fallen as a result.

There is a tendency for an increasing proportion of the children in the schools for the deaf to be dually or multiply handicapped. A figure often quoted by headmasters in Britain and the u.s.a. is that one-third of their children have one or more handicaps in addition to their deafness. This makes results more and more difficult to achieve.

Within the deaf schools, there is a tendency among some teachers to feel that their schools are obsolete and unit classes in ordinary schools are more 'modern' and 'socially acceptable'. This feeling is shared by a number of teachers in units, in the visiting teacher services and by many of the medical profession.

There are difficulties in a number of the units in ordinary schools (a) because of incorrect siting, (b) through incorrect placement of children in them – e.g. too wide an age and ability range and occasionally the inclusion of socially and emotionally maladjusted deaf children – but also (c) by inadequate staffing and (d) too little supervision and guidance being given to inexperienced teachers.

A number of young, inexperienced teachers of the deaf have been employed as specialist visiting teachers and thereby been asked to accept

much more responsibility than their experience warrants. The consequent errors made in counselling parents and recommending school
placements, etc., have occasionally brought this very important service
into disrepute.

*If schools for deaf children, units in ordinary schools, and visiting teacher
services are co-ordinated on a regional basis, the following advantages have
been found:*

1 All the abilities, experience and skills available in a certain area
may be drawn upon at any time – they represent a form of team
teaching.

2 Children can be offered a variety of educational placements and
placements can be made with much greater accuracy.

3 A promotion scheme for teachers within the service as a whole
can be established which offers numerous graded and interesting steps
of advancement. In time this ensures that senior officers have had wide
experience in the field and are thus well qualified to administer this
more varied service. The promotion scheme might run, for example,
from class teacher in a school for deaf children, to a teacher in a unit
class, to senior teacher in the unit, to specialist visiting teacher, to deputy
headmaster or headmistress, to headmaster or headmistress.

4 Attaching teachers in the units, and visiting teachers, to the staffs of
the schools for the deaf lets a great deal of light into the schools when
supervising the work of unit and peripatetic teachers. These teachers
also come into the schools for the deaf regularly to staff meetings, for
professional courses, for equipment, and on social occasions.

5 Not only the salaries, but also the self-respect and the enthusiasm
of head teachers and other teachers in schools for deaf children are
maintained.

*Administrators cannot be urged too strongly to consider this type of regional
provision most seriously.*

The school for the deaf (or for 'children with language disorders'
as some American educators feel it may ultimately be called) is now
envisaged as a *centre* where in addition to catering for a nucleus of
boarding- and day-school children, new teachers will be trained and
guided, where teachers in units and specialist visiting teachers will

receive supervision, encouragement and stimulation, where information regarding the educational treatment of deafness can be assembled and sent out, where research can be conducted, and experimentation in improving teaching techniques can take place, and where all deaf people will always find understanding, respect and kindness. In short, the school for the deaf becomes the mainspring of the educational services for the deaf children in an area. This, of course, has been the aim of many schools for deaf children over the years, but the regional organization outlined here represents a tangible way of making this ideal a reality.

No two regions can be organized identically – density of population, the incidence of deafness, the staff and finance available, personalities of the various workers, and local boundaries are just some of the factors which influence the type of facilities which can develop. From my own experience in New Zealand, and from observations in Britain, Australia and the United States, however, I have drawn up what I believe could represent a satisfactory and flexible service for many regions. (See opposite.)

Specialist visiting teachers of the deaf

Without doubt, one of the most valuable services for deaf children developed in recent years has been that involving the use of 'itinerant' teachers. In New Zealand, there are eight specialist visiting teachers – four attached to each school for the deaf and each has an area for which he or she is responsible. These visiting teachers are usually, but not always, recruited from the staffs of the deaf schools. In Britain a similar service operates under nearly all education authorities. The duties of British visiting or peripatetic teachers are almost identical with those outlined below, except that no assistance is given to children once they leave school and visits are not made to the homes of children attending schools or classes for the deaf and partially hearing.

The two main functions of specialist visiting teachers are to help parents in the home training of their pre-school deaf children and to assist children in ordinary schools who wear hearing aids. I believe all schools for the deaf should have specialist visiting teachers attached.

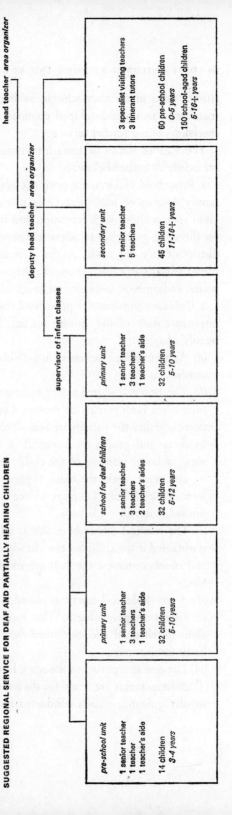

Figure 4

SUGGESTED REGIONAL SERVICE FOR DEAF AND PARTIALLY HEARING CHILDREN

head teacher *area organizer*

deputy head teacher *area organizer*

supervisor of infant classes

pre-school unit
1 senior teacher
1 teacher
1 teacher's aide

14 children
3-4 years

primary unit
1 senior teacher
3 teachers
1 teacher's aide

32 children
5-10 years

school for deaf children
1 senior teacher
3 teachers
2 teacher's aides

32 children
5-12 years

primary unit
1 senior teacher
3 teachers
1 teacher's aide

32 children
5-10 years

secondary unit
1 senior teacher
5 teachers

45 children
11-16+ years

3 specialist visiting teachers
3 itinerant tutors

60 pre-school children
0-5 years
150 school-aged children
5-16+ years

(Just as units in ordinary schools, as described later, would help tremendously in underdeveloped countries, so too would this type of specialist visiting teacher service.)

The various duties of specialist visiting teachers in New Zealand are briefly described below:

1 Pre-school children are normally referred to visiting teachers by family doctors or otologists. Only in exceptional circumstances is a child seen without such reference, and in such cases there is an onus on the visiting teacher to advise the medical officer of health for the district of any test made. As far as possible, testing is conducted in group sessions at a suitable centre. Diagnostic tests and, where appropriate, audiometric and speech tests are administered.

2 Guidance to parents of pre-school children is regarded as the most important duty of the visiting teacher. The following procedure is usually adopted:

(a) As accurate an assessment as possible of the child's hearing loss is obtained.

(b) The home is visited at the earliest opportunity, preferably at a time when both parents are present. On this visit the visiting teacher notes whether the parents are reasonably well adjusted to the child's handicap and gauges the potential of the home from the point of view of home training of the child. She demonstrates how to talk to, and work with, the child, suggests that the parents enrol with John Tracy Clinic Correspondence Course and leaves pertinent printed material.

(c) The medical officer of health is informed, an otological report is obtained if the child has not already been referred by an otologist and observations on the visit are recorded on the child's personal file.

(d) A psychological report is obtained from the local Department of Education psychologist. This report will provide information about intellectual and emotional factors and about aspects of the home environment.

(e) The case is reported to the school for deaf children.

(f) Arrangements are made for the mother to bring the child to the regular guidance session conducted by the visiting teacher. In the early stages of guidance these visits are frequent. Where necessary (usually in the areas remote from the visiting teachers' headquarters), the help of speech therapists or other suitable people is enlisted to supplement the work as part of the total guidance programme planned by the visiting teacher.

(*g*) Every severely or profoundly deaf child is seen by the visiting teacher at least twice each term even in the remotest areas, but of course in the cities they may be seen twice each week if necessary.

(*h*) Where three or more pre-schoolers can get to a kindergarten play centre, a teacher of the deaf is employed on a part-time basis. Generally, three-year-old children attend on three mornings each week and four-year-olds attend four mornings each week but there is nothing hard and fast about this. Lessons similar to that described in Chapter 7 are taken and a story is told to them in addition to the children engaging in constructive play and associating with normally hearing children.

3 When deaf children are enrolled at nursery schools or play centres, those in charge are regarded as substitute mothers and given similar guidance by the visiting teacher.

4 Visiting teachers assist children with defective hearing in ordinary schools but only children with hearing losses in excess of 25 db. in the better ear are the concern of these teachers. The handicap is assessed with special reference to (*a*) the *degree of hearing loss*, when pure-tone and speech tests are administered; (*b*) *educational attainment*, when reading(21), arithmetic(22) and speech ability is tested as explained in Chapter 10. Further relevant information is obtained from the head teacher and/or class teacher and from the child's record of progress and achievement card; (*c*) *intelligence*, when results of any standardized tests are noted and the teacher's rating of the child is also obtained. *Any other handicaps*, physical or environmental, are noted.

An assessment of the child's social adjustment is made. Appropriate guidance is given to those concerned with the deaf child. Visiting teachers help teachers and pupils to accept the deaf child by explaining some of his interests and abilities, and by demonstrating how to speak to him and involve him in activities. The home is visited if the case seems a sufficiently serious one, the medical officer of health is notified, or reported to, if he has referred the child, and the case is reported to the principal of the school for the deaf in the monthly report. Tutoring is arranged where necessary. (See below.)

5 Each term, the four visiting teachers of the deaf have a two-day conference at the school for deaf children. At this, new trends and developments within the school and within the field generally are made known to them and the areas of responsibility or functions of the visiting teachers are discussed in turn. In addition, the specialist teachers visit every classroom in the school and talk to the children from their particular areas – they also discuss progress and difficulties with the class teachers and are then able to talk to the parents more profitably next time they meet them. They are encouraged to bring snapshots, or a toy, or some other treasured possession from the child's home.

6 Children who have spent all or most of their earlier school life in a school for the deaf are in some cases transferred to their local secondary school at an appropriate age. It is a function of the visiting teacher to prepare the way for a transfer by providing the post-primary school with information about the child and his likely problems and needs. Appropriate advice is given to enable the staff and pupils of the post-primary school to make the most suitable arrangements for the education of the deaf pupil among hearing children. Regular visits are made while the child remains in the post-primary school. Correspondence school lessons in the verbal subjects are organized and help from an *itinerant tutor* is arranged as required.

7 It is an important function of the visiting teacher to help deaf school-leavers to adjust to working conditions and assist employers and fellow-workers to understand and communicate with them. It is usually easier for an 'outsider' to discuss a child's abilities and limitations with employers than it is for parents – although, of course, parents should maintain a real interest in the child's welfare when he starts work.

Visiting teachers are not able to help a great deal with the placement and general care of adult deaf people. Our experience with this group has been that there seems to be a 'hard core' of deaf people – about nine or ten of the four hundred in this area – who have a great deal of difficulty obtaining and keeping jobs. Finding work and accommodation for this group can be very time-consuming and it is becoming increasingly clear that a full-time welfare officer for adult deaf people is very necessary.

8 Wherever possible visiting teachers take opportunities to give information about the special problems of deaf children and adults and to enlist public support in projects for their welfare. Rotary Clubs, women's groups, Red Cross organizations, etc., usually appreciate talks very much.

9 Specialist visiting teachers can be a wonderful help in passing on useful information about the homes of the children. This is particularly true of the homes which are a long distance from the school and a visit by the class teacher is not possible.

It can be seen from the above that the nature of the work of a specialist visiting teacher can be both varied and complex. In addition to intelligence and experience, qualities of tact, integrity and understanding are called for. A twelve-week training course, both theoretical and practical, covering the above duties is necessary before specialist visiting teachers begin working, and continued support from senior staff is usually very much appreciated.

Itinerant teachers for individual tutoring

A second type of visiting teacher, here called an *itinerant tutor*, is required for children with hearing losses who attend ordinary schools and are sufficiently handicapped in their learning to require a limited amount of additional individual assistance. (If they are so handicapped that they require daily help, then they should be enrolled in a unit in an ordinary school – as described later.)

The itinerant tutor visits a certain school at a specific time each week and the hearing-impaired child comes from his classroom for a period of up to one hour. Hearing aids are checked, and an inquiry made about specific difficulties in the previous week's work. Work in speech and reading is given. (Ability in reading, of course, assists all subjects.) As far as possible, other subjects such as mathematics, history and geography, science, botany, etc., are briefly checked. The extent to which the tutor is able to assist the child with such specific subjects depends largely on the cooperation gained from the class teacher.

Itinerant tutors report that they are well received in the school as soon as it is shown that the handicapped child's reading and general work improves.

Parental cooperation can, of course, be of critical importance, and the tutor must be careful to inform them of the work done each week, so that if the class teacher is unable to find time to assist the child, the parent often can.

For this work some of the best tutors seem to be able and experienced class teachers from ordinary schools who, either through retirement or family commitments, are unable to undertake full-time teaching. They need not, of course, be ex-teachers of deaf children, and they can be employed on an hourly basis. This work should most certainly *not* be undertaken by the specialist visiting teachers of the deaf – they are too valuable to be engaged on such straightforward assignments. They select cases for the tutor, and are responsible for the general oversight of these children, but weekly tutoring sessions are the work of a much less skilled person. Where peripatetic tutors are not available, some visiting teachers are undertaking a limited amount of this work but, ideally, they should not.

Assistance from teachers in ordinary schools

Most cases of hearing impairment in children are now detected by the audiometric screening tests, but not all are, and class teachers might suspect some degree of deafness in children exhibiting one or more of these characteristics:

1 Speech defects – particularly defective consonants like 's', 'sh', 't' and 'k'.

2 Behaviour problems and poor social adjustment.

3 Unusually low scores in dictation work.

4 Difficulties in oral mental arithmetic, but good results in written work.

5 Frequently misunderstanding or 'ignoring' instructions – e.g. continuing to write when the class is asked to stop.

6 Often seeking assistance from their neighbours.

7 Frequently having running ears or a cold.

8 Showing a reluctance to speak, e.g. nodding or shaking their heads rather than saying 'Yes' or 'No'.

9 Watching the speaker much more intently than other children do. Such children should sit at the front of the class, and if they have no hearing aid or for any reason are not wearing their aids, they should sit with their better ear to the teacher. In class they should be encouraged to turn round so as to see the face of a child who is speaking. They should also be allowed to turn round to lipread when the teacher is not in front of them.

Teachers and children are requested to talk to the handicapped child as often as possible, both in and out of school, without making it too obvious. When speaking to them one should face them and speak a little more slowly than usual, emphasizing important words. Abbreviated speech should be avoided such as: 'English – finished?' – i.e. one should speak naturally – 'Have you finished your English yet?'

These children should be encouraged to speak in sentences and phrases, not in single words. It is appreciated that teachers will not have a great deal of time in class to assist in this but it is important for them to do all they can.

If children have hearing aids they should wear them as comfortably and inconspicuously as possible all day long, except when engaged in boisterous physical activity, swimming, etc. Parents of these children should send them to school each day with hearing aids that are working. Occasionally, however, teachers are required to help in this respect. The specialist visiting teachers for the deaf children should be notified.

The more time that can be spent individually on these children the better it will be for them. This is very important and can often be the deciding factor in whether a child can remain in an ordinary school or will have to be given full-time special educational treatment.

Some teachers are prepared to give them a little time out of school hours, particularly for extra reading and language work; in secondary schools some teachers give up to ten minutes or more of a spare period to give individual coaching in school subjects and in general language and remedial work.

A friend (preferably a bright one!) who sits beside the hard-of-hearing child can be a tremendous help to him by explaining instructions or work which has not been fully understood. Sometimes this responsibility is given to the weekly monitor and the children quite enjoy taking their turn.

Deaf children should be given opportunities to be leaders.

Interest in music should be encouraged as even very deaf children are able to hear the melody of music and in practical and creative subjects – woodwork, physical education, art and craft, etc. – deaf children should hold their own well and if they can excel in any of these it is a big help psychologically.

If speech therapy is given, one should try to arrange it at a time when it will not interfere too much with the child's school work – out of school hours if possible.

Accommodation for deaf children

There is general agreement among teachers that deaf children's basic educational need is a *language* with which to communicate ideas. It is also recognized that the need for them to be helped to achieve adequate language development is more urgent than for any other group of children, except perhaps these who are both deaf and blind. Studies have shown, however, that faulty institutional care of handicapped children, even those with normal hearing, can seriously affect language growth(23, 24). The information presented in Figure 5, for example, shows very dramatically the influence on language development of good and poor residential facilities for children who are educationally subnormal.

Results such as these emphasize the tremendous responsibility placed on administrators to ensure that those deaf children who are required to live away from home receive the very best care that the community's resources can provide.

Compare, for example, the language opportunities afforded deaf children at meal-times in two schools visited recently by the writer. In the first, a deaf child sits at a table with five other deaf children and a teacher or supervisor who has been trained to speak carefully and encourage the children to do the same. In the second school, twenty

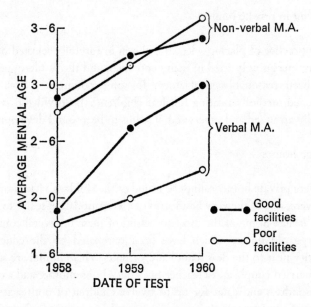

Figure 5 Intelligence test results of children in residential care

deaf children sit at a table (in a dining-room for no fewer than 280 deaf children), where the only people with normal hearing and speech are the waitresses who distribute the food to them (as quickly as possible). Similarly, in some schools, staff have groups of ten or twelve children to supervise – in others the groups may be as large as forty-five or even more.

Residential child care is a tremendously important aspect of special education and there is no doubt that it has received far too little attention in the past.

Some Departments of Education today are assisting parents of handicapped children by means of removal expenses and preferential housing allocations to move near to special educational facilities so that the children may live at home and attend school daily. In a large number of cases, however, it is impossible for parents to make such a move, and residential accommodation must then be provided.

Boarding in private homes

The practice of placing selected children in carefully selected homes is being increasingly tried in many countries, and the results appear to have been reasonably satisfactory. In some countries it is a well established method of caring for deaf children(25). Provided it is very carefully arranged and supervised, it seems to be a sound development.

Cottage homes

Where private homes cannot be found or the children's handicaps are too severe, one of the very best forms of accommodation seems to be in *cottage homes*. Some of the most successful of these in several countries are large old houses which have been purchased by the education authority near to the deaf school and/or units. These homes are staffed by a married couple and a teacher or deputy housemother and a cook-cum-laundress and cater for up to twelve children of both sexes and usually of varying ages. It is sometimes made a condition of admission that every child can get home (or to friends or relations) every weekend. This is felt to be extremely important if it can possibly be arranged. Apart from the value of the children getting home regularly, it is also much easier to obtain good staff when they can be assured that their weekends will be almost completely free.

Residential schools

At the present time, the most common form of accommodation for deaf and partially hearing who cannot live at home is in residential schools.

Three factors seem important in achieving the best possible hostel care of deaf children: the *physical conditions* must be stimulating, the *organization* must be effective and the *staff* must be able, knowledgeable, kind and energetic. The following is a description of how one school tried to meet some of these requirements:

Eighty children live in residence, and twenty of these go home at week-ends. By most boarding-school standards, there are excellent

Plate 5 Learning to be independent in the hostel (p. 104)

Plate 6 Pets
are most important (p. 97)

Plate 7 Specialist lessons in the deaf children's own room (p. 110)

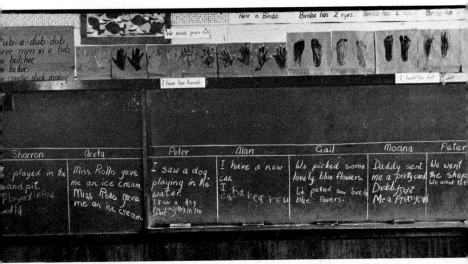

Plate 8 (*above*) Children copy teacher's writing (*Stage 1*) (p. 138)

Plate 9 (*below*) Writing news without copying (*Stage 3*) (p. 138)

facilities: very generous staffing (ten supervising staff and six teachers doing residential duty), interesting activities out of school which include gymnastics, fencing and dancing classes, television, hobbies evenings, sport of all kinds, Scout and Guide groups, films and filmstrips, a swimming-pool, indoor games and regular visits to places and events of interest. Pets for the children to play with and care for include a horse, a donkey, goats, geese, ducks, small birds, a dog and a number of fish. The parents have built a camp at a beach where up to twenty children go at week-ends. There is a homework period each night for children over the age of nine years, and every child has suitable reading material by his bed. Before the children go to sleep each night, someone has a word with them personally and writes a sentence or so in the home/ school notebook.

An effort is made to ensure that the sixty children who live all the term in the hostel are not cut off too much from normally hearing people. Sixty-five of the sixty-seven staff members have normal hearing and everyone – housemaids, cooks, gardeners, etc. – is encouraged to speak carefully to the children.

Middle and senior classes go out to the local schools for woodwork, metalwork, cooking, dressmaking and typing, rather than have such facilities set up in the deaf school. They also go out to the dentist and dental nurse.

Sports teams play home and away games with ordinary schools. Girls go out to Girls' Life Brigade (they won the shield for grooming and good manners last year), and all go out to Sunday schools each week. Some of the big boys have joined local rugby clubs. Local residents are also encouraged to take the children out for afternoons and sometimes week-ends with their own families. Rotary and Lions Clubs, local church groups, the local Young Jewish Society, the Maori Women's Welfare League and about fifty local residents have all helped in this way.

Local groups are encouraged to use the assembly hall and other facilities when they are not required by the children. The local fencing club meets there each week and the League of Mothers each month. A number of sports bodies have their annual meetings in the school. This helps local people to get to know the children and staff who in their turn have fresh faces to look at and different things to think about.

The hostel is a happy place – everyone is genuinely fond of the children, and in consequence a great deal of thought is given to each child's particular needs. Check lists such as the following help to direct the supervising staff's attention to the type of care required for the children:

Check list for supervisors (beginning of term)

1 Do I know the ages (birthdays) of all the children in my group?

2 Do I know the names and ages of the other children in each family?

3 Have I written to the children in the holidays?

4 Have I welcomed all members of my group back warmly?

5 Have I *listened* patiently and questioned them carefully on all they did at home?

6 Do I write in their notebooks every night?

7 Have I checked all the available equipment and noted any that needs replacing?

8 Have I looked in books for ideas of activities, games and hobbies for the children in my group?

9 Have I made my dormitories as attractive as possible?

10 Have I made my playroom as attractive as possible?

11 Do I use the blackboard in the dormitory for group reading practice and for explaining things to the children?

12 Have I planned my programme (*a*) roughly for the term; (*b*) carefully for the week; (*c*) meticulously for tomorrow?

13 Have I kept in mind that visits should be made frequently to places and events of interest?

14 Do I spend some of my time off each day preparing apparatus?

15 Do I ever visit places like the wharves, the museum, the railway station, etc., on my days off and think about taking the children there when the opportunity arises?

The recruitment, training, and retaining of suitable staff for hostels and cottage homes, for example, seems to be a vexed problem in most Western countries. There are numerous factors to consider. Siting of accommodation is important. If this is located in remote districts, the recruitment of any staff, let alone capable people, can be extremely difficult.

The broken hours which supervising staff are required to work are unsuitable for many people. Frequently they see a group of children up, breakfasted and made ready for school, and then are off duty until perhaps 3 p.m. when they come on duty again and their day ends at perhaps 8 or 9 p.m. In some schools it is even necessary for the staff to come on duty at lunch-time so that there are three periods of duty on most working days. At week-ends, when other people are relaxing, the housemasters and supervisors are busier than ever. It is not uncommon for them to work eight hours on Saturday and five on Sunday or vice versa. Sometimes they arrange between themselves to do a full thirteen- or fourteen-hour day on one day at the week-end so that they can have one completely free day, but the standard of the care given to the children towards the end of these long days cannot be the same as when the supervisor is properly rested. The hours to be worked are difficult at any time, but with poor time-tabling or inadequate staffing, conditions can become almost intolerable with a consequent drop in staff morale.

No supervisor should work more than forty-eight hours per week. When hours in excess of eight hours on any weekday and those after 12 noon on Saturdays are credited as time and a half, and Sundays at double time, this of course usually reduces the actual hours worked to something under forty. In some schools, however, supervisors are required to be on duty for over seventy hours per week and this is inexcusable. As anyone knows who has worked in a residential school, there are numerous calls on one's time throughout the school term which necessitate working longer hours than are officially time-tabled. Events such as sports days, parties, parents' days, fire practices, epidemics and staff sicknesses, make extra demands on the staff which nearly everyone shoulders willingly. It is important to the efficient running of the hostel, however, that at normal times staff do not work too much in excess of their hours.

There are also disadvantages in staff staying on duty when they should be off. They are not refreshed and so are less able to present themselves to the children in a buoyant and interesting manner. Sometimes the whole tempo of the work slows down whether they are on duty or not. While complaining about the excessive amount they find it necessary to do, they, at the same time, do not in fact work very hard at any time. A third factor is that if they stay about the hostel, children will often go to them rather than to the person officially on duty. Apart from the supervisor not knowing where members of her group are, this can also have an undermining effect on her authority. There is, as a result, a loss of the sense of responsibility so necessary in any supervisor and often a consequent loss of interest in the work as a whole.

There are so many ways in which an interested and thoughtful matron and headmaster can make the lives of housemasters and supervisors more pleasant and worth while. It should be remembered, as Tizard(24) has so well put it 'that slippers make less noise than shoes in a house; and that children get dirty out of doors and need frequent changes of suitable clothing – these things, so obvious, tend to be forgotten by administrators. Yet having to make do with an inadequate supply of clothing for the children can easily become the major preoccupation of an overworked housemother.' There is a tendency sometimes to regard these positions as unimportant: 'Anyone can look after kids' is the attitude of the less well informed administrators. In fact, of course, in addition to a natural affection for and ability to manage children, quite extensive knowledge is required if the best possible care and training is to be given to the children.

In one school each Tuesday morning a meeting is held of housemasters, supervisors, matron, sub-matrons, nurse, senior resident teacher and principal of the school. At these meetings the coming week's events are discussed; any new or interesting developments in the school or in the field of deafness generally are mentioned and current procedures are reviewed as necessary. Meetings usually last one hour. It was interesting that at these meetings to begin with, only the senior staff were inclined to speak, but after a time it became quite common for every person present to make some spontaneous comment.

The Home School Association pays fees for two staff members each year to attend a thirty-hour lecture course conducted by the Residential Child Care Association. Lectures are given one evening each week by specialists in child development, child psychology, institutional management, diet, physical education and religious instruction. Some of the staff were disinclined to attend but, when persuaded to do so, all have said that they were pleased they had gone. It is evident that this course has made the staff more thoughtful regarding the needs of children in particular and the school in general.

At the beginning of each term, a one-day course is usually held at which policy is discussed for the coming term and one or two outside lecturers such as art and craft and physical education specialists, inspectors of special schools, the local doctor, a parent of a deaf child, etc., are asked to talk.

From time to time, the Department of Child Welfare conducts national one-week courses for matrons and sub-matrons or housemasters. In Great Britain, the National Deaf Children's Society conducts annual courses in residential child care.

Supervisors of deaf children have two main functions: one is to give the children all the care and attention they need for their physical health and hygiene and to train them in habits of courtesy and kindness, etc.; the second is educational – to help them to use what hearing they have, to lipread and to speak. Frequently, supervisors are better at one aspect than the other and they should try to strengthen that side which is less effective.

Excellent opportunities for teaching exist outside the classroom and headmasters should appreciate this and give the supervisors guidance and encouragement to make the most of them. This is not always the case – one very capable class teacher in England who was also the headmistress of a residential school was asked why there were no examples of the children's art or craft or language work on the bare walls of the dormitories, and replied: 'Oh, the classroom is the place for that sort of thing.'

Not everyone – in fact very few people – are capable of keeping a group of very deaf, very lively five- and six-year-old children happily and busily engaged throughout, for example, the whole of a wet Sunday. These practical suggestions on physical, social and emotional care may prove helpful to other supervisors.

When I walk into the dormitory, I smile and wave to the children and say: 'Hello, everybody' and most of the children come and give

me a hug. I leave the children who are asleep until the last and take
their clothes over to them and give them a cuddle and sometimes tell
them to hurry up, but with a smile.

I let the children have some latitude in where they put things. Their
pyjamas may go under their pillows or in the drawers but they are
never permitted just to drop clothes or towels, etc., on the floor, even if
they are not able to fold them and put them away. Later on I teach them
not to drop their shoes anywhere and to change into their slippers.

The little ones especially like bright things. I have to watch what
they wear. Some of the children will put on as many clothes as they
can – singlet, blouse, dress and cardigan, even though the weather is
quite warm. It seems important to me that the children's likes and dislikes should be taken into account. Most of the little girls, for instance,
hate square-necked things because their underwear shows.

The supervisor's example is very important in teaching manners.
The children watch everything I do – whether I use a serviette or not –
even the way I wipe my mouth, or blow my nose.

On wet Saturdays and Sundays I spend quite a lot of time in preparation before going on duty and have plenty of crayons, books, glue,
needles, thread and newspapers on hand as well as their toys, and other
play apparatus. I carry a pair of sharp scissors in my belt or in a pocket.
Felt is very good for making animals and the children love cutting them
out and sewing them. They often draw a very strange shape, then say
it is a cat or duck and I let them make what they have drawn.

I think a supervisor must be ready for continual change – about
every half-hour. When they get bored, I make them sit on chairs and
I sit on a chair too for perhaps two or three minutes. Gradually they
get up one by one and go to another activity. Sometimes they pretend
they are in hospital, some go to school and pretend they are the
teacher, and one little boy last week even went off to work!

During the week, I take my group of twelve or sometimes fourteen
children on little outings whenever possible and I let them mix freely
with other people. One of our favourite walks is on the day they
have sixpence to spend. We go to a milk bar where I line them up in
two rows and they each have a turn at the counter. In this way they
do not annoy other people who are in the shop. It also lets other people
see that they are not different just because they are deaf. At this time I
teach them not to throw their lolly papers down in the shop or in the
street.

Another outing the little ones like is to private homes. I think it
reminds them of their own homes. They love to see the flowers and
perhaps be allowed to pick one for themselves. When we look in shop

windows, the children point out all sorts of things they are familiar with, and I show them the foods we eat at school and try to tell them that they have to be bought before we are able to eat them.

Our children's good behaviour is often demonstrated to me when escorting them home at the end of term. Even with a group of mixed ages, and after hours of travel by train when they must be tired, they never attempt to race up and down or show off, even though we see some children do this who are not deaf and are with their parents.

When the second factor, language, is neglected, deaf children can grow up very ignorant of basic everyday vocabulary. A class of eleven-year-old children, for example, were asked once how to make a bed (which they did beautifully each morning) but their equivalent of 'turn the mattress' was 'over the soft' and 'sheets' were referred to as 'whites'. They had been trained well in the art of bedmaking, but the language had been overlooked. As well as *talking* to the children about what they are doing each day, supervisors can help by revising much of this language in little lipreading games in the bedroom such as: 'Where is your sandal?' 'Show me Bill's handkerchief' 'Bring me John's slipper' 'Throw me your comb' and for more advanced children: 'Where is Peter's left gym shoe?' or 'Show me the largest of the three pictures on the back wall', etc.

These phrases and sentences can be printed on cardboard and used as flash cards at another time.

A handful of plastic counters or ticks on the dormitory blackboard under each child's initials is usually all the 'reward' required –and sometimes not even this. It is important that the activities are kept well within each child's comprehension to begin with, and gradually increased in difficulty. Parents, of course, can devise similar games at home.

Despite the pleasure which the work brings the staff and the fun the staff and children have together in residential schools, however, one cannot say that these children are receiving the best possible educational and social training to fit them for life in the hearing world. A good home is the best place for that.

Hostel children can, of course, be better off than some who live in homes which, for one reason or another, cannot be classified as 'good'. There are not many, but every teacher knows them. In some the children are neglected and grow up with little or no training; in others they are over-protected or spoilt to such a degree that they do not develop attractive personalities and can become selfish, lazy and unpleasant company for most of those they meet. Where the deaf child is the only child in a family and there are not good companions for him in the neighbourhood, the child can be very lonely and several adult deaf people have said that they much preferred boarding in the deaf school.

A short period of residence in the hostel has been found very beneficial for children, and there are quite a number, who have been somewhat over-indulged at home. Parents have noticed that the children are more appreciative of their homes after experiencing the more ordered routine of hostel living.

Everyone is convinced of the tremendous contribution which parents of deaf children can make. Teachers are encouraged to bring them actively into the work being done in school and so enable them to work as members of a team. *Parent guidance* should not be given only at the pre-school level. Teachers need regular counselling and encouragement and teachers need the parents' opinion and their encouragement throughout the child's school life. Chapter 4 gives an indication of some of the things parents can do to assist their school-aged deaf children.

It must be faced, however, that some parents seem not to have the ability or in some cases the facilities to give satisfactory educational assistance to their children at home. We all know of children who could 'make the grade' in an ordinary school, for example, if the parents would only encourage them to wear their hearing aids regularly and give them some assistance with school work at home. For some of these, we are considering the possibility of their boarding in boarding schools for normally hearing children.

6 Deaf Children in Ordinary Schools

Whenever possible a child with a hearing loss should, of course, go to his own local school for normally hearing children. In Great Britain 714 children in ordinary schools in 1958 had been issued with hearing aids. In 1965 the figure was over 5,000. Of all the children issued with hearing aids today, over half are able to attend ordinary schools, the only special assistance being visits from specialist visiting teachers – in some cases one each week but in others as infrequently as twice each term.

When deaf children require this daily special educational treatment, in seven or eight cases out of ten, units in ordinary schools (as described here) seem the best placement for them. It is important to remember that not *all* the children will profit from attendance in a group at an ordinary school. A few deaf children do not respond well to the large and exciting classrooms of today's ordinary schools. They seem bewildered by them and, even with their own teacher at hand, they are never completely at home in a large group. Almost one-third of the children at present enrolled in schools for the deaf have another handicap in addition to their hearing problem: they may be dull, brain-damaged, cerebrally palsied or psychologically maladjusted. Many of these children seem better catered for (for a time at least) in a school for deaf children where they receive complete acceptance from everyone and the groups are small. Some find it hard to make friends with ordinary children and often are very much happier and learn better when they are grouped together with other deaf children. The enthusiastic integrationist should remember that it is just as unkind to deny many deaf people the company of others who are deaf as it is to deny them the company of those who hear normally. The parents of an intelligent, very deaf girl had not allowed her to go to the Adult Deaf

Society in Auckland because they wanted her to mix only with normally hearing people. When someone finally persuaded them to let her go, she said on the way home: 'Tonight is the first time I've laughed for two years.'

The more successfully we teach them at home and at school, the fewer deaf people there should be who are ill at ease among the normally hearing, but as long as there is deafness there will always be such a group and they should be recognized, accepted and respected just like all other children and adults. The most recent trend, in many countries, is to try as far as possible to keep handicapped children in their own homes and to make special provision for them in ordinary schools rather than to segregate them. While it is appreciated that some handicapped children are best educated in special schools, in the field of education of the deaf far more children have been found able to be taught well in units in ordinary schools than was at first believed to be possible.

Myklebust(26) considered that a number of children who failed in ordinary schools could be successfully rehabilitated in those schools after being provided with a hearing aid and given a year or so of specialist training in a school for the deaf.

Harriet Montague, who ran the Correspondence Course at John Tracy Clinic for so many years, discussed the social adjustment of deaf and hearing children in an article in the *Volta Review*(27). The majority of parents had told her, she said, that pre-school deaf children 'got along well' with hearing children of their own age or a little older, but she considered the problem became more difficult the older the child grew. Teenagers did experience difficulty in adjusting to hearing groups but 'the problem is less in proportion to the amount of experience they have had associating with children who hear.'

This point of Miss Montague's appears to be of paramount importance. The integration must be regular and active for it to be of any great value. It is frequently observed, for example, that a deaf child's younger brother or sister often understands what he is saying even better than his mother does. This regular association is the great virtue of the classes for deaf children in ordinary schools which are being set up in New Zealand (described below). Working together in selected subjects like needlework or games is not sufficient. The hearing children do not learn to know the deaf group or vice versa, they do not feel at home with them; their friends are the friends they sit with in class for hours each day. In one of the units which we established, although the deaf children were spending three hours each day in the large room with the normally hearing ones, all the deaf children had been placed at one table so that the teacher of the deaf could speak to them all at once. This, of course, was not really 'integration' and the deaf children might almost as well have remained in their own room all day. It is best if the deaf group can be split up and each child placed between two who hear normally. If the normally hearing children are given this opportunity of spending a great deal of time in really close association with a deaf boy or girl, many of them learn (just as teachers, parents, brothers and sisters have learnt) that deaf children can be very interesting and lovable. The deaf children are accepted quite casually in these cases.

It must be emphasized, however, that if the child is very deaf and does not lipread really well, although he is accepted casually, there is nothing casual about a conversation with him. It usually requires effort on his part as well as on the part of the person to whom he is speaking. This is one of the fundamental problems of really deaf people, if not *the* fundamental one. It takes more effort to speak to them than to people who hear normally, and in consequence it is often difficult for them to make *close* friendships with normally hearing children. Close friends, of course, spend much time talking to one another.

This establishment of classes for deaf and partially hearing children in ordinary schools has become increasingly popular in most countries in recent years. In Britain, for example, there were twenty-four such classes for partially hearing children in January 1955 and 149 classes by January 1965. In the United States, Britain and Australia, where these units have been observed, the most common practice at the primary school level is to have the handicapped group taught in one classroom, and to integrate them with normally hearing children for certain periods during the week. Sometimes this is done by the class combining with another class for such subjects as physical education or handwork. Sometimes the teacher of the deaf accompanies her group but frequently she sends some of her class out while she works with the remainder. When this latter method is adopted, its success depends to a large extent on the attitude and personality of the teachers, and the encouragement and interest shown by the headmaster of the primary school, and even then the handicapped children must be particularly well behaved. It is not uncommon, for example, to hear the teachers of normally hearing children make statements such as: 'I have got forty-three of my own, and then every Tuesday and Thursday afternoon I get these three partially deaf ones foisted on to me – while Miss Jones "grapples" with the remaining four!'

It appears that the benefit which most of these children in units derive from lessons as taken in normally hearing classrooms is not as great as when they are taught by qualified teachers of the deaf, even in subjects like handwork. A Ministry of Education survey in 1962 of children transferred from special schools and special classes to ordinary classrooms, tends to confirm this.

At the Alexander Graham Bell School in Chicago, one-third of the 750 children attending have either sight or hearing defects (fifty and two hundred respectively). Sixty-five professional staff are engaged and of these two-thirds have specialist qualifications to deal with these two handicaps. This means, of course, that when deaf children go to an integrated class for, say, mathematics, the teacher of the whole group is likely to be a qualified teacher of the deaf. It is very clear that excellent work is done in the school and even many profoundly deaf children have been educated very happily there during the past thirty years.

It appears, however, that even with very skilled teachers normally hearing children and deaf ones at the primary school level cannot be satisfactorily taught many of the verbal subjects together by one teacher. The presentation is either too rapid for the deaf ones or too slow for those with normal hearing.

The New Zealand units appear to be the only ones where two teachers work in the one classroom for over half of each day and for that reason they are described in considerable detail.

THE NEW ZEALAND UNITS

A scheme for the teaching of deaf and partially hearing children in very close association with normally hearing ones has been given a fairly full trial. Beginning with a placement in 1960 of a class of deaf children and their teacher with a normal class and teacher, the experiment has been extended and fifteen similar classes have now been established in six primary and secondary schools in the North Island.

The usual pattern is for a small room to be built on to an existing classroom and a doorway made between the two (Figure 6).

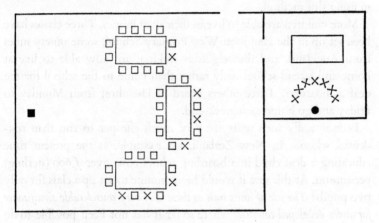

■ Teacher of children with normal hearing
● Teacher of deaf children
✕ Places for deaf children
☐ Places for children with normal hearing

Figure 6   Plan of classrooms for deaf and normally hearing children

To a class of not more than thirty normally hearing children a group of six or eight deaf children is added, together with a teacher of the deaf.

The deaf children spend roughly half the day with the hearing children and the two teachers work in the one room. For the 'activity' period (when children choose their own activities and then talk and read and write about them—see page 176), reading and number activities, printing, music, rhythmic work, art, physical education, nature study and class visits, the two groups are usually combined, the two teachers working mainly but not exclusively with their own group. At table work, the deaf children sit, as far as possible, between two hearing children though not necessarily performing the same tasks. (See page 176).

Subjects for which the deaf children need specialist help, e.g. speech, language, news sessions, story or, say, the teaching of a new process in arithmetic, are taken in the small room. (See page 97).

There are a number of educational, social and economic advantages in using this method.

More children are able to live in their own homes. Three classes have been set up in the Hamilton West Primary School, some ninety miles from Auckland, and thus eighteen children are now able to live at home and attend school daily rather than come to the school for the deaf as boarders. Three others board in Hamilton from Monday to Friday and go home each week-end.

Economically such units are very much cheaper to run than residential schools. In New Zealand, for example, at the present time educating a deaf child in a boarding school costs over £600 (sterling) per annum. At this rate it would be economic to set up a class for only two pupils! *The use of units such as these is of very considerable significance for under-developed countries* where so far it has not been possible to do very much about educating handicapped children.

There is a normalizing effect on the deaf children – socially they become more mature through observing the behaviour of hearing children of their own age. One class, for example, when taught at the school for the deaf, were still at the baby stage of pushing and quarrelling over who was to be first in line when going into school. They stopped doing this almost immediately after arriving at the ordinary school. The deaf children become more 'oral'. The temptation to use the hands in communication is reduced, and there is less gross facial movement when talking than usually occurs when deaf children are educated in isolation.

There is also a normalizing effect on the teacher of the deaf! She has

an excellent opportunity of observing daily the behaviour, the thoughts
and the language of normally hearing children. As teachers of the deaf,
we are sometimes criticized by outsiders because we are too insular –
our levels of aspiration are too low and so on. When her class of bright
eight-year-old very deaf children were first introduced to an ordinary
school, a teacher remarked: 'How far removed I've become from the
ordinary lessons – even in three years! Is our attitude to deaf children
too pleasant and over-anxious? Do we "baby" them too much? It
seems so when I look at the other children and the way the other
teachers speak to them.'

The teaching of language is easier because speech and language
seem so sensible when one has numerous opportunities to practise the
phrase or sentence with hearing people and find it working. When
the deaf children see the others speaking, reading and writing, they are
stimulated to do the same. Sometimes when both groups have been out
together to see something of interest, e.g. a bulldozer at work, they
return to the classroom to draw and write about the experience. From
the hearing children as many as thirty pages of interesting sentences are
pinned around the room. A wall story is built and makes excellent
reading material for both classes.

Making comparisons between themselves and normally hearing
children is considered to be one of the very real advantages of the deaf
unit and associate hearing class. The children have an opportunity to
adjust to their deafness about twenty times each day. They can learn, for
example, that although they cannot write as much as the hearing children, they can run as fast, they can draw perhaps better, they can build
more interesting things, they can do mechanical arithmetic just as
well, etc. This is life for a deaf person and it is better for them to learn
early what it is like to live in a hearing world with a handicap rather
than have to make a very big adjustment when they leave a special
school for the deaf.

A number of headmasters, doctors and parents have made the point
that it is good for those of us without a handicap to learn at first hand
about those who have one. One cannot imagine the hearing children
who are at present growing up with the deaf ones ever feeling afraid,
embarrassed or antagonistic towards a deaf person. This often does

occur as a result of ignorance, but these normally hearing children and all the teachers in those schools will accept deafness in people quite casually throughout their lives just as they are doing now.

Parents of the deaf children are usually very enthusiastic about units. They like the idea of having their children attend a normal school if it can possibly be arranged. Only one complaint has been received from parents about the educational or social progress of a child in a unit since the classes began. These parents were given the option of sending their boy back to the deaf school if they wished but after weighing everything up they have now decided to keep him in the unit class.

Teachers' reactions have been one of the most convincing factors in deciding to extend the scheme. At the outset, in nearly every case, both the teachers of the deaf and the teachers of the ordinary children have been somewhat apprehensive about attempting this form of teaching. Quite understandably, if one is teaching successfully in one situation, one does not take kindly to having a very different system thrust upon one. Without exception, however, the teachers have become convinced of its merits. They have had problems, of course, but they feel that the advantages far outweigh the disadvantages. Several of the teachers have said that they have enjoyed teaching in this atmosphere more than they have done when teaching alone in a room. It represents a sort of 'team teaching'(28) and this can be very stimulating.

When two teachers are required to work for over half of each day in the one room, it is imperative that they 'get along' together. It can be said that so far teachers of very different ages, personalities and teaching styles have been found to work well together and respect one another's abilities. There is always a possibility, however, that there will be a clash of personalities and this is one of the reasons why the teachers of the deaf have been retained on the staff of the deaf school.

ESTABLISHING UNITS

It is important that the deaf classes are introduced to ordinary primary and secondary schools as smoothly and pleasantly as possible. It goes without saying that the full cooperation of the education authority is obtained when a suitable school, as near as possible to the school for the deaf, is first considered, but an informal meeting between the head teachers of the two schools to discuss the scheme will be helpful *before* any formal approach is made through the education authority. Equally important are meetings with the parents and teachers of the deaf pupils to explain the scheme to them, meetings between the staffs of both schools with the head teachers and one or two senior members of staff of the school for the deaf available to answer questions, and meetings with parents of children in the associate hearing class where the head teachers of both schools might give a short talk, with a film, if a suitable one is available, followed by questions and discussion. It is important that these meetings between the various groups should take place within a day or so of each other, so that the people who will be directly concerned are all informed at approximately the same time, and are not disturbed by 'second-hand' versions of what is to happen.

Setting up isolated classes should normally be avoided. It frequently seems desirable to establish a class wherever a suitable group of deaf children exists. For several reasons, however, this has often proved unwise. If, for example, the group happened to be in a very small town, as sometimes occurs, it can be difficult to find a teacher of the deaf to serve there. If a teacher was appointed and then was ill or had suddenly to leave, a replacement might be extremely difficult to obtain; the parents of some of the children can move to another district and the drop in the class enrolment thus makes it impossible to justify the retention of a specialist teacher; additions to the class after a year or two can upset the grouping and make it extremely difficult to teach. Pressure is sometimes brought to bear to admit a child of widely differing age, and ability from the remainder of the class so that he or she will not have to go away from home. As suggested elsewhere,

H

however, much unnecessary difficulty can be caused to the teacher of the deaf if this happens and the whole group's education can suffer in consequence.

At least three classes in each school would seem to be sensible. This not only overcomes the isolation problem but it also enables a child to move right through the primary school; it creates a senior position for one teacher in three; it makes the supervision from the deaf school easier, and it enables much more team teaching to be done.

In every school where a group of deaf children is attached, the preliminary period of discussions with headmaster, parents, teachers and children, the films shown and the alterations made to class enrolments and the structural alterations to the classrooms all create a great deal of interest in the coming of the group of deaf children. When they finally arrive, they are usually besieged by kindly, curious children who want to 'talk' to them, show them round the school and to play with them. This intense interest is found to die down quite soon, however, and the deaf children are then treated much more normally.

Indications of this initial interest are evident in statements and questions such as the following:

'Even when Graham (65 db.) looks at me he doesn't know what I'm saying. What shall I do?' (nine-year-old boy)

'That's one of the deaf girls, but she can play all right. You watch.' (nine-year-old girl)

The hearing aids, being the only outward sign that the deaf children are different, always attract attention in the early stages, e.g.

'Can I try his hearing aid? . . . No wonder he can't talk if that's what he hears. I'm glad I don't have to wear one of those things.'

'You know that box thing and the things you put on the deaf kids' ears? I want to try. Can I have a go? I'm a bit scared, though. What's it like? Is it very awful?' (nine-year-old boy)

Interest in the unit programme shown by the staff in the ordinary school should be fostered. It can be great or it can be negligible, depending on the attitude of the headmaster, the personality and ability of the teachers of the deaf children and their attitude to the running of the school as a whole and, to a certain extent, by the interest shown in the project by inspectors of schools, medical officers, etc., and, of course, the senior staff of the school for the deaf if they are supervising the scheme.

After six weeks one nine-year-old girl said: 'It's better when you see how deaf children talk, isn't it? I was kind of scared of them before, but I'm not now – not any more. It's good fun.' Another nine-year-old boy said: 'I see now how you talk to deaf kids. You go slow and wait all the time to see if they know.'

Statements such as the two above indicate, of course, a growing awareness of the problems of deaf children and it cannot be emphasized too strongly that this understanding and acceptance comes about primarily as a result of *close* association. As suggested earlier, simply placing a class of deaf children in an ordinary school and allowing them to mix with a normally hearing class for one or two periods each week is not sufficient. This is the most common practice in Britain and the u.s.a. A recent survey of facilities for deaf children in the u.s.a. by the Department of Health, Education and Welfare reported that 'integration was more imaginary than real' and that although they sat in the same halls at lunch time and so on there appeared to be a glass wall between the two groups of children. Other comments which indicate the growth of a warm relationship between many of the ordinary and the deaf children in the New Zealand type units include:

'Robert, Meina and Graham can lipread me now. I'm going to try Lucy next but it is hard for her. She won't watch. I don't think she wants to. I wonder why?' (eight-year-old girl)

'Yes, I'll help Lesley if she gets stuck with her arithmetic. Ochi can sit on the other side and we'll both help.' (nine-year-old boy)

'I play with Richard (100 db.) at school. He is my friend. He came to stay with me and now I know him.'

'I like Richard because he laughs and is full of fun.'

'Is Ellen at school today? Thank goodness! She is our pitcher (in the softball team) and she hits sloggers as well. We wouldn't win without Ellen.'

After two years' association with a group of severely and profoundly deaf children, the children in the associate class were asked in a written questionnaire whether they liked the deaf children, and all except two replied that they did. These two gave as their reason that they could not understand them or be understood.

Of the others, eight said that they liked teaching deaf children and/or talking to them, two said they were good to play with. One said they were friendly, another that they were kind and a third that they were 'not nosey'.

This question was also put: 'What is the worst thing about the deaf children?' It is interesting that only five had any real objection. Of these, three mentioned their fighting, another said: 'They tell lies and cheat' and the fifth said that they could not understand when he spoke to them. One girl replied: 'They don't like you at first'; another: 'There's nothing wrong with them' and a third: 'They are just like us.'

Teachers of the associate classes should have an introductory course of instruction which includes observing a unit in operation and at a school for deaf pupils, lectures and discussions on language development, speech improvement, elementary audiology and the psychology of deafness with demonstrations and discussions on how to encourage speaking between normally hearing and deaf children.

It is the responsibility of the associate teacher to prepare the class programme with its centres of interest, etc., and the teacher of the deaf will cooperate in this. When deaf children are to be catered for, an *active* programme with plenty of outside interest is particularly important. This will include visits outside school and receiving visitors in the classroom with plenty of language work based on such activities.

Teachers of the deaf and the associate teachers should visit the school for deaf children at least once a year on a weekday to observe new methods, to compare syllabuses and children's progress with other teachers and to see new filmstrips, books and pictures and other teaching aids.

One of the most important duties of the associate teacher is to help the hearing children understand something of the difficulties which the deaf children have to cope with. In 'the deaf game' for example, the hearing children have to lipread as the teacher will give commands by moving her lips but using no sound of voice. She might say: 'Go to the corner, Jane', and Jane has to understand and obey exactly as a deaf child would. 'Mary can't hear anything so you have to help her' is an obvious way of approaching the problem but what is also important is to show appreciation of the deaf children's efforts to speak in front of the hearing ones: 'We can understand John quite well now, can't we?' Hearing children should be shown a hearing aid and how it works, and what to do if there is acoustic feedback.

If the deaf children want to attempt the hearing ones' work, they should be allowed to do so, even if this is sometimes beyond them from the point of view of language. Conversely, to copy some of the activities used with the deaf children in their speech work can be helpful to the hearing ones in phonics, rhythm and voice quality.

As deaf children are inclined to dominate, it is important that 'class leaders' for each week should be appointed so that both deaf and hearing children take turns. It seems that deaf children (often the brightest ones) are inclined to direct the normally hearing children so that they 'know what is going on', i.e. if someone else gives the instructions, the deaf child frequently misses them and the game or activity becomes less fun. There seems no simple solution to the difficulty, but explaining the reason for the apparent 'bossiness' can be helpful, and so too is ensuring that the normally hearing children *do* take turns at leading – particularly in those activities where following the instructions is relatively easy for the deaf child.

The units should be sited near the centre of the school, if possible, so that the children will integrate more readily. The school loud-speaker system should be fitted in the units as well as the main classrooms.

In the main classroom, the deaf children should sit in mixed groups with hearing children, and face the front of the room as far as possible.

Interesting apparatus and materials which will attract other children should be kept in the units and the deaf children allowed to invite the others to see them. Such apparatus should include a typewriter with large type for making reading material in the infant class and a camera and tape recorder.

Photographs of the staff and other regular visitors to the school should be pasted on to a large-scale wall plan of the school so that the deaf children get an idea of the layout and where various people may be found.

Parents of deaf children should be encouraged to attend the general meetings of the local parent/teacher association, although occasionally special meetings should be held for them.

Time-tables

No two deaf and associate classes work to exactly the same time-table. The numbers of children in each class, the abilities of the children, the facilities available and the interests of individual teachers all affect the programme and teachers may modify their daily time-tables. The following are two time-tables in use in two junior classes; they are not intended as models of what every time-table should be – indeed, in the nine- to ten-year-old group, the last hour each day being devoted to integrated programmes appears to me excessive, but teachers have been allowed a fairly free hand during the initial period.

(Five- and six-year-old children)
Twenty normally hearing children, eight deaf children
⋆ Separate   = Together
9·00– 9·30 ⋆ Class Discussion, Weather, News, Centre of Interest
9·30–11.00 = Directed Developmental Activities
11.00–12.00 { ⋆ Instructional Reading (Assoc.)
            { ⋆ Language (Deaf)

1·00– 1.40 = Number (group work)
1.40– 2.00 = Physical Education
2.05– 3.00 = Aesthetic Appreciation

(Nine- and ten-year-old children)
Twenty-four normally hearing children, seven deaf children
* Separate   = Together

9.00– 9.05 * Religious Education

9.05– 9.15 * Class Organisation, Banking, Lunch Orders, Completion if necessary of previous day's Reading Assignment, Silent Reading

9.15– 9.35 * Oral Expression, Group and Individual News, Topic Discussion

9.35– 9.55 = Spelling

9.55–10.30 = Arithmetic

Interval

10.45–11.30 * Language

11.30–12.00 = Physical Education

1.00– 2.00 = Music   = Films = Writing = Music   = Writing
             Writing = Films   and   = Writing * Broadcast
             Reading = Films = Reading = Reading = Reading

Interval

2.05– 3.00 = Social Integration – Social Studies, Nature Study, Art and Craft, Project Work, Sport, Centre of Interest

The following report was written at the end of the first year of a deaf unit working with a class of hearing children.

This class comprises twenty hearing children, and is the associate class for a deaf class of seven children. The children were selected at the end of last year – their selection being based on personality and stability rather than on intelligence.

They were told that they had been especially chosen for the class and why they had been chosen. A discussion then followed on the best ways to help the deaf children, both inside and outside the classroom.

The children were introduced to their 'second' teacher who explained some of the problems of deafness and demonstrated ways of communicating with deaf people.

The children soon became familiar with the classroom routines, some of which were, of course, different from anything they had known before. This was especially so with regard to the *social integration period* which became a regular feature of the day's programme. Four activities were planned, and each group spent a week on each with one group working in the deaf children's room and three in the associate room.

By the beginning of the second term, this social integration period was covering art and craft, nature study, and social studies, and to a lesser extent oral and written expression, drama and mime. Integration of a more formal nature was limited to handwriting, physical education, films, sport and reading (although the deaf children had different work in the latter).

A progression is now planned from social type integration to more integration in formal subjects: arithmetic, for example. For a start two of the deaf children who are coping with more advanced work will work with an arithmetic group who are working at nearly the same level. Gradually more children will integrate with other groups in the same way. The daily time-table has been changed to allow for full afternoon integration daily and partial integration in the morning. It is felt that the hearing children's programme will not suffer in any way.

As part of the individual file kept on each hearing child in the class, a section has been devoted to *integration*, and from the beginning two girls in particular showed a real interest in, and ability to communicate with, the deaf children, and assisted them greatly throughout the year.

Some normally hearing children are much more interested in deaf children than are others. There have been some quite remarkable instances of children befriending deaf children, asking to sit with them and talking carefully to them both in and out of school. We hope soon to conduct a research on these children. Some of the children, on the other hand, show no interest at all and these too should make an interesting study. We are only just beginning to learn how best we can tap the potential for assisting language growth which is represented by the normally hearing children in every class.

The opportunity to mix freely and regularly with normally hearing children helps some children more than others. The extent of the hearing loss is, of course, an important factor but there are instances of even the deafest children profiting very considerably – personality and intelligence are clearly two other important considerations.

Although, generally speaking, deaf and partially hearing children have fitted in well to the ordinary schools, there seems to be quite a group whom it would be unwise to include in such an integrated scheme – perhaps 20 per cent of the children at present enrolled at the deaf school would not be likely to profit. Some are of low intelligence, others have additional problems, either physical or psychological. They can lead a more sheltered life in the deaf school than is possible in the hurly-burly atmosphere of a big day school. One or two seriously maladjusted deaf children among a group could do considerable damage to the normal school's attitude to deaf children in general. Two children out of the eighty who are attending units in New Zealand have proved not to be sufficiently mature socially to justify their continued attendance in a unit class. One of these was returned to the school for the deaf but the other remained in the ordinary school. One feels, however, that leaving him there was not in the best interests of the other deaf children in the unit. This type of remark by a small boy: 'Hey, Miss! See that kid over there with the thing in his ear? Well, he's bashing us all the time and smashing our tunnels. Will you stop him?' led to this type: 'I'm not scared of anyone in this school 'cept the deaf kids. I'm scared of the deaf kids.'

Children (as well as adults!) do tend to generalize from a specific case, and the presence of a really badly adjusted deaf child in an ordinary school can do considerable damage in a relatively short time to the 'image' of the group as a whole. In this particular case, perhaps a term or two terms' residence in the school for deaf children might have been the wisest procedure. Out-of-school supervision is much closer in such schools than is possible in ordinary schools, and the daily routines develop a sense of security which often has a steadying effect.

The last thing one wants, of course, is for the 'image' of the deaf school to become one of a school for 'naughty children' – mention of it should *never on any account* be used as an aid to discipline. It has been found that visits to the deaf school by all the unit and associate classes have proved most helpful in removing any fears either group might have felt.

What has been learned so far? Undoubtedly the most significant thing is that *many profoundly deaf children can be successfully educated in such units in ordinary schools.* We teachers who have had most of our teaching experience in schools for deaf children are often inclined to believe that such units can only be successful with partially hearing children, i.e. those whose deafnesses do not exceed about eighty decibels. For this reason I was most apprehensive about the class established in Wellington in 1960. On the first morning when the period from 9.0 to 10.30 a.m. had been conducted reasonably well, I remember vividly thinking: 'So far, so good, but what on earth will happen now? It is playtime and what will become of these profoundly deaf children if they go outside?' At this moment the deaf group saw the normally hearing children going out to play, so they got up and ran off to join them. They did not appreciate, as I did, that their hearing losses exceeded eighty decibels, nor that they were unable to speak properly, nor that a deaf school was the only place for a deaf child.

A second very significant and encouraging factor appears to be that when deaf children spend *a very considerable proportion of time in the main classroom,* many of them do seem to form warm relationships with the normally hearing group which make them feel like playing together outside. The fact that the handicapped children receive nearly all their teaching in their own classroom is felt to be a major weakness in nearly all other classes for deaf and partially hearing children in ordinary school in other countries. Children tend to play with other children in their own class, even if their hearing is normal. Even in the New Zealand units there is a tendency for the deaf children to play together out of school and this is natural enough, but they do also play quite regularly with the children in the associate class.

It is better if the hearing children in the associate class can be fairly normal in their own social adjustment and *the deaf children should be of approximately the same age and ability.* Problems occur when the teacher of the deaf tries to manage two or more levels of ability within the one class.

SECONDARY SCHOOLS

There are several ways in which a child with a hearing loss can attend secondary school. He may enrol with other children and be the only deaf child at the school and, with assistance from the visiting teacher of the deaf, his parents and the staff and children of the school, have a very stimulating and worthwhile time there. Secondly, he may do that but in addition go out for speech therapy work for one or two periods each week. Thirdly, he may, in addition, take his verbal subjects like English and social studies through a correspondence course but do all other subjects with the other children. The correspondence school sends assignments to the deaf child and while the rest of the class are tackling more advanced work he is able to work at his own level on practical and worthwhile material. Frequently coaching is beneficial out of school hours in all school subjects but especially the verbal ones. It should be borne in mind that deaf and hard-of-hearing students must be prepared to work as few hearing students must, to achieve the same educational standards and background.

When daily specialist help is necessary, unit-type provision is indicated and works extremely well with almost all deaf children. An excellent group such as this was first observed in Adelaide, Australia, in 1960. In this technical college, a teacher of the deaf and a little classroom were provided for six deaf boys and seven deaf girls. They spent most of the day in ordinary classes for the technical subjects, but went to their own room for language and speech work for about two of the seven periods. The children were deriving a great deal from their contact with normally hearing children in the classrooms and on the playing-fields and without exception said they were very happy there. Another of these classes in an ordinary school has been functioning well in Sydney for a number of years, and such provision has recently been made at Kelston Boys' and Girls' High Schools. The Alexander Graham Bell School in Chicago, mentioned earlier, represents perhaps the best example of this type of integrated programme at the secondary level. There are numerous classes for partially hearing children attached to secondary schools in England. It is extremely helpful if simply written, well illustrated synopses of lessons given by the specialist subject teachers can be provided for the deaf children well before the lessons take place. These should be prepared by the teacher of the deaf in collaboration with the specialist teacher of the ordinary children.

During the last six years several different types of integration have been tried in a partially hearing unit in London in addition to the obvious ones of physical education, games, outings, swimming, art and handwork.

In school assembly all partially hearing children are present with aids switched to the 'loop' plus microphone position, so that responses from the school are heard as well as the headmaster's voice through the microphone. Preparation for this is done in the unit by a weekly practice of prayers and hymns. This is very difficult in the early stages but by the fourth year all are participating.

For drama there are twelve normally hearing children plus six partially hearing ones. Plays are prepared by the unit teacher in the quiet room and then transferred to the hall stage. On one occasion the leading speaking part was taken with considerable success by a boy with a very severe hearing loss.

In French the group is limited to ten children, eight normal and two partially hearing with fairly normal speech and language. The group is kept small so that the unit teacher can cope with two groups at once, the third year with the teacher using records and the fourth year using headphones and tapes in the corridor. The two groups alternate each day.

Again, the importance of an interested and energetic headmaster is emphasized. The principal of the very large school in Adelaide knew all the deaf children by name and even interpreted some audiograms for me. The young teacher of the deaf said that he was grateful to the principal because at staff meetings he invariably asked him how things were going and inquired if any assistance was needed with any of the children.

A number of intelligent deaf children have made their way in ordinary secondary schools with very little help from teachers of the deaf. The following reports, one by a teacher on a deaf boy about to enter an ordinary school after several years in a school for the deaf, may suggest the kind of help which deaf pupils need.

John is considered to have the ability to continue to the General Certificate Examination at the end of the third year. This is desirable both from a general education-broadening viewpoint and from his vocational interests – tentatively, accountancy, draughtsmanship, surveying or some other form of clerical work. Should he manage to cope in a hearing school with a reasonable measure of academic and social success, his adjustment to the adult world will be infinitely easier.

Personal characteristics

John is a lad of superior intelligence, good manners and of quite high principles, although of necessity immature. Without the easy communication of the normally hearing person and the give and take of everyday life in a large group, deaf people are always immature. He accepts his deafness well and is an industrious lad. Physically he is strong and well coordinated. He is, however, really shy and sensitive. While hoping to make the grade in English he is naturally more than a little worried about it.

Suggested subjects

The headmaster has agreed to five subjects only, owing to the added difficulty for John and the extra time which will be needed for coaching and study: English, Mathematics I and II, Economics and Ancient History.

Coaching

Experience with the comparatively few deaf-born children with almost total loss of hearing has shown that coaching in all subjects is necessary at least until they prove that they can manage without.

While lipreading is a very useful means of communication within a small group, it is quite inadequate in the classroom, particularly in senior work. Every mouth is different and some people are virtually impossible to lipread. In class discussions the lipreader is quite at a loss. He does not even know half the time who is speaking. Any teaching given while the teacher is writing on the blackboard is lost. It is impossible to look at a book and lipread at the same time.

At every stage and in every subject there will be words, idioms and forms of expression that are new. It is often thought that reading is easy for the deaf student but this is only true within the limits of his command of language and, even for the hearing student, English must grow rapidly during the senior school years. Without coaching this would not happen for John. Both for teaching and testing it is necessary for the deaf student to have the practice of much additional work; only coaching would make this possible. It is therefore suggested that John be coached in all subjects.

Friendship help

It is suggested that boys be asked to volunteer to give some help in the various subjects, and out of school: (*a*) see that he knows what to do, where and when, give him a brief résumé of announcements, etc.; (*b*) assist with note-taking. (John could provide carbon paper and paper of the size of the exercise-book used, so that copies of the notes could be made, studied and used as a guide for the coach.) The volunteers could perhaps be changed from time to time so that he would not become a burden.

A general talk about deafness could help to overcome some of the common difficulties, such as the mistaken notion that he can lipread every word spoken and is therefore spying on the boys, so making him an object of too much curiosity. The boys could be asked to help him settle in, to talk to him only when he can see them and then to accept him as one of themselves, without fuss.

Sport clubs and responsibilities

John is interested in cricket but has had no senior matches. Athletics, gym, rowing and chess, camera or philately clubs – any of these would be of interest to him. Time will prevent him from participating in too many activities but he must have some. It would be good if some sphere could be found where he could take some responsibility and be of service, again within the limits of time. Maybe he could help with the library or some similar activity.

The second report was written by a very intelligent girl (I.Q. 120–130 WISC Performance) who was severely deaf (75–80 db.) and came from a very good home. Her criticism of the school for the deaf emphasizes the importance of stimulating the best children to the full rather than just teaching the whole group at the level of the least able in the class.

At last, after all those simple lessons, being taught by only one teacher in one classroom for nine years in the school for the deaf, I was getting a really satisfying education. At the beginning I found it rather bewildering having seven lessons a day – three quarters of an hour per lesson – walking from one numbered classroom to another through all the long corridors, all the girls chattering away, carrying all our books in our cases, noises of the footsteps everywhere. I now saw about nine teachers a week. All had different characters, ways of teaching, voices and mouths and were in different classrooms. Gradually I settled down to this strange system. I eagerly took in the wide range of lessons, learning something new every time – at the old school we sometimes had the same old thing for a few days at a time.

Teachers were really good to me when they could be. Most of them spoke well enough for me to catch most of what they were saying. The textbooks gave me plenty of hints in what teachers would say at certain times. One English teacher was very talkative but nevertheless I enjoyed lipreading and listening to her as she made no effort to talk differently.

I began to try to talk as well as the others. At the same time I watched my speech so I would not be misunderstood. If I made a mistake, they wasted their time (and mine) when they said 'Beg pardon?' so many times that I lost interest in what I meant to convey and they lost theirs too. Sometimes they burst out laughing when my words didn't come out quite right – perhaps a wrong meaning. I would be told of what they thought I had said, then I would correct the meaning.

I would easily copy one of the girls scribbling notes while she jotted. Girls were used to having me look over their shoulders for notes. Perhaps when at times I could not follow what the teacher had been saying, one or two would scribble a sentence or two at a time on to my scribbling-pad. Sometimes I would pretend to ask a question and I would really be jotting down what I'd been doing the last night or week-end. We would converse on paper right under the teacher's nose! There were times I was frankly bored – not being able to follow the teacher on a boring subject such as laundry, clothing or science. I would do a sketch or two and I had no worries because I could go back and read the notes in my exercise or textbooks. At last I could compare my capabilities with others and found I could keep up reasonably, which gave me a little confidence.

The assemblies I remember with mixed feelings. In some ways I used to hate going as we had to sit still while the headmaster talked. It seemed ages but was only ten minutes or so. (I've just realized that I had no idea what he usually talked about.) I was so painfully self-conscious when I had a bad cold or bad cough during that time. We would sing a hymn or two on certain mornings. I welcomed the singing as a relief from sitting and the silence. I enjoyed listening and following the words on the song book. Sometimes I sang when I felt like it – shyly and quietly.

My desire to learn English as well as others was somewhat hampered by my limited written and spoken English. English was then somewhat beyond my reach. It was rather a mixed bag of poems, metaphors,

Shakespeare, language and essays. I was not ready for Shakespeare – not 'old enough' to understand the meanings. I didn't dig in very deeply but some words and sentences, so cleverly and beautifully written, did attract my attention.

Although I was getting a wonderfully satisfying education, I had some personal problems. I ignored them as far as I could, but I couldn't help noticing that I was unable to be completely 'in' with the girls at times. I was reserved and self-conscious of my handicap. When the girls were excited they often talked to one another quickly so I missed some understanding of everyday occurrences. I did not blame them, only at times I wished I was more adaptable with them. At that time I was terribly shy of boys and remembered not a word spoken to them during three years.

My main aim was to obtain a school certificate pass to prove to myself and others that a deaf girl could get it if necessary and this I managed to do.

Although the academic and linguistic attainments of this girl at the high school cannot be questioned, one cannot be complacent regarding her failure to establish completely happy relations with her classmates. Several factors may have contributed to this. Firstly, of course, it is a natural effect of deafness in an intelligent person – not knowing exactly what people are talking and laughing about causes insecurity in most people – and when one is severely or profoundly deaf, this occurs very frequently.

Although most deaf people (including this particular girl in later years) learn to live with this very frustrating state of affairs, it is clear that some adjust to living among a group of normally hearing people much more readily than others. This is, of course, true of normally hearing individuals also. It must be remembered, therefore, that there are personality differences among deaf people quite apart from those imposed by their hearing handicap.

A third factor which might be very significant is that this girl had spent nine years in a day and residential school for deaf children. When she was informed of the new units in ordinary schools (as described earlier), she immediately commented: 'I wish I could have gone to a class like that.'

Finally, had a visiting teacher of the deaf been available who could have spent a considerable amount of time talking to the girls in the class as well as to the teachers and arranging 'friendship help' as suggested above in the first report, this girl might have been drawn more wholeheartedly into the other girls' activities.

All teachers agree that sport is an excellent field in which deaf children can compete on almost equal terms and that this assists greatly in their being accepted by the normally hearing pupils. They also make excellent instructors. One deaf boy at a technical college in Sydney had become New South Wales schoolboys diving champion the previous year and this had given all of the deaf children there a considerable fillip.

Another point which has become clear is that in large schools there are usually one or two teachers who, without any special training, show a particular flair for handling deaf children and enjoy having them to work with as much as do good teachers of the deaf.

The following statement is made by the mother of a profoundly deaf boy who attended, without help, a secondary school for normally hearing children for four years. Few deaf children could, however, cope so well unaided.

At school John settled in happily, enjoying the company of boys of his own age, mixing well and loving the greater opportunities for sport. He was very good at book-keeping and woodwork and this boosted his morale for his other subjects. English was especially difficult and considerable help at home was required. We found the days were not long enough nor the human constitution strong enough for all we would have liked to do. How proud John was to be in the first rugby fifteen for his last two years at school! I think we tasted the ultimate in happiness when we stood on the sideline and heard his schoolmates call: 'Good old John.' He could not hear them but they were obviously so proud of him.

7 The Development of Language in School

There are various ways in which language can be presented to deaf children. Two common ones are the formal structured method and the genetic or developmental approach. The former is characterized by language schemes setting out exactly which words, phrases and sentences are to be taught at each stage. The latter relies on working from the activities in which the children are interested and giving them the conventional language forms associated with them.

A disadvantage of the first method is that it is very easy for lessons to become deadly dull. The teacher does not think so much about what the child is interested in but tends to restrict herself very much to the words or sentences in her master scheme.

A disadvantage of the second approach – the purely developmental one – is that, although good individual lessons can be taken, the language forms are often not presented frequently enough for them to become established as part of the child's active vocabulary. This is particularly so with inexperienced teachers.

At Lexington School for the Deaf, New York, these two essential ingredients of learning – *interest* and *reinforcement* – are provided by means of a language *check list* for the various levels. Here teachers are expected to take their normal interesting lessons but also to know the check list words and phrases well and to give them added emphasis whenever the occasion arises. This gives a teacher freedom to take lessons on all sorts of topics largely as the interests of the children dictate but, while covering such topics, opportunities are taken and occasionally contrived to introduce and reintroduce the check list words and phrases. Check lists are discussed further in Chapter 10.

In presenting language lessons, it has been generally believed that 'the oral should precede the written form'. In consequence, lessons are prepared using apparatus in such a way that a situation is created in which a word or phrase becomes necessary to describe it. For example, a doll is taken from a bath dripping with water and the child, now knowing that a drying operation is afoot, is asked: 'Where's the towel?' or 'Bring me the towel, please.' The word 'towel' thus becomes meaningful and alive and after using it in several sentences the teacher writes one on the blackboard and proceeds to the next step. Gradually a written summary of this acivity lesson is built up.

The *listening-reading-speaking* method (LRS), as described briefly below, involves much of the above practice but contains two major differences:

1 Much of the basic language is written up in sentences *before* the lesson begins.

2 There is tremendous emphasis on listening alone, as well as on listening plus lipreading.

The LRS method (see page 192) is extensively used in group situations at a school for deaf children in Essex(35) and is being increasingly used in other schools and classes. It has been described by Lady Ethel Ewing(57) for individual children, and we have also found it very helpful to student teachers in training. The Ewing method includes ten minutes of individual training each day, reading in continuous sentences while indicating the words with a pencil, speaking close to the microphone of the hearing aid, and the child concentrating his visual attention on the written words rather than on the teacher's face. It was concluded that the technique 'assisted the children to read, to hear, to comprehend and to say words which were new to them.' The method is considered to be of real significance to parents when hearing their children read at home. Reading has this advantage over lipreading. In a sentence like: 'He goes as soon as his sister is six', for example, virtually nothing is clear when spoken normally. The written material focuses everyone's attention accurately and serves as a central theme from which further oral and written language can be developed as widely as the particular needs of the children seem to warrant and their abilities will allow. It is very stimulating for the children to puzzle out meaning from a written passage. Teachers encourage them to worry away at each phrase and sentence until the meaning becomes clear. With plenty of such practice, the children develop confidence later to tackle passages in books.

Asking the children to say some words and phrases after the teacher which they do not fully understand may seem strange, but it is in fact similar to that which parents of normally hearing children do orally, when teaching a baby to speak. I think we have been a little too conscious in the past of ensuring that every single word must be meaningful to the child. 'The idea must precede the language', but not every word of the language.

There are three main sources of material for language lessons: activities, material brought by the children and material prepared by the teacher.

Developmental activities

The following extract is a very good description of the aims and practice of what is often called the *developmental* (or *activity*) *period*(29). The smallness of many of the traditional classrooms for deaf children can make its introduction difficult but, given reasonable physical conditions and energetic and imaginative teachers, it can prove very effective. It usually runs nearly all day at the nursery level (three to five years) and for over an hour each day in the infant school (five to seven years). Recently we have been introducing it a little in the upper school and again, when carefully planned, it has proved very stimulating.

Most infant rooms begin the day with a period when a variety of materials is set out and children can choose their own activities. Here we practise all of our guiding principles: that growth in language is a part of children's whole development; that language is a form of behaviour rather than a series of subjects to be taught; that there must be a lot to do, to talk about, to think about, to read about and to write about; and that teachers must provide situations that challenge children to use language well. Here, too, the children learn as they did before they came to school. A well-planned developmental period offers scope for all the children in a class to work at their own best level of concentration and skill, a situation which is rare in 'teaching' periods conducted by the teacher with a large group where as a rule the lesson is really useful only to a few children in the group.

Some teachers are worried about this period and are uncertain about their own role in it. Certainly, unless we are able to provide the right kind of stimulation through the environment we create and the material we set out, the free choice period can become as monotonous and as rigid as the most stereotyped lesson. There can also be aimlessness and real waste of time. Planning is required to meet the needs of children widely different from each other in ability and experience and constant opportunities for further development must be provided. Children will become bored unless we are ready to help them on to the next stage. We face these problems, of course, in all our teaching but we are much more aware of them when we play an apparently less direct role.

The following suggestions bear upon these problems. They are based on the principle of providing materials, which children have been observed to choose whenever they had the chance. The same children will use the same materials in more individual ways in several succeeding years.

Reading and writing will develop through any well-planned period of this kind but we will defeat our purposes if we make reading and writing our sole aim. Often the most valuable and significant results are those which cannot be measured or tabulated. How can we measure the ways in which making and acting and planning lead to greater understanding and use of spoken language? Only by our own observations. This will convince us that where activity is vital and creative there is no need for mere practice in listening and speaking or reading and writing, and that to spend time on such practice is to waste time.

The materials children need for their full growth are those which offer most scope for creative activity, for resourcefulness, and for independence.

The natural play of young children is dominated by:
   Joy in movement;
   Delight in experiment with natural materials;
   Pleasure in make-believe and in playing a part;
   The satisfaction of making things;
   A developing interest in books and writing.

The more deeply imagination, feeling and bodily sensation are involved in a child's play, the more important this play becomes in his development.

In the course of school life other interests and activities will suggest themselves, some coming with the seasons – harvest festival, Christmas, Easter – others as the result of neighbourhood events and the interests which individual children bring to the class.

During the early months of their school life children should be free for a good deal of the day within a carefully planned environment, where they are busily engaged on self-chosen tasks. In such a classroom a teacher's observation will help her to select the right time and the right kinds of materials for introducing the skills which all the children must eventually master.

At the nursery level, especially in America, a form of 'freedom with order' operates in a number of schools for the deaf. About twenty children, aged between three and five years, play in one large room. One teacher and two teacher's helpers supervise the play and talk to the children about the interesting things they are building, drawing, making or doing – a type of developmental or activity period. In two small adjoining rooms, two teachers take individual children for specific language work.

Observations of a lesson taken in one of these sessions ran as follows:

A bright little boy of four years nine months who has been at school for fifteen months sits at a small table opposite the teacher. His hearing averages 100 db. (American standard) over the speech range 500, 1,000 and 2,000 c.p.s, but he has very good hearing for the frequencies below 500 c.p.s. He uses a speech-training hearing aid.

1. Thirty different pictures, photographs and objects are taken out of a basket and placed on the table.

> Teacher: Show me a boy and a towel.
> Show me a cow and a dog.
> Where are a man and a girl?
> Can you see a baby and a ball? etc.

The form of the instructions at this stage is varied deliberately so that the child has practice in lipreading a variety of language forms. Then follow:

2 Some tongue exercises – the child copies the tongue movements made by the teacher.

3 Recognition of sounds written on cards – ar ow o-e b;

4 Copying sounds –

Teacher: ar   Child: ar
         oo   oo
         dada   dada
         m   m   etc.

5 Grammar —

(a) Teacher: (*picking up an object from the box*) I have a dog.
     Child: You have a dog.
     Teacher: I have a bird.
     Child: You have a bird. (*Two more objects are taken.*)

(b) Teacher: (*giving child a picture of an apple*) What do you have?
     Child: I have a apple. (*'a' was not corrected.*)
     Child then says: 'I have a bus, I have a comb, I have a house'
     as the objects are given to him.

(c) Teacher: (*holding up a picture or object*) What do you see?
     Child: I see a horse, I see a man, I see a doll, etc.

(d) Teacher: (*looking at the basket*) What do you want?
     Child: I want a Santa, I want a flower, I want a table.
     (The remainder of the objects are removed from the basket in
     this way.)
     Teacher: Do you want some candy? (*short rest here*)

6 Commands —

Teacher: Shake hands with me.
           Shake hands with the man.
           Turn off the lights.
           Get a handkerchief and blow your nose.
           Take off your coat.
           Brush your teeth. (*There are about twenty of these.*)

7 Reading —

(a) Teacher: Fall.
     (*Child falls on the floor.*)
     Teacher: What did you do?
     Child reads from a card: *I fell.* (*The card is turned.*)
     Teachers shows picture of a dog falling and the child reads:
     A dog fell. (*A picture of a baby falling is shown, and so on.*)

(b) 'Run' is then dealt with in the same way, and this concludes
     the child's individual lesson.

Liaison —

(a) The teacher and supervisors in the large room are informed of progress so that opportunities can be taken to reinforce it during the day and in future days.

(b) A note is made in the home/school notebook of this material so that parents or supervisors can revise it in the evening.

Every child should receive an individual lesson every day.

The lessons may be of ten or twelve minutes or may extend to even forty minutes if time permits and the child is enjoying it. (The session above took twenty-five minutes.)

It will be clear that the individual lesson just outlined could not be taken unless the child had been carefully prepared for it. This little boy had built up gradually to this stage over a period of fifteen months.

The process of *revision and extension* goes on continuously and, if imaginatively and sympathetically applied, brings great satisfaction and happiness to the child, to the teacher and to the parents. It can, of course, be deadly dull and of very little value if applied unimaginatively.

Mildred Groht(30) deplores the dull and lifeless manner in which *lipreading boxes* are used by some teachers, and suggests that such boxes of common objects should be banished from classes for deaf children. While to use the box of objects purely for naming exercises can be detrimental to the child's interest in language, it does appear that in the hands of some imaginative teachers excellent work can be done with groups of objects. A teacher at a school in Sussex, for example, uses three boxes with her four- and five-year-old deaf children and working with them in pairs, she *does* things with the objects which make them come to life, e.g. 'The aeroplane goes up, up, up, doesn't it? And now it's coming down, down, down; isn't it lovely? Don't you wish you could fly like that? Up, up, up. And now look out – it's going to come under the table and chase you – watch – down, down, down and *under* the table. Oh, isn't it a funny plane? Now I'll put it over here on this side table and it can have a rest', and so on.

Another teacher uses objects connected with *one* subject particularly interesting to a particular child. Daily language work is given with dolls or trains or horses or a toy kitchen forming the centre of interest.

The following activities are suggested for normally intelligent, older deaf children during the activity period: (Some of them, e.g. checking the car tyres, battery, etc., are best introduced in set language times as group activity lessons, and then included in the developmental programme. Activities should be of short duration – 'knitting a sweater' for example, is *not* a good topic.)

Care of classroom pets, fish tanks, guinea-pigs, mice, birds, etc.

Mowing a lawn

Mending a puncture

Pumping up a football or basketball

Oiling a cricket-bat

Playing various card games

Removing stains

Cleaning a bicycle

Making model farms, aerodromes, power stations, etc.

Soldering

Making a kite

Dismantling and assembling old home appliances, toasters, irons, hot water jugs, vacuum cleaners, radios, clocks, etc.

Cleaning shoes

Washing hair

Ironing a shirt or blouse

Checking the water, oil, battery, petrol and tyres of a car

Making properties for plays – e.g. bows and arrows, pistols, a lamp, costumes, etc.

Making a rabbit-hutch or birdcage

Making toys for other children

Listening to recorded songs and speech

Pitching a little tent

Taking a photograph

For backward deaf children, the activities listed here and those referred to at the pre-school level can be excellent. The age-level at which these children are able to undertake a particular activity may well be four or even five years behind that at which a normally intelligent child would be ready to attempt it. The equipment should not, of course, look too babyish. Magnets, compasses, spirit-levels, egg-timers, magnifying glasses, bicycle pumps, locks, pulleys, cranes, clocks and spring balances can be used to stimulate scientific interests or a special corner can be set up with a bed, toy stethoscope, bandages, etc., for the children to play hospitals. Tizard(24) has an excellent section of suggestions for adapting pre-school apparatus to the needs of older educationally subnormal children.

Language material brought by the children

Often children bring interesting items of news from home which make excellent language material for the whole class, e.g. 'Daddy went to a farm yesterday. He brought home four baby ducks. We put them in the hot water cupboard last night. I love them.'

The home/school notebooks (see page 60) are a wonderful help here if intelligently used. Parents and supervisors are encouraged to write in these books the most interesting and vital things that happen to the child the previous evening or before coming to school. The entries from school to home or hostel each day should be of the same type – points or events which the teacher has noticed have been really significant to that particular child during the day.

As each child 'tells' the class his news, the teacher prints it on a sheet of paper (Figure 7), and it makes excellent reading material as well as giving practice in the pleasant business of talking.

These daily 'news' sessions can also be an excellent means of getting the deaf children started on writing. We have found that four steps are often necessary. First the teacher writes each child's news on a blackboard (or piece of paper), and the children copy their own (see page 97). At the next stage, the children copy their news from the teacher's sheet of paper. Thirdly they write their own news without copying at all, and finally they are able to write little sentences without having them written anywhere.

When they have written their news once, the teacher sometimes comes along, ticks it if it is correct and then rubs it off so that they can practise doing it again. They seem to enjoy seeing how many times they can write it in five or ten minutes.

One teacher gets excellent language work from seven- and eight-year-olds by asking them to write their news each morning on a section of the main blackboard. The emphasis is on spontaneity and

Room 4's news

It was Edwin's birthday on Wednesday. He's 7 now.

Paul lost 1 of his shoes in the park.

Barry has lost his swimming trunks.

Poor Hui has been ill
He stayed in bed.

Mark likes water-melon.

Henry has a letter. It is 2 pages long.

Penny gets all her sums right every night.

$$6 + 2 + 1 = 9 \checkmark \qquad 2 + 4 + 2 = 8 \checkmark$$
$$3 + 4 + 2 = 9 \checkmark \qquad 7 + 1 + 1 = 9 \checkmark$$
$$1 + 0 + 1 = 2 \checkmark \qquad 6 + 2 + 1 = 9 \checkmark$$
$$6 + 4 + 1 = 11 \checkmark \qquad 3 + 1 + 3 = 7 \checkmark$$
$$5 + 2 + 3 = 10 \checkmark \qquad 4 + 2 + 4 = 10 \checkmark$$

Figure 7   Weekly news sheet for infants

interest in the child's attempt. To begin with perhaps only one or two words can be written, and the child's mime and gestures must be interpreted and written for him. Fairly soon, though, as the children realize that they can communicate by means of written words, and they read what their friends have written, vocabularies and syntactical English improve markedly.

An excellent way to get assistance from visitors to the school, and at the same time to help them appreciate the children's difficulties and achievements, is for each child to keep a little collection of photographs in his desk. Snapshots of people, pets and objects at home are ideal, and form a splendid centre of interest for discussion.

Language material prepared by the teacher

Deaf children do not learn all the natural little phrases which we use unless they are taught them. Phrases like 'It doesn't matter', 'I can't see', 'That's all right', etc. (Appendix 2) which are learnt by normally hearing children without being taught must be presented specifically to deaf children.

These are the lessons that test our skill as teachers of deaf children. Some teachers never learn to present language effectively. They 'talk' to the children who sit passively – smiling when the teacher smiles, frowning when she frowns, etc., and comprehending next to nothing. The children then copy from the blackboard into their language books a summary of what has been poured over them, this summary being almost incomprehensible to most of them.

The acid test of language teaching is the extent to which the material presented is used spontaneously by the children at a later date.

The following are suggestions to promote this:

Choice of topic

A cardinal principle of language work has been stated earlier: that 'the experience must precede the language'. Trying to tell very deaf ten-year-olds, for example, about the function of UNESCO or the importance of higher education would be uphill work for the most able of teachers. To mend a puncture in a bicycle tyre and get the children to lipread, read, say and write and learn little sentences and phrases in connection with it, however, would be fairly straightforward. *Interest,* then, is a basic ingredient and the teacher who chooses an uninteresting topic immediately makes her task difficult.

Preparation

It is tremendously important for teachers (and parents and supervisors) to be able to look ahead – to anticipate in training a deaf child (or any child, for that matter). They should anticipate on both a long- and a short-term basis. What will this child need for life? What will he need this year? This month? This week? This day and this next hour and even minute? If one frequently asks oneself these questions it is likely that careful planning and preparation will result. Lessons and activities are likely to be made interesting and worth while because they will meet the children's needs. The best teachers do two hours' preparation each day; all should do at least one hour.

The children, too, must be helped from an early age to anticipate in their language work and in nearly all life's situations. For pre-school children, an excellent way of enabling them to look ahead to some event is to draw it or draw the sequence of events involved. Before her nursery school class went to see Santa Claus, one teacher drew a bus and a big department store, Santa Claus and a child shaking hands with him and receiving a present. Arrows connected the items up and it was talked about. The children had very little idea of what it was all about. The next visit, however, was to the zoo, and when she showed the children the little sketch of the bus and the animals in cages the class became excited and began pulling at their chins, i.e. making the Santa Claus sign. If used thoughtfully, this technique can be invaluable. It is possible, for example, to arrange the visit, say, to the zoo, for Thursday or Friday and talk about it every morning so that by the time the children go, they have a great deal of information about the zoo and what they will see when they visit it.

Presentation

A teacher must be animated and a personality in the room. The more deaf the children are, the more dynamic one's teaching must be. There is little place for the casual 'academic' type of presentation of material to young, very deaf children. One must teach as though one meant it – with verve, drive, dramatization and humour.

As a rule it is as well to keep most apparatus out of sight until it is needed during the lesson. Deaf children love a 'secret' and are kept interested if they know something has been hidden in the cupboard or in a paper bag or behind the blackboard.

It is a good idea for the children to sit near the teacher so that she can take their hands for a moment's speech work when necessary. A little table in the middle is helpful where there is apparatus to show.

Jotter pads are excellent at these times – or alternatively a piece of chalk each and a space marked for each on the blackboard. During a lesson the teacher may say: 'On my table there is a yellow box.' Some of the children may not be paying attention, so the teacher will say: 'All write what I said.' There will be pained expressions and mutterings about it being 'too hard'. The teacher then says: 'Well, you watch again. On my table . . .' One should be sure to give them short phrases and very easy material to write down to begin with.

The advantages of this are that they show teachers how little some of the children really understand of the lessons; they give the children a break from watching all the time; and they 'perk the class up' and stimulate them to watch more carefully.

Content

For older children, the daily newspaper (read carefully by the teacher before school starts) can be the main source of language lessons.

Some suitable topics for language lessons are listed in Appendix 4. Generally those listed last in each group are more suitable for the older children. Here is an outline for a month's work on the specific language topic 'Illness' with very deaf twelve- to thirteen-year-olds.

Sometimes people become ill. Often they are unfit for school or for work. If people feel off colour, they go to bed, and if they get worse, they usually send for the doctor.

When the doctor comes, he usually feels your pulse, examines your tongue and takes your temperature. Then he writes out a prescription for some medicine.

Sometimes people get a headache or a sore throat or stomach-ache or they feel shivery.

If people are very ill they go to hospital. There are always a lot of patients in the hospital. Some of them are seriously ill but most of them get well.

Years ago people had to pay the doctor and also pay when they went to hospital. Nowadays the Government pays the doctors and the public hospital is free.

Do you ever feel 'off colour'? What is the best way to cure a headache?

Have you ever been in hospital?

Have you ever had an operation?

Do you know much about your body?

What is the heart for?

What work do the kidneys do?

What is the normal pulse rate?

How many minor illnesses do you know of?

What about serious diseases?

Have you ever heard of leprosy?

Find out about Ronald Ross, Louis Pasteur, James Simpson, Father Peter Damien, Marie Curie, St Vincent de Paul, Joseph Lister, Alexander Fleming, and Salk. (Although time will not permit a full coverage of the work of the people named, some interesting lessons can be made from their work and achievements.)

Find out some rules for good health.

New vocabulary: Unfit, 'off colour', get worse, etc.

Colloquialisms and idioms

A dictionary of *Idioms for Deaf People* is being very carefully compiled by Dr E. T. Boatner at the American School for the Deaf, in Hartford, Connecticut. It is hoped to include 4,000 common idioms in this publication and it could be very helpful for older deaf children and adults.

A number of these (Appendix 2) can be taught to the children in the natural day-to-day language and reading situations as they arise. It is useful (especially with slower-learning deaf children), however, to contrive situations which will give opportunity for using the colloquial phrase or sentence and, after teaching it thoroughly, to consolidate it during the everyday situations.

When language is introduced in this way, it can be lipread, read, said and written by the deaf child several times over. The slower the child, the more this repetition and reinforcement is necessary. It should be made as pleasant as possible – little dramatized lessons are good. A child comes into the room pretending to cry. One of the class perhaps says to him: 'What for?' The teacher first tells the class and then writes the question 'What's the matter?' The child replies: 'I fell over and hurt my knee.' The second child is then taught to say: 'Too bad – I'm sorry' or 'Bad luck – it will be better soon,' etc.

Most of the class can have turns at playing the patient and the sympathizer and the colloquial language is recorded in the home/school notebooks. Gradually a number of these little plays can be built up and the children enjoy using the appropriate language when the real situations occur.

Nursery rhymes and jingles

A very good infant teacher in an ordinary school once said that she took all her language work from nursery rhymes. *All deaf children should learn lots of them.* (There are some four hundred different words in the common nursery rhymes alone.) They contain dozens of good conventional sentences and phrases, e.g. 'went up the hill', 'was white as snow', 'have you any wool?' 'how does your garden grow?' 'sat on a wall'.

Children love to have little 'concerts' once they have learned a few rhymes and jingles. When visitors come into the room the rhymes can be a good way to entertain them. Repetition of the language is done in a happy atmosphere in this way and hand movements, finger plays (see Chapter 3) and so on help the enjoyment and the rhythm.

Nursery rhymes are learnt by all hearing children so this is just another way of making our deaf ones as normal as possible. Some teachers have a flair for making up their own poems and jingles and songs. These are especially good because they usually contain vocabulary and phrase units that are known fairly well by the children.

Popular songs are also excellent for language and speech work. Many (but not all) of the songs sung currently by the children's teenage idols are worth using. The basic interest is there and the repetition of the language is so easy and natural. If possible, these should be tape recordings of a bass singer accompanied on an organ and they should be played through a group hearing aid while the children watch the teacher point to the words on the song sheet.

The reinforcement comes mainly from repeating the material over and over but some songs and poems can be found which contain the same phrases within themselves. Teachers should look for these.

Proverbs

For older children proverbs can be very popular and worth while. A deaf woman said recently, when I had commented on the fact that she often used proverbs and adages, that her teacher had taught her proverbs twenty-five years ago. These are a few common ones that appeal to deaf adolescents:

People who live in glass houses shouldn't throw stones.

The early bird catches the worm.

Pride goes before a fall.

More haste, less speed.

Time and tide wait for no man.

All that glitters is not gold.

Too many cooks spoil the broth.

Look before you leap.

A rolling stone gathers no moss.

Absence makes the heart grow fonder.

Many hands make light work.

A drowning man will clutch at a straw.

There's no smoke without fire.

It's a long lane that has no turning.

It's an ill wind that blows nobody good.

Dictation

The Australians seem to do a great deal of dictation work and in some American schools it is taken regularly from six or seven years of age onwards. Even quite little children can and should do some dictation work – just a few words and phrases. Later on it can be varied by letting one of the children play 'teacher' and read the material for the rest of the class.

With older children, a simple story can be selected and two or three times each week an 'instalment' given as dictation. The paragraph is first read right through and then repeated one sentence at a time. Dictation work should only take up a fraction of each school week.

Verbs and adjectives

Sometimes, with both teachers and parents, there is a tendency to place too much emphasis on nouns. Lists of nouns should be avoided like poison. The sentence and phrase are the thought unit. Learning lists of single words have been found to *inhibit* rather than promote language use(31).

Particularly with young children, there is a great deal of merit in concentrating on verbs and adjectives without over-emphasizing nouns. Professor Priscilla Pittenger, of San Francisco State College, has given the example of a lesson using a ball where one can bounce it, roll it, throw it, catch it, etc. One can do so much more with a ball than just name it. These verbs are interesting and can be used in all sorts of situations with objects, to teach their names which are not known to the child.

Language for daily routines

A teacher (or parent) should deliberately vary the language used in routine daily situations, e.g. she should not always say: 'It's time for lunch.' She could say: 'It's lunch time now' or 'I'm hungry; let's go to lunch' 'How about some lunch?' 'It's twelve o'clock: let's go and have something to eat', etc. Once a basic language form is known in a routine situation, one should introduce other common ways of saying the same thing, and thus acquaint the children with these forms natur- ally, easily, and regularly.

Wall calendars

Another way of presenting meaningful language and constantly revising common forms of it is by using a wall calendar. These are found in a large number of American schools for deaf children. Again they must be kept imaginatively to be really helpful. A long strip of paper (brown or newsprint), is placed along one wall at the beginning of each week or fortnight. On it the days of the week are marked and under each day the most interesting news items are entered. Pictures and photographs can be included to make it more meaningful and attractive.

It is important, to begin with, to remember that news about one day should be entered under that day, e.g. 'We shall have a surprise on Thursday', although mentioned on Monday for the first time, should be written under Thursday rather than Monday. It can become very confusing for the children if this is not done.

When well kept, the wall calendar represents one of the best ways of learning about verbs and seeing how they change according to time. 'We shall have a surprise tomorrow' becomes 'We had a surprise yesterday'. If not overdone, wall calendars are excellent for simple analysis work. 'Who can find the verbs in the news?' 'Who can find the wheres?' (to the library, to school, to Jim's). 'Who can find "when"?' (today, yesterday, last Wednesday), etc.

At the end of the week the strip of paper is cut up and stapled together as a news book. When this is placed on the book table it is interesting to note the number of children who will take it to read during free reading, rather than choose one of the more attractive reading books.

Word and sentence study

As far as possible words used for word-and-sentence study should be taken from reading or language work rather than selected out of the blue from a scheme or check list (or a teacher's imagination).

With bright children especially, a short word-study period each day or two or three times each week can be of benefit. There are, of course, bad and good methods of presenting new words. One teacher simply listed six words on the blackboard and then tried to explain them to the children. The first word was 'corkscrew' and he drew a cork-screw beside it and said: 'That is a corkscrew' and proceeded to the next word. A much better method would be to take a bottle into the classroom with a cork jammed down the neck of it and say to the children: 'How should I get the cork out?' In a matter of seconds they will be excitedly making twisting motions with their hands. The teacher then should say: 'Yes, that's right – but what is the *name* of it?' 'Tease' them a little longer with it and then when they are almost 'gasping' for the word, give them the name.

In the main, words being studied should be learnt in sentences and phrases rather than singly, e.g. 'George brought a corkscrew' is better than just 'corkscrew'.

With children of average intelligence, only about two new words should be introduced each day, and perhaps four other words be in-cluded for revision.

With slower children, just one new word in a sentence each day is often sufficient for the study period.

At the Berkeley School for the Deaf, near San Francisco, four new words were written up on little boards around the senior section of the school each week. Staff (and visitors) were asked to try the children out to see if they had learned the meanings of these words, and it seemed that the majority had! At Kelston two or three colloquial phrases each week were used recently in a similar manner and a number of children seemed to benefit from it. At St Joseph's School for the Deaf in St Louis *bright* senior classes are given as many as thirty words a day, two days each week, and are asked to look up the meanings in their diction-aries. They seemed to enjoy doing this, and to realize that they can extend their knowledge and vocabularies a great deal in this way.

In Australia thousands of immigrant families from non-English-speak-ing countries have arrived in recent years. It has been found that the young children of these families are able to learn to speak quite fluent (Australian) English within six months. Their parents, however, despite countless 'grammar lessons' often have extreme difficulty in mastering the language. The value of formal English work should not be over-rated. Often very interesting and quite helpful exercises in the use of words and phrases can be found in grammar or English textbooks written for normally hearing children and for foreign students wishing to learn English. Simply to take such a textbook and work through it from beginning to end, however, is rarely of benefit to the majority of deaf children. As suggested above, the work must fit in with what is currently undertaken and encountered in other subjects and no textbook can be so arranged. Brief follow-up exercises to be done at home or in the hostel are very important for consolidation and to encourage the children to use the words in everyday situations. No teacher, for example, should imagine that he or she will teach deaf children all their language this way. The bulk of the language will be learnt in the active programme of reading and language, and many difficulties will be dealt with on the spot. Word and sentence study just give a *little* help in clarifying a few details. Words like 'such', 'if', 'must' and 'just', although being encountered regularly in everyday language work, can profitably be isolated and briefly studied. A list of useful texts for suggestions and ideas is given at the end of this chapter.

Films and filmstrips

Films and filmstrips are an excellent means of getting ideas and the language surrounding those ideas across to deaf children. With film-strips it is helpful to have the positives pasted on cards. A teacher can then quickly scan the text and the photographs without the incon-venience of unravelling the filmstrip.

A good synopsis of a film can be of much assistance in choosing a suitable one and preparing a lesson or series of lessons involving it. Better still, the sound script (or selected parts of it) can be taken as a basis for discussion before the film is shown.

Letter-writing

Little children, to begin with, can often send a labelled painting together with a copy of the 'school newspaper,' but quite soon they should try to write things that interest them and that they think will interest their parents. Teachers should give a great deal of thought to getting the idea across that 'letters tell us things'. An excellent way of doing this is by encouraging parents and friends to take a great deal of time over *their* weekly letter to the child. One mother, for example, spent an average of four hours each week preparing the one-page letter to her little daughter. If care is taken to include photos of well-known people and things at home, and little sketches and cut-out pictures, these letters can be very stimulating and meaningful to the child and the child then wants to communicate in a like manner.

An example of how meaningless letter-writing can become to children is this letter home by a deaf boy (in 1933):

> My dear Parents,
>> Brush your hair. Clean your boots.
>> Your affectionate son,
>>> John

Little better is the 'Dear Mum and Dad – How are you? – I am very well – on Saturday we played football – on Sunday we went to church – Love from Peter' type of letter. (Normally hearing children, will, of course, write like this unless encouraged to do otherwise.)

The notebook from hostel to school and the daily diary can be extremely useful when children wish to write home but again the letter must not just become an automatic copying out of the week's activities. As far as possible a discussion with the child should precede his attempt to write, to ensure that he understands what is in his notebook and diary and that he does appreciate that he should try to write things that will be of most interest to his parents and brothers and sisters.

Items from the newspaper and from magazines can be collected during the week and saved up for inclusion in the letter.

Pen-friends, often in other schools or classes for deaf children, can be very useful for encouraging the day pupils to write interesting letters.

Asking and answering questions

It is vitally important that deaf children learn how to ask questions. The following are some points raised in a lecture given by a very experienced teacher of the deaf:

'I have six faithful serving men
Who taught me all I knew.
Their names are Why and What and How
And Where and When and Who.'

If deaf children can ask these questions, if they can even answer them
first, they have gone a long way. By expansion they can say 'How far?'
'How high?' 'How do you do that?' and 'How do you know?' and by
expanding 'What' into its many variations: 'What time?' 'What
colour?' 'What do you think?' 'What's your opinion?' and so on. If
the children can do that, they really have got a gold mine – and our
children have gone a very long way to living (as against just being alive)
and continuing to learn while they live.

Firstly we must make the children want to know. You know how curious
little hearing children are. We need to develop this ability to be eager,
to be anxious to know, to try to find out and to be willing to make a
tremendous effort – for a tremendous effort it is, always, for deaf
children, and I am talking of profoundly deaf children.

How do we develop this? I think through living; by being eager and
enthusiastic; by using natural situations; by being ready to put aside
the lesson we've prepared so carefully, grasping something that the
child has brought and saying: 'Where did you get this?' and talking
about it, and 'How does it work?' etc. We must somehow create a
situation by always asking the children although we know the answer –
just using natural questions and using them over and over and over
again.

Daily discussion on news items is very valuable. Fill out the facts by
first asking and then listing questions. If the news lesson is really alive,
the children will want to know something more: 'I have a little item
of news – So-and-So has a new frock.' Somebody will want to know
what colour it is: 'Did Mummy make it?' or 'Was it from the shop?' So
we will find out these items by question and answer. If the child does
not know a word he might, if he is six, seven or eight, go and hunt in the
dictionary, especially a picture dictionary. Again, he might draw
something. We accept any of these ways, but the child who is eager to
learn will gladly try to remember the word you give him for he is now
aware that words help him to find out what he wants to know.

For children from seven to nine questions do not come easily –
make the habit of soliciting two or three questions about each news
item, taking care each child has a chance to be first some time – the
first question is, of course, the easiest one.

*We cannot develop in our profoundly deaf children sentence construction
usages that can become fixed and readily usable, not even in bright children,*

without drill. We must continue using all types of question forms in free incidental situations, but side by side we plan formal rules in first answering and then asking all the different question forms.

From about eight years of age until the end of primary school, I have a weekly general questions lesson. Skills in asking questions are not easy to develop but they are by no means impossible. Write 'Today is Tuesday' and somebody with some help will write 'What is today?' and so on. There are all sorts of other things. It can get more involved as you go on – colours, birthdays, dates, what things are made of, when something is going to happen, and so on, always revising and expanding.

Then at all stages, in the classroom or with visitors, we try to have some lively, bubbling-over questions for the outgoing able child. They often want to know the name of the ship, or what kind of plane or something. There will be somebody else in the same age-group who will hardly be able to ask whether the visitor came by boat or plane, and they have to be helped.

Some reference material in the form of questions, turnover charts or question books is worth while – something to which the children can refer and which helps them consolidate their language learning.

Conversations

The following technique has produced excellent results in a partially hearing unit in a London primary school, and is useful with severely deaf children also.

There must be two people with normal speech so that the correct sound and speech patterns of question and answer follow each other closely. All participants sit in a circle with the two adults wearing microphones sitting facing each other and all the children's aids switched to the loop plus microphone position. The visual aids are on a central table. First the teacher questions a child. If he fails to reply, she then questions the other adult and all children watch and listen for the answer. The child is then questioned again and must use the correct words in his reply.

Several parents have watched the method in order to use it at home.

Stage 1 – Nursery and infants

(*Small group of from four to six children. Time – fifteen to twenty minutes. Visual aids – models of four rooms of a house, contents, people, etc.*)

The first must be limited, usually with the questions and answers decided beforehand. These will be suggested by the various difficulties observed in classroom situations. Three short periods a day could be used profitably.

e.g. *Nouns*

What's that?	That's a chair.
What's this?	This is a table.
Who is it?	It's a girl.
Where are those?	Those are in the box.

Pronouns

Who is it for?	For me, you, him, her, them.
Whose is it?	It's mine, yours, his, hers, theirs.
Who did it?	I did it. You . . . He . . . She . . . They . . .

The children soon see that they can rearrange the words of the question to help form the answer. This develops a listening attitude and a positive response so that they acquire new words and practise them.

Stage 2 – Juniors

(*Visual aids – contents of shops, real and dummy goods. Scales, money, measures, etc.*)

At this stage the sentences are longer and more complex. The conversation should be allowed to wander around the subject matter to encourage versatility of thought and to give opportunity for the idioms to arise and to be understood in context. The questions should range from price to weight, to shape, to texture, to simple calculation, etc., e.g.

What did you buy?	I bought . . .
What does it weigh?	It weighs . . .
What is the price of this?	The price is . . .
What is it wrapped in?	It's wrapped in . . .
What did he charge you?	He charged me . . .

The two teachers constantly exchange the questioning role and as fluency increases they seldom have to appeal for a correct answer.

Stage 3 – Conversation without visual aids

By this time fluency has been established and more children can be included without the conversation flagging. For example, suggestions for the fancy-dress party lend themselves to:

Who would you like to be?	I should like to be . . .
What will you wear?	I shall wear . . .
What material will you use?	I shall use . . .
Who are you going to come as?	I am going to come as . . .

After the party was over a further talk was held commenting on each other's choice of costume. The tape dealing with the special vocabulary on clothes was used for practice.

These talking sessions should be followed by practice on tapes using the new vocabulary. After a visit to the zoo and a conversation using model animals, a tape was made using a picture book on the zoo as a visual aid. The sound track had three stages of difficulty: (*a*) naming process – a penguin, a brown bear, etc.; (*b*) short sentence – Here is an elephant. The Polar bear is white; (*c*) long sentence – The hippopotamus likes playing in the water.

Each sound pattern has a space following to allow repetition and is repeated twice. The child follows Stage 1 through the book and when he has become fluent, Stage 2 is attempted, and so on. The tape must be prepared with the child and followed up with questions and answers. The tape recorder used is fitted with twelve sets of headphones so that several children can practise at once. They like working on tapes and can be left practising in the corridor.

Teachers' helpers in language work

A fairly recent development in many schools and classes for deaf children has been the employment of non-professional staff, known as teachers' aides or teachers' helpers. In most districts there appears to be a large group of women who, for family reasons, are unable to undertake full-time employment. They are, however, free during school hours and are keen to undertake part-time work.

Teachers' helpers can be so helpful and encouraging to teachers and children alike. Officially, they are employed to assist with all the hundreds of little non-professional duties which teachers otherwise must spend teaching time doing: preparing and putting out materials, taking nursery children to the toilet, escorting them to the dentist or doctor, helping prepare reading materials, cutting up cardboard, mixing paints, collecting lunch money, cyclostyling and spirit duplicating, etc. Increasingly, however, teachers are finding that *some* teachers' aides can be very helpful in assisting with classwork. One must be careful, of course, that this is controlled so that the aides do not become teachers. One should never ask them to do more than one asks parents of deaf children to do.

In one nursery class the help of nursery aides is used very effectively during the morning language period. One lesson observed ran as follows:

The teacher of the deaf sat in front of the semi-circle of twelve three- and four-year-old very deaf children. The two teachers' helpers sat immediately behind the children.

The teacher said: 'Good morning' and immediately asked the three or four children in front of her to say: 'Good morning.' At the same time, the teachers' helpers asked the children near to them to say: 'Good morning' also.

Next minute, one of the children arrived late with his mother and the teacher said: 'Oh, and who's this? It's *Roger*, isn't it? Who is it?'

She then asked her little group to say: 'Roger, Roger, Roger' and the aides did likewise. Some of the children spoke very indistinctly and were only able to move their lips and make a sort of 'woewoe' sound for 'Roger'. This type of approximation was accepted by the three adults.

Teacher: 'And who's this with him? It's his *mother*, isn't it?'

The same process was gone through again. When a little child did not attempt to vocalize, his hands were placed on the teacher's or helper's face while she said it, and as is often the case with profoundly deaf children, an attempt was then made to imitate the teachers' pattern.

Then the teacher said: 'Roger and his mother came in the *car*, didn't they? How did they come? They came in the car.' A car was sketched on the little blackboard by the teacher, and then all said the word again.

The whole lesson was kept happy and animated and the children seemed to derive a great deal of pleasure from attempting to speak. The meanings of most of the words and phrases which they were asked to say were fairly clear to them, i.e. Roger, mother, car, etc., but sometimes the words were not well understood. This did not seem to affect these little children's enjoyment of saying them. In much the same way, of course, normally hearing babies will 'parrot back' phrases which parents say to them without really comprehending the language used. (At all levels there is a danger of becoming over-conscious of the need to make every word meaningful for deaf children.)

It was interesting that after observing the above lesson for about five minutes there was the sound of continual chatter from these twelve very deaf three- and four-year-olds – and, of course, from the three adults working with them.

At Central Institute for the Deaf in St Louis teachers' helpers are also used in more educational roles than is customary elsewhere. The teacher, for example, would take a language lesson with half of her class and the helper would then revise it from a blackboard summary and supervise reading seatwork made earlier under the teacher's direction. The teacher would work with the other half of the class while this was being done.

In a number of schools, parents are either employed, or assist voluntarily as teachers' helpers. There are, of course, arguments both for and against parents being so closely involved in the life of the school but many teachers feel that the pros outweigh the cons. The headmaster of one day school for deaf children has parents of the children in his class rostered so that one comes each day to help him. Other teachers in his school are also free to arrange such assistance from parents if they wish and about half do so.

The 'conversation' period described earlier could well be conducted using a competent teachers' helper as the other normally hearing speaker.

Suggestions for textbooks

Carter, V. (1961) *Find Out* (Books 1 and 2) Cassell
Filipovic, R. and Z., and Webster, L. (1962) *Méthode Audio-visuelle d'Anglais* Didier, Paris (distributed by Harrap)
Lack, Agnes (1955) *The Teaching of Language to Deaf Children* Oxford University Press
MacIvor, A. (1949) *The New First Aid to English* Gibson
Meade, F. H. M. and Kerry, F. (1960) *Look, Think and Write* (Books 1 and 2) Chambers
Ridout, R. (1963) *International English* (Books 1 to 5) Macmillan, New York
Thorpe, E. G. (1963) *Complete English* (Books 1 to 4) Heinemann Educational (for nine- to twelve-year-olds and particularly good for parents' use)
Walters, D. W. (1964) *Preliminary English* Collins
West, M. (1958) *Improve Your English* Longmans

A series of filmstrips produced by Camera Talks Ltd, 23 Denmark Place, London W.C.2, entitled *Language* (Nos. 1–12) have been found useful for children from about the age of eight years.

Suggestions for reading on play and play materials may be obtained from the Nursery Association of Great Britain and Northern Ireland, 89 Stamford Street, London S.E.1.

8 The Teaching of Reading

After observing methods of teaching reading to deaf children in several countries it can be said that widely differing methods are obtaining good results. There must, therefore, be some features common to them all which assist children to read. Some of these are discussed later.

METHODS AT THE PRIMARY STAGE

In Detroit a technique is used which emphasizes silent reading a great deal, particularly in the early stages – children are not expected to pronounce the words, but only to recognize them and comprehend their meaning in sentences and paragraphs. This differs from the well-known sequence of 'direct experience to *oral symbol* and then to written symbol'.

At the California School for the Deaf in Berkeley(32) a short story is carefully chosen, or two pages in a reading book, and then introductory material is meticulously prepared. The language concept involved is then taught with activity methods, and tested. Next, comprehension of the phrases and sentences is tested by drawing, and the children are then asked to compare their drawings with the one appearing in the book. Only then are they permitted to read the story from the reading book. (Pages ahead are sealed down with rubber bands.)

According to a method used in South Africa(33) the children are taken through a graded progression of language forms – which holds things like tense, length of sentence, and type of sentence static – so as not to confuse the children. Even by five and six years of age, many children are said to read well using this technique.

A fourth method is that used at Lexington School for the Deaf, New York(34). This approach is based on two types of reading practice: *skill building* and *free reading*. The basic reader used in the school and carefully selected library books are part of skill building. Under skill building also are teacher-made exercises for developing sight vocabularies and word, sentence and paragraph reading. (It is a requirement of several teacher of the deaf training courses in the U.S.A. that students learn to type.) Under free reading a wide variety of material is included: attractive trade books, periodicals, readers supplementary to the basic readers, workbooks, diaries, daily news, reading in all lessons, and incidental or functional reading, e.g. newspapers, bus time-tables, advertisements, television, letters, games, notices, menus, maps and films.

At Woodford School for the Deaf in Essex(35) no basic readers or supplementaries at all are used until the children are about eight years of age. All reading prior to this time is of the 'experience' type. Little books are made which describe (often under the children's illustrations) what they have been doing, e.g. 'We went to the shop. We bought some plums. We took turns carrying them back to school,' etc. (See facing page 192.) At the nursery level, these 'books' may consist of only two pages with one sentence on each page, but by the time the children are six or seven, the book will consist of five or six pages with four or five sentences on each page. In addition to an increase in length, there is an increase in the complexity of the sentence and the vocabulary becomes more varied, e.g. replacing 'good' and 'bad' are words like 'delightful', 'beautiful', 'messy' and 'naughty'. The sentences are repeated at the end of the book without pictures and so form little stories which the children soon learn to read. These books are taken home and apparently very few parents are unable to cooperate by hearing their child read – usually over and over again!

As the children progress to the junior school, the experience reading continues but now the blackboard is used a great deal more. This 'listening–reading–speaking method' has been discussed more fully in the previous chapter.

Factors in learning

Factors common to all methods seem to include the old psychological 'laws of learning' – *primacy, frequency, recency* and *emotional congruity*.

The first presentation of a word or sentence can be crucial. It is therefore most important that the material which is initially placed in front of the children should be as *interesting* as possible. The example of the two ways of teaching 'corkscrew', in the previous chapter emphasizes this.

There is absolutely no doubt that the more frequently children have the opportunity to read, the more progress is likely to be made. Nothing improves reading ability more than reading. They should be bombarded with print which is of interest to them at every opportunity throughout their waking hours. The nursery school children in Primary School 47, New York, 'read' while they stand and wait in their classroom for the bus to come to take them home. If children hope ever to learn to read, they must practise and practise and practise in as many *pleasurable* and *meaningful* situations as possible. Gates(36) draws attention to this in the following table giving the average number of repetitions necessary for normally hearing children to learn words in reading:

I.Q.	Repetitions
120–129	20
110–119	30
90–109	35
80– 89	40
70– 79	50

The number of repetitions for deaf children is no doubt very much greater owing to their language deficiency.

Recency is, of course, often related very closely to frequency. If a child sees a new phrase one day and does not see it again for six months, it is unlikely that he will recognize it. If, on the other hand, he sees it again at home the same night when his mother writes it in the family diary or points it out in another book, then it is much more likely to be remembered. The more frequently he reads, the more opportunities he will have to recall new words.

Emotional congruity is basic to success in all subjects, and no matter what method is employed, good teachers present the material in such a way that it is enjoyable, or at least interesting to the children. When one sees half the class surreptitiously stifling yawns, one can be sure that not a great deal of learning is taking place. The choice of the topic, the material prepared and the length of the session all affect the child's emotional approach to the task. Roma Gans in *Common Sense in Teaching Reading* says: 'One cannot over-emphasize the importance of a 'peppy' creative teacher – no matter what reading theory is involved.'

There must be a happy atmosphere in the classroom, so that the child feels secure and confident. The teacher must know her children and appreciate such things as individual differences, each child's hearing loss, the variability of home backgrounds, physical and emotional differences, language development, native intelligence and rate of learning.

The classroom environment must foster a desire to learn to read. The room must be neat, clean, orderly, bright, interesting and stimulating. Books need to be arranged so that they invite children to become acquainted with them. This is a day-to-day job – a housekeeping task. A 'book corner' is essential to every classroom and children must learn to handle books with care. Books that are torn or falling apart, that are carelessly piled together or stacked in any old place do not encourage children to read.

'Reading is part of the development of language and language is not an isolated subject. It is part of the whole process of growth and development. Language is speaking, listening, writing and reading.'(29)

Experience reading

In the reading scheme used at Kelston, we pay great attention to 'experience reading'. This covers a wide range of reading activities. The developmental period in language development in the primary school is fully described in the previous chapter and during this time the teacher will make much use of captions: she will, for instance, write the child's name on his painting or drawing, a caption for the painting itself, e.g. 'Peter went for a swim' and labels for the child's constructions 'Eddie's big garage'. She will write a description of a particular activity on a piece of paper, e.g. 'Janet is pushing the pram' which may be enlarged later to 'Janet pushed the pram: the doll fell out.'

The child watches the teacher say the caption before she writes it. Then the teacher reads it to the child who attempts to repeat the caption, which is of interest, is meaningful and is used for language and reading later in the day, e.g. 'What did you do, Janet?' 'I pushed the doll's pram.'

The use of captions can, of course, be extended to other studies: one for the nature table might be 'John found a lizard. It is slippery.'

As well as the home/school notebook (see page 60) a news board offers excellent opportunities for reading experience. Class news may be written by the teacher about any interesting class event and excursion news (excursions being most necessary experiences for deaf children) may be written by the children themselves: 'We shall go to the shop; we shall buy some meat', etc. Items of interest may be brought by the children, teacher or parents and the children can display such news as: 'On Thursday we shall go to the show', with illustrations. The news board is also the obvious place to display notices about school events – Parents' Day, the school picnic, Christmas party, etc. – and letters to be sent home or to other classes and schools.

Good presentation of all work is important. The words must attract attention and good-sized, even lettering is necessary for notices and captions. Teachers must make every effort to present reading as attractively as possible. An overcrowded, carelessly arranged news board or wall display with old notices or work has no meaning.

Weekly newspaper sheets (see page 139) are excellent and so are 'wall stories'. These may be based on shared experiences like a trip to the beach. Each child draws a different picture and the teacher pastes the pictures side by side in sequence on a length of brown paper. She then prints captions under each picture so the story might read: 'We went to the bus. We went to the beach. We played in the sand. We found shells and crabs. We had a swim. The water was cold.' The same captions are then printed separately so that the children can match these to the wall story. They are encouraged to isolate words by pointing out the word 'bus' or 'shells'. These stories should be read each day for several days and, when they are taken from the wall, they can be made into books for the book table. Simple stories such as 'John's Toys' can also be made into wall stories, which should always be placed low enough for children to reach when matching captions.

To enable a deaf child with limited or no spoken language to recall an experience in order to talk, write or read about it, teachers have found the camera an invaluable teaching aid. Photos are taken of the children in the class (who soon recognize each other's names) and the teachers, house staff and helpers around the school are also photographed and the photographs made into wall stories and later into books. The children are interested in themselves and the pictures are interesting, meaningful and topical.

Once or twice each term teachers can stimulate interest in reading in the older children by writing all instructions on the board instead of saying them. Usually one morning is sufficient for this, and it should be conducted as a game.

Teachers should patiently provide words and repeatedly draw the children's attention to them, showing real interest in the children's news, letters, etc. They must seize every opportunity to stimulate and encourage question forms and conversational language.

In addition to this very important 'interest reading' (based on real experiences) children should also be introduced to easy and attractive trade books from the reading corner. Some suggestions for these will be found at the end of the chapter. Each day nursery and infant classes are told a story from an attractive book and this increases their interest in reading.

Basic readers

When the child has had this kind of meaningful reading experience and is picking out words, remembering them and recognizing them in other contexts, he will be ready to start on a basic series of readers. Since children learn best when they are interested, it is necessary to have a wide variety of books.

The basic readers used at Kelston are New Zealand's *Ready to Read* series. These books do not use isolated words. Deaf children have to be taught to think and talk in sentences and the New Zealand readers use the sentence method. Many of the basic sight words will have been used during the preparatory stage. Much of the new language is taught during earlier language periods – e.g. visits to the airport and the fire station precede the books *Grandma Comes to Stay* and *The Fire Engine*. Children will eventually need to build up a basic sight vocabulary of words they recognize immediately. Many of the words like 'the', 'at', 'on', will be learnt purely through their frequent use in context until they are finally recognized by themselves.

If children are having difficulty with a word such as 'here' they may make a booklet about it. Each child cuts out a picture of an animal to paste on a sheet of paper. The teacher then writes the caption for each: 'Here is an elephant – Here is a lion.' The pages are stapled together and on the back page teacher prints 'Here' in isolation.

With each *basic reader*, several *supplementary readers* are used. In these, different stories have been specially written using the same vocabulary. This consolidates the reading done in the basic reader and the children get pleasure from being able to read a little story straight off. We often find that several series of basic and supplementary readers are needed – e.g. Book 1 plus supplementaries of four or five series – before the children are ready to proceed to Book 2 of the main basic reader. Complications occur, of course, because the vocabulary for each series is not exactly the same. We select as carefully as possible and sometimes paste more suitable wording over the least suitable pages.

READING IN THE JUNIOR AND SENIOR SCHOOL

The experience type reading for older children consists largely of an extension of all the points mentioned above. Both the vocabulary and the type of sentence construction becomes more complex. Compare for example, these sentences taken from the weekly 'school newspaper' of the eight- to nine-year-old and twelve- to thirteen-year-old children, with those of the six-year-olds on page 139.

Junior School

Peter brought a plastic garage to school.
Dennis made a leather case for his gun.
Stephen said: 'I have new sandals' very nicely.
Charlie reads the school magazine. He thinks it is very interesting.
Caroline made a chocolate pudding at cooking.
Seena is very lucky. She got two parcels and a birthday card.
Glenn is trying hard to be a good boy.
Freddie has been to the dentist twice this week.

Senior School

Rakai – Some of the seniors played bowls and badminton in the hall tonight and I was tired after all the running about.

Weather permitting, Brenda is going to visit Lorraine's place tomorrow.

Lorraine – Today my cousin Robbie is going to get married. My family is going to the wedding.

Terry – Terry has a paper round now and will deliver 150 papers each day.

Pao – Last night we played in the gym. Next Wednesday will be the finish of gym at this school, but I hope to keep it up at high school.

Jennifer – I have made two exciting dresses – one blue and one green. The green one is for the Christmas party and the blue one for the play.

Parents and hostel staff are encouraged to keep *family* and *dormitory diaries*. In these there is now much more writing and much less drawing and use of pictures.

When they reach about seven and eight years of age, deaf children often seem to enter the 'doldrums' in both their language development and their reading ability. Progress seems negligible and some words are even forgotten. Wrightson and his colleagues(37) administered reading tests to all the 5,307 children in schools for the deaf in the U.S.A. and Canada in 1959, aged ten to sixteen years inclusively. Their depressing results showed that between the ages of ten and sixteen there was an increase in reading age of less than ten months; the ten-and-a-half-year-olds had reading ages of eight years seven months and the reading ages of the sixteen-and-a-half-year-olds had increased to only nine years five months. A. S. Neill(38) allows the children in his school (a normally hearing one) to come to lessons if they wish and has noted that during the eight- to ten-year-old period, they seldom avail themselves of what is offered in the classroom. The boys, particularly, seem to love the outdoors, playing cowboys and Indians and so on. As adolescence approaches however, an interest in schooling again becomes apparent and Neill says his children, of their own volition, usually study extremely hard.

This innate desire to be on the move for a large part of each day could be a possible explanation for the deaf children's apparent disinterest in much of the school work they are asked to attempt at eight to ten years of age. Another reason, however, that certainly does contribute is the fact that while the children are in the beginners' classes the work tends to be fairly concrete, clear and tangible, such as the names of things and people, adjectives and verbs and a few articles. Later, the child's horizons begin to expand – he looks farther afield than just his own feelings about his own things and the people in his home and school. He learns about other places, other experiences, more subtle emotions, and he runs head on into the varied and complex language we use to describe them.

'The boy had no money. He was sad,' for example, is much easier to comprehend than 'If we haven't got enough, we'll just have to make do.'

One way of making the breakthrough into abstract work easier is by ensuring that the children are familiar with the tricky little words that creep into reading work at this stage. Many of these words, like 'is', 'as', 'has' and 'can' are not easy to lipread, and their comprehension is not critical in lipreading the whole sentence. In 'John has an apple', 'John' and 'apple' are the two most important words. 'Has' can be skipped over for a long time without its being fully understood. In reading, these words can cause a great deal of trouble. By drawing attention to them, and *constantly* reviewing them in reading, their significance gradually becomes apparent, and children are helped to read more advanced material which otherwise may be beyond them.

Sight words

Dr E. W. Dolch(39) has compiled a list of 220 words which are contained in 50 to 75 per cent of all reading material (Appendix 3). The basic sight vocabulary is divided into eight columns. When the first four columns are known, then use can be made of the Dolch Basic Readers. These readers have worthwhile story value as well as containing the first hundred and ten sight words and ninety-five commonest nouns. Knowledge of these words, of course, assists in the reading of any basic reading series.

When teaching the sight words, teachers are recommended to concentrate on one column at a time and *test* the child by using flash cards. The words not known should be recorded and taught in sentences.

The sight words should be used in as many ways as possible in the speech, reading and language programme. The new words can be used in simple comprehension exercises. Each list of sight words can be tested by flash cards or lipreading tests.

Points to remember

1 Flash cards should be used a great deal for testing and checking but not for *teaching* purposes.

2 Children must not learn sight words from lists of words but through sentences and phrases.

3 The sight word must be recognized instantly.

One teacher of deaf children suggests that the Dolch readers should be used in the following way:

Select a reader *to suit the child's interest*, or even better, let him choose it. He will also need a notebook to do comprehension exercises after each reading lesson. A daily oral reading period from five to ten minutes should be set aside for each child. In the initial stages one page is sufficient but this can be increased when reading skills improve. Make full use of the speech training aid or the induction loop.

When the child is reading orally he sees the word, says the word, and hears the word and even though the last two skills have been acquired imperfectly, *he is using them*. If he is unable to say the word or does not recognize it, give him as much help as possible through lipreading, listening and speech. Once he can say the word, continue; do not delay too long to perfect it. This can be done during the individual or group speech lesson. At the conclusion of the oral reading, discuss new vocabulary with the child. This will help to establish meaning and recognition.

The next step is to set some simple comprehension exercises to do in the notebook. At first these should merely be to test his understanding of phrases and thought units, e.g. draw the bird flying down from the tree; draw the blown-down tree. Encourage the use of coloured pencils as this helps to maintain interest. As the reader develops proficiency, set (a) simple questions followed by (b) more detailed ones; e.g. (a) Where was the wolf's den? (b) When the wolf woke up, what did he do?

In the evening the child should read the extract from the basic reader prepared by himself and the teacher to his parent or supervisor in the hostel. The comprehension exercises can then be done. It is essential to enlist this help. Generally speaking it can be obtained willingly. Teacher–pupil or parent–child oral reading holds the learner's interest, increases his self-confidence, alerts him to word recognition, assists phrasing and gives him an appreciation of punctuation signposts for meaningful reading. The teacher particularly during these lessons is able to get on-the-spot information on: (a) his pupil's attack on unknown words; (b) his ability or inability to see similarities in word structure; (c) his strength and weakness in relating the written form of sounds to the spoken sound; (d) his knowledge of sight words; (e) his skill in understanding words, phrases and sentences.

To give every child in the class five to ten minutes of individual reading each day (and a similar amount of speech) can be a problem if there are eight or more in the group. 'What can I do with the others?' one is frequently asked. Keeping them *usefully* employed can be difficult, especially for an inexperienced teacher. The younger or less intelligent the children, the more pressing does this problem become.

One suggestion is to increase the staffing so that each teacher is freed to do an hour and a half of individual (clinical) work each day(39) while another teacher takes the remainder of the class, but this is not usually practicable.

Another solution is to employ teachers' helpers to supervise simple projects and games, in written language, arithmetic, reading, arts and crafts and so on. This is much cheaper and can be excellent, but again, has to be very carefully planned to be successful.

A third method is to work up a host of useful activities which the children can profitably do without a great deal of supervision. They do, of course, need some supervision and usually soon run into difficulties if not given any.

There are a number of books(40) which contain good activities which the teacher can adapt if necessary and introduce to the children in group lessons (no individual work that day). They can then be practised by the children individually on subsequent days.

Individual work does not have to be done in one long session. Some teachers snatch short periods throughout the day. Two children can be taken before school, one more gets five minutes at lunch-time and three more can be squeezed in during the 'seatwork' period described below. One child does not do physical education, so he can be taken for two half-hour sessions each week at that time, and so on.

It is easier in some classes and schools to arrange individual work than in others, but 'where there's a will, there's a way' and it is surprising what can be achieved. The important thing is that it be done regularly and imaginatively. If it is really difficult to arrange, it is probably better to take two children for four sessions each per week than eight children for one session each. A teacher might select the two children who need her help most (not necessarily the slowest in the class), and give them a few weeks' tutoring, then select another pair.

Reading activities

Some excellent suggestions for reading activities are contained in an article in *Volta Review*(41) and extracts from it are given below. The teacher is not of course just using this individual work as a means of keeping the children busy. Her primary aim is to provide revision of material taught in a variety of ways, and at each child's individual rate. These activities give him meaningful drill to assist in mastering reading and language skills. They also give excellent training to help the child become independent. Most of the following exercises are suitable for lower second grade (eight-year-old) children, but they could all be adapted for other ages.

A simple type of individual reading activity stressing *sentence comprehension* is matching sentences to pictures. Teaching materials for use with the class include large pictures set on the chalk tray, and large sentence strips telling about the pictures. A sentence is given in speech-reading. A child finds the sentence and places it by the proper picture. The same type of thing can be done using expressions or dialogue sentences suggested by the pictures. After having presented the material in class, stressing speech and speech-reading, individual materials are handed out. Now each child must think for himself. Each one receives an envelope containing four pictures and about sixteen sentences. All the pictures and sentences are different. The children are to place the sentences below the most fitting picture. Everyone sets to work, leaving the teacher free to give individual help.

Arrange the sentence strips in sequence

Jack and Julie played leapfrog. Julie jumped over Jack.	A frog jumped over Julie. Julie was very surprised. Where did the frog come from ?
Jack jumped over Julie.	
Julie jumped over Jack again.	

It helps also to make some duplicated seatwork for each type, using the same idea but different vocabulary. Then the children can take the finished product home and show the family how smart they really are! This is also an incentive to use the new learning at home.

'*Where' phrases* merit a lot of meaningful drill. A picture is shown of a boy on a horse, and the question asked: 'Where is the boy?' Four or five appropriate pictures are pasted on a chart, with about twenty 'where?' questions typed beside them, and a line for each answer. Answers are on cards in an envelope clipped to the chart. To make checking easy, the teacher has the answer cards correctly arranged and marked in alphabetical order. The children never catch on to the checking system because they don't yet understand alphabetical order. Besides, always start with a different letter and mark the answers from the bottom up. It's foolproof!

For meaningful drill on correct *adjective sequence*, place pictures on the chalk tray, and have descriptive phrases cut into separate words and scattered on a desk. Pupils arrange the phrases according to how many, what kind, what colour, what, and place them by the proper picture. Each descriptive phrase has been printed on a different colour paper to avoid confusion. After sufficient drill, objects are placed on the chalk tray, and a pupil comes forward to describe an object – a funny yellow rabbit, a silly clown, etc.

Further meaningful drill is provided on charts. About eight pictures of objects are pasted on a cardboard sheet. Descriptive phrases, each typed on a different colour cardboard, are cut apart and placed in an envelope. The children enjoy sorting the words into colour groups, then arranging these scrambled phrases in correct order under the proper pictures. Sometimes they use the phrases in sentences. There is a definite carry-over to original language periods, and to spontaneous usage.

To make children more aware of the correct *sequence of words* within a sentence, as well as the meaning of the sentence, these teaching materials are helpful. Sentences typed on different coloured strips of paper and cut into words or phrases are placed in an envelope together with small pictures illustrating them. The pictures are numbered 1 to 10 in order to facilitate checking. The youngsters put the pictures in order first, then arrange a sentence correctly and place it by the correct picture.

Sequence work is found in many reading workbooks. It is usually quite difficult for the children to understand. So this was tried: in each envelope are four pictures cut from a workbook page stressing sequence. There are also four or five sentences telling the story. Children arrange the pictures in correct sequence, and then fit the sentences to the pictures. A bit later we remove the pictures and the children arrange the sentences only in sequence. This lays a foundation for later work where only sentences are given to be numbered in correct order.

Classification is important to facilitate straight thinking. Forty work cards are placed in an envelope for the youngsters to classify under Food, People, Toys and Animals. These classifications are so different that they are not hard, but it sets the stage for harder classification later on.

Comprehension

Redgate(42) analysed the errors made by 144 deaf children aged eight, nine and ten years when they were asked to attempt his Graded Directions Test. Several of his findings have direct application for teachers. A large group of the children, for example, showed complete ignorance of the negative form – i.e. when they read: 'Do not pick up a pencil', 36 per cent of the children *did* pick up a pencil. Similarly, a lack of understanding of the pronoun 'it' was displayed by no less than 32 per cent of these 144 children, and confusions between 'on' and 'in' were not infrequent.

'Children in the early stages of learning to read were often found to make mistakes which were probably attributable to misinterpreting or failing to notice the indefinite article "a".'

It is suggested therefore that teachers should recognize that such errors occur when anyone is learning a language, and give more attention to helping children with them.

In the Perth School for Deaf Children the technique set out below is used in teaching reading to older children to suit the children's vocabularies, so that there are not too many unfamiliar words. Instalments of between two and five hundred words are studied at one time.

Word	Pronunciation	Meaning	Sea Hunt – Episode 5
Electra	e-lek-tra	a name	The *Electra* was a ship used by
used	ewz-d	employed	the American Army to track their rockets when they were fired over the sea. On board
electronic	e-lek-tro-nik	apparatus like a radio, a TV set	was an electronic instrument called a Micro-Finder which recorded the speed, height and
instrument	ins-tru-ment	a radar an asdic	position of the rocket.
torpedo	taw-pee-doa	under-water bomb	One day the *Electra* was sunk by a torpedo explosion
explosion	eks-ploa-shin	blown up	and two skin-divers from a
Micro	mie-croa	electronic	boat went into the wreck and
Finder	fien-du	instrument	took away the Micro-Finder.

Word	Pronunciation	Meaning	Sea Hunt – Episode 5 *(contd)*
wreck	rek	a sunken ship	One diver's air-pipe caught on
jagged	ja-gid	uneven edge	a jagged piece of metal on the
			hull and tore it so that he had
surface	sur-fis	outside area	to come to the surface quickly.
			When the *Electra* did not
port	port	town on the coast	come back to port the Army
			started to look for it with a
naval	nae-val	of the navy	speedy naval launch. Mr John-
			son, the captain of the naval
engaged	en-gaej-d	employed	launch engaged Mike Nelson
radar	rae-da	electronic	to help him. The launch was
asdic	as-dic	submarine radar	fitted with radar and asdic but
			the radar screen only showed
crew	c-roo	those who sail a ship	a small boat and the crew said
			they were fishing.

Reading comprehension

1 The *Electra* was a ship for
   (*a*) fishing   (*b*) skin-diving   (*c*) tracking rockets
   (*d*) patrolling.
2 The Micro-Finder was
   (*a*) on the quay   (*b*) in the water   (*c*) in the ship
   (*d*) on the rocks.
3 The *Electra* was sunk by
   (*a*) a bomb   (*b*) a torpedo   (*c*) a shell   (*d*) a storm.

(Care must be taken here to set questions which cannot be answered simply by copying out the sentence in the prose containing the principal noun in the question.)

Meaning of words

1 'on board' was an electronic instrument;
   'on board' means
   (*a*) on the floor   (*b*) on the mast   (*c*) on the ship.
2 Two skin-divers went on the 'wreck';
   'wreck' means
   (*a*) sea-weed   (*b*) a rock   (*c*) a sunken ship.

3 The asdic screen indicated something under the water;
   'indicated' means
   (*a*) recorded   (*b*) exploded   (*c*) lit-up.

About ten *comprehension* and *meaning of words* exercises are given on each instalment.

Some schools adapt ordinary books in a similar manner to the above. Known vocabulary is pasted over very difficult phrases, and at a later stage the text is left untouched but explanations of difficult words are given in the margin.

By the time deaf children reach the age of thirteen years, one of two things seems usually to have happened to their reading. Either they are reading well, and in many cases voraciously, within a year or two of their mental age level, or, in very many cases, they are floundering about somewhere on the eight-and-a-half-year-old reading-age bar.

It is interesting that many normally hearing children also have difficulty at about the eight- to nine-year-old level. This is usually ascribed to a lack of independent word attack and is compounded by a self-image of failure as a reader. For deaf children these are probably contributing causes. The main one, however, seems to be associated with their general lack of adequate language. No matter how clearly a phrase is heard, for example, it still means virtually nothing unless a number of the words are already known to the reader.

An article in *Volta Review*(43) puts this well: 'It should always be kept in mind that reading requires taking something to the printed page rather than just getting something from it.' When you read the word *korero* you probably have no idea of its meaning. If it was said to you carefully and clearly, you would still have no idea of its meaning, i.e. the language is quite unfamiliar to you. If the word was placed in a sentence the context is not a great deal of help unless one knows most of it. For example, *Korero te wahine e te tamaiti* does not make the meaning of *korero* a great deal more clear. If one has more vocabulary, however, one might be able to read the above sentence as: 'The woman *korero* the boy.' Now it is possible to guess that *korero* is a verb and may mean 'spanked' or 'kissed' or 'washed' or something like that. In other words, the unknown word takes on *some* meaning. (*Korero* incidentally is the Maori for 'talk' or in this case, 'talked to'.)

It seems that the burgeoning vocabulary and the increasing complexity of the language forms at the eight-plus age makes reading increasingly difficult.

What can be done about it? The programmes at home and in school such as the 'listening–reading–speaking' method which have been referred to earlier, do much to overcome the problem. Remedial work based on the lines of these programmes but scaled up in interest level, can be very helpful. More and more books are being published for adolescent children who read badly. The National College of Teachers of the Deaf in England, largely through the efforts of Mr A. E. Heys, has produced a very fair selection of books, the texts of which have been compiled by teachers of the deaf to meet the above need.

READING SCHEMES

In recent years, there has been a revival of interest in raising standards of reading in the general field. Although these approaches are designed specifically to mitigate the difficulties encountered by normally hearing children, adoption of a method which has been objectively shown to be successful might well reduce some of the complexities of the task for deaf children also.

New methods must at the outset, of course, be treated with caution. Success, for example, appears to be ensured whether one is using Stott's Programmed Reading Kit(44), Moxon's Remedial Reading Method (45), Webster's Visual-Verbal Method(46), Gattegno's Words in Colour (47), Jones's Colour Story Method(48), Pitman's i.t.a.(49), or one of the linguistic approaches. Yet this may be merely a matter of partiality. Innovators are certainly highly motivated to succeed. The children too may become highly motivated and so learn more effectively. The conviction with which a new reading scheme is introduced helps to give children confidence, and confidence is such an important factor in learning to read. Innovators and teachers who are keen to try new methods are often among the most capable and efficient teachers. It is difficult to separate out effects due to the above factors from those which may be solely due to the scheme in use – unless vigorous and objective scientific testing of the method is undertaken, using experimental and control groups.

It can, of course, be argued that one should take advantage of whatever 'novelty' and 'Hawthorne' effects(50) one can obtain if they show that children's reading is aided in the short run, but what is really required is a clear answer to the question – does this particular approach *of itself* help children to read?

Two of the approaches mentioned above will be considered very briefly:

The initial teaching alphabet is a standardized system devised for use in the early stages of learning to read so that difficulties caused by the irregularities of English spelling may be eliminated. Pitman(51) suggests that children become confused either because of the lack of consistency in single words or because of the lack of systematic relationships between the individual characters of the alphabet and the phonemes of the spoken language. Pitman's alphabet consists of forty-four characters, each standing for one phoneme only – thus 'c' for example, does not represent both 'k' and 's'. The same phoneme, however, may be represented by more than one symbol – e.g. 'c' 'k' and 'ck' all represent the 'k' sound – so that the difficulties of traditional spelling have not been removed; i.t.a. is thus a *medium* and not a *method*. It is a system of printing and writing that may be used with any method, global, phonic or eclectic.

Downing(52) has made a study over a one-and-a-half-year period and has found that 413 children who had been taught on the i.t.a. were significantly better readers than were a matched group of children using the ordinary alphabet. These are only interim results, and, as Downing states, 'it is still too early to form any definite judgements or firm conclusions'. He is of course very cognizant of the factors mentioned earlier which may affect results in such experiments. It certainly would seem wisest to await more final assessments of this interesting approach before its general introduction should be considered. If it *is* proved

Plate 10 At table work the deaf children sit between hearing children
(p. 110)

Plate 11 Activity period in the infant department (p. 132)

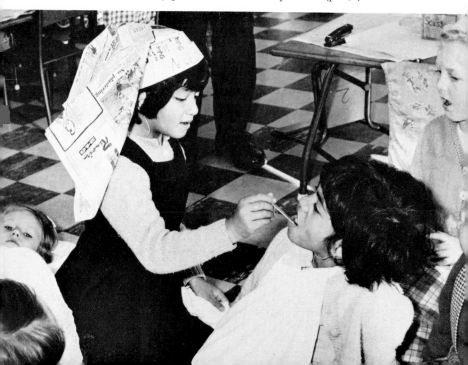

Plate 12 Deaf children can be
excellent instructors (p. 129)

Plate 13 Responsible deaf children can learn to use power tools

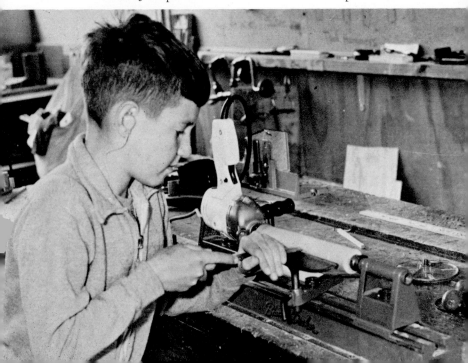

beyond doubt to be beneficial, and if the i.t.a. of Pitman *is* proved to be the best possible simplified alphabet, then it would seem very worth while to try to assess its value to deaf children. *Phonics* (or more correctly, perhaps, *kinaesthetics*) does seem helpful to a number of deaf children in attacking unfamiliar words, and a system which will enable them to do so more easily should be considered carefully.

Another extensive two-year study is being made by Jones(53) of the 'Colour-Story Method'. This system, like i.t.a., claims that the use of these coded scripts helps children to solve their reading problems in a natural way and encourages the development of their reasoning abilities in other problem-solving situations. Any aids of this kind to intellectual growth obviously deserve serious consideration.

The main purpose of phonetic colour is to provide additional tools and clues for independent reading and accurate spelling. The reading books are not intended to replace black print books, and the two systems of reading can go on side by side.

If this method is proved of distinct advantage to normally hearing children, it might well prove effective if adapted for those with impaired hearing. In theory, it could well prove beneficial to older (slow learning) deaf children, and to the less severely deaf.

PROGRAMMED LEARNING

Programmed learning techniques which are being increasingly tried in all subjects(54) may eventually have some application for many deaf children. Reported work in this field to date, however, using either programmed texts or teaching machines with deaf children, does not indicate that revolutionary changes are likely in the near future(55). The Lexington School for the Deaf in New York made a fairly careful study of the programmed material existing in the United States in 1961–2 for normally hearing children and decided not to begin ex-perimenting with it for the next five years. By this time, the staff felt that the techniques could have been improved very considerably. Again, carefully planned research using imaginative programmes is

M

indicated before any mass introduction of such a method should be contemplated.

Suggestions for further reading

Cory, P. B. (1964) *School Library Services for Deaf Children* Volta Bureau, Washington D.C.

Groht, M. A. (1958) *Natural Language for Deaf Children* Volta Bureau

Newton, M. G. (1962) *Books for Deaf Children* Volta Bureau

University of Bristol Institute of Education *A First Survey of Books for Backward Readers* (1956) and *A Second Survey of Books for Backward Readers* (1962) University of London Press Ltd

Richardson, J. A., and Hart, J. A. (1954) *Books for the Retarded Reader* Australian Council for Educational Research, Melbourne

Trevor, R. (1959) *Suggestions for Teaching Backward Readers* New Zealand Department of Education, Wellington

9 Speech Teaching

To avoid confusion, 'speech' teaching in this book means developing intelligible utterance, i.e. helping the children to say more clearly the words they know. It does not mean the teaching of new words – that is *language*. Often, of course, speech, language and reading are so closely related to and dependent on one another that it is hard to differentiate between them.

THE PROBLEM

As was stated earlier, we speak as we hear. Children born in Italy hear Italian speech and, when they begin to talk, they attempt to say Italian words. In the same way, accents are passed on from one generation to another. Profoundly deaf children hear so little of speech that they are unable to speak themselves unless given special help. For this reason, their first attempts to copy speech are often merely lip and jaw movements with no sound produced at all. The problem of the deaf child in speech, then, is essentially a *monitoring* one. Normally hearing children in many cases speak very approximately for several years. Speech therapists usually ignore most of the inaccuracies in the speech of these children, knowing that by the time they are six or seven years old, they will have refined their speech through listening until most of these little errors have disappeared. The grossly defective speech of deaf children cannot, of course, be ignored in this way.

The effect of not being able to monitor one's speech is illustrated clearly in the case of *the adventitiously deaf*. A person who becomes profoundly deaf at, say, twenty years of age, may well have perfect speech. In such cases, the speech always remains intelligible but within a year or so the voice usually shows signs of losing its natural quality and difficulty is, of course, experienced in keeping it at the appropriate level of loudness in noisy and quiet conditions.

THE EFFECT

Just as there are hundreds of different degrees of hearing loss, so there are hundreds of variations in the way deaf people speak. With severe or profound deafness, however, there are certain features which are frequently present. The vowel sounds are longer and the speech generally is slower and more laboured. Much more breath is used by the deaf person. Pronunciation of consonants and combinations of consonants is often defective. Voices tend to sound monotonous, and vowel sounds have a hollow 'wooden' quality. Owing to the above factors, it is not uncommon for the speech of many deaf people to lack rhythm.

It must be said that the speech of many of the children who leave schools for the deaf at the present time is by no means intelligible. Reports such as the following give some cause for real concern regarding many of the methods used in teaching speech(56). In 1962–3, 359 children, aged between fifteen and sixteen who were attending schools for the deaf in England, were interviewed to establish whether their speech had developed intelligibly. The average hearing loss of the group was approximately 85 db. and the mean I.Q. was 97.08.

The report states: 'It is difficult to assess success or failure in this sort of interview and fine assessment did not in any case seem to be appropriate, so that the children were divided into three broad groups based on speech ability.' By this means, 22·3 per cent of the children were considered to have intelligible speech and 23 per cent had speech which was regarded as unintelligible.

Results do vary from school to school. It is felt that if some of the most successful schools were rated in isolation, the distribution of figures in these groups would be considerably different. Two head teachers, for example, felt that 70 per cent and 75 per cent of the children in their schools could reasonably be said to have intelligible speech. Unfortunately, no really objective data of these sort seem so far available.

Unless given good speech teaching, the speech of severely and profoundly deaf children is usually unintelligible to anyone who has not mixed frequently with deaf people.

THE TREATMENT

One of the most interesting recent contributions to the teaching of speech to deaf children has been the development of the 'listening-reading-speaking method (see Chapter 7). It is highly significant that when hearing aids are used properly, and listening practice is given so consistently, it is found that there is much less need to spend time teaching the children individual speech sounds. Many of them are learnt without being taught at all through the most natural medium of all - hearing, and in most cases rhythm and intonation is strikingly natural.

A very useful piece of research by John and Howarth(58) has also drawn attention to the importance of the 'non-articulatory' aspects of speech, i.e. concentrating on achieving normal rate of utterance and stress, rather than the clear articulation of individual speech sounds. When a group of deaf children was taught by concentrating solely on improving the time factors in the speech, a 56 per cent improvement in word intelligibility was achieved, and an even greater improvement in the listeners' ability to recognize the children's utterance of complete sentences. It was concluded by the writers that the information carried in the time factors could be critical in the interpretation of speech which was grossly defective in articulation.

The method used by John and Howarth was as follows: the teaching was individual and a speech training aid was used. The children were encouraged to comment freely on toy or picture material appropriate to their age. Any one of the child's spontaneous phrases or sentences was then selected for special attention. Not more than three or four minutes of teaching time was spent on each sentence. The phrases used ranged between three and eight words in length, because longer phrases were found to have an inhibiting effect when the child made the effort to recall the sequence, and thus defeated the purpose of the teaching.

The teacher repeated a selected phrase three or four times at his own normal speed of utterance. The child was asked to listen and then to imitate the pattern. He was reminded to listen attentively to his own and to the teacher's voice. The teacher commented on the child's efforts as too slow, too jerky, too fast, etc., as seemed appropriate. After listening to several further repetitions of the phrase by the teacher, the child then tried again to make the necessary improvements.

The ideas which we tried to communicate to the children, both by the techniques used and by explanation, were that they should regard the sentence as a whole and try to reproduce the teacher's pattern as closely as possible. We also emphasized the continuity of speech, encouraging the children to run words smoothly together and discouraging their learnt tendency to pause between words whilst they thought how certain sounds should be articulated. There was some resistance to the breaking of this habit but, once overcome, the children's response to a quicker-moving type of speech lesson, with a less analytic approach than they were used to, led us to think that the new emphasis was psychologically sound and, if it were also productive of good results, very worthwhile continuing. It will be seen that the teaching method depends primarily on the presentation of many normal speech patterns and on the child's using his residual hearing to perceive them and to match his own attempts to them. It relies heavily on the cumulative effect of auditory experience.

Of the twenty-nine children in the group, ten were between the ages of six and eight-plus, ten between nine and eleven-plus and the remainder between twelve and fourteen-plus. Fourteen of the children had a hearing loss of 100 db. or more, five 90–99 db., five 80–89 db. and the remainder a loss of under 80 db. Age of onset of deafness was so early in life that none would have spoken without special help.

It is interesting that although the whole group improved markedly as a result of this treatment, no statistically significant differences were found in the improvement scores due to either age or hearing loss. The writers conclude:

When speech becomes laboured or tedious to the speaker and listener the result may be a rejection of speech. Repeated failure by deaf children to get a message across may result in the substitution of gesture language or of writing for speech. It seems to us, therefore, that prior attention must be given to those factors in speech where improvement brings quickest reward for effort. When habits of speaking smoothly, of running words together and of using natural stress and intonation patterns have been firmly established and when the resulting speech, though not wholly intelligible 'sounds like English' to the listener, then is the time to press the children for more accurate pronunciation of particular phonemes within words. To attack the problem the other way round is rather like insisting on correct spelling before the child has any facility in writing.

INDIVIDUAL SPEECH TEACHING

In many American schools speech work begins somewhat earlier than in England – from about three and a half years of age, it seemed in many schools and clinics to be started in earnest. The Ewings(59) emphasized that speech teaching should not begin before some language had been developed and this is an excellent point to bear in mind. They suggested that readiness to begin speech work (or as they call it 'articulation readiness') was usually achieved at about four or five years of age but might be as late as seven years.

When one sees a child being taught speech before he is ready, it is usually fairly obvious. His eyes 'glaze over' after a minute or two and despite 'candy' or 'coercion', boredom is the only observable result. It appears that some of the children who lipread and speak so badly may be the victims of such premature enthusiasm on the part of a teacher or parent.

While teachers should be careful to take note of the Ewings' advice to delay speech teaching until the child has shown some comprehension of what language is, one should also be careful not to delay it longer than necessary. The greatest encouragement a deaf child can have to speak is to see action on his command. For example, if a child went to his father and said: 'Wa', his father might not understand him. He might then put his hand up and twist his fingers as though he is turning on a tap. When supplied with the water, and supposing he had the vocabulary, the child might well think to himself: 'Well, talking is not much use, but the old gestures always seem to get results.' If, on the other hand, he says: 'Water' fairly plainly, and his father gives him a drink of water, he is stimulated to try speech for other things. It is, therefore, very important that we as teachers help the children to speak as clearly as they can as early in their lives as possible.

Five cardinal rules apply to specific speech work:

1 The material used should be meaningful.

2 It should be carefully selected from a speech point of view so that it is not too easy and not too difficult.

3 The lesson should be pleasurable.

4 A record should be kept of material that has been successfully taught.

5 Children should select words and phrases that they particularly want taught. This helps them make the essential transfer from the speech lesson to everyday living.

For the above reasons, a word which might be taken very early in a young child's speech programme, might be 'Mum' or 'Mummy' (or 'Mom' or 'Mommy'). It is likely that this word will be meaningful and interesting to a little child. It is a relatively easy word to say – if not perfectly, at least with fair approximation. Consonants produced at the front of the mouth are often the first to appear(60). By using a photograph of the child's mother and numerous pictures of other little children with their mothers, it could well be made an interesting part of a speech lesson. By pasting the photograph in the child's speech book, with the word printed beside it, it would be excellent for showing to the family that night and to visitors on other occasions. Another photograph of the child's mother could be kept with the ones at school and shown to visitors.

Next day 'Mum' is revised and another word is introduced. Gradually, by this process of revision and extension, each child compiles a little list of words and phrases that he can say clearly. As far as possible, all the people who come in contact with him should know the words and encourage him to say them as nicely as he can whenever a situation requires them.

The regular revision is of great importance. We found at Kelston that, without it, many of the words and phrases were soon forgotten and the speech book became of very little use. If carefully kept, however, with clear and colourful illustrations of the words and phrases, it can become an exciting book which is treasured by everyone. It is also of importance that only words which the child really does say intelligibly should be recorded. One does not want him to go away and practise an error, and then be frustrated by finding that when he says the word it is not understood by most people. 'If in doubt, leave it out' should be the teacher's maxim.

GROUP SPEECH TEACHING

No one ever contends that group speech teaching is as effective as individual work. Ideally, every child would have at least one session of individual speech work every day. The question, of course, is *how* to arrange it. Most schools are just not sufficiently well staffed to enable this to be done. We look forward to the day when they will be.

In the meantime, I believe good group speech teaching is very important.

The five rules stated above apply equally to group speech work. It is just more difficult to achieve the precision that is possible when planning speech work for one child at a time. When a teacher takes over a class of deaf children, she usually consults previous records and then administers speech tests which help her diagnose each child's main difficulties (see Chapter 10). Bearing in mind the dangers noted earlier regarding the too early emphasis on individual sounds, it can be said that improving them at the appropriate time is perhaps the most straightforward task. When all the results are set out it can quickly be seen that perhaps six of the eight children cannot say an 'ng' sound, five are having difficulty with 'z' and five with 'k' and 'g'.

The teacher might decide to take a little poem or jingle containing several 'ng' sounds as the basis for group speech work for the following week. She would then introduce the poem as a language lesson. When it was used for speech work a day or two later, it would thus be meaningful and, one hopes, interesting. Alternatively she might choose a very interesting phrase from a news session or any other source which contains an 'ng' sound and use it for group speech work. The children who can already pronounce 'ng' would be included in the first part of the lesson, but some other defect such as faulty accent, emphasis, rhythm or pitch, might be stressed when it was their turn to speak. When the actual 'ng' sound had been isolated and was being explained and taught, these children would go back to their places and go on with other work. The last steps are to replace the sound in the word and the word in the phrase and, when well established, to record it in the home/school notebook and the speech record.

Another feature of group speech lessons is that the teacher must be particularly active and animated. Lady Irene Ewing emphasized that these lessons had to be 'nippy'. If a teacher starts from one side of her class and patiently works around the semi-circle to the last child, listening and correcting speech as she goes, she soon finds that the remainder of the class begin to fidget and before long are indicating their displeasure in all the various ways known to them. If, on the other hand, she gives all the class an opportunity to say the phrase or word or sound in chorus, and then quickly asks three or four children in random order to try it, all pay attention because they are not sure when it will be their turn. They also enjoy the lessons and, if really well taught, will ask the teacher if they can have speech, if for some reason she was not intending to take it.

Taking individual speech sessions regularly is perhaps the best means of training a teacher to become skilful in group speech technique. One learns when a sound or combination of sounds is well beyond the ability of a child or is almost established. The various progressions teachers use to correct defective speech(59, 61) become well learned and one can get much quicker results. When group speech is taken, one has to work quickly and the work done can be very superficial unless the basic progressions are thoroughly known by the teacher.

It is not possible in this book to describe all the basic procedures used by teachers of the deaf to develop good speech in their children. Sibley Haycock, *The Teaching of Speech*, Ewing, E. C. and A. W. G., *Teaching Deaf Children to Talk*, already referred to (see Bibliography) and Agnes Lack, *The Teaching of Language to Deaf Children*, provide a good deal of this information. Factors such as voice quality, pitch variation, intonation, accent and emphasis, rhythm and the production of individual phonemes, are all discussed in some detail. There is, however, a great deal more to be done in this field to achieve more reliable results.

The following is a description of the procedure and the techniques a teacher might adopt in teaching one sound. 'K' as in 'kitten' can be a difficult sound to teach. (K and g, s and z, and ng, can all be awkward.)

'K' is produced by drawing the tongue back and up against the hard palate, building up air pressure and suddenly releasing it by 'flicking' down with the tongue. 'K' is thus described as a *voiceless, velar, plosive consonant*.

To teach it, the steps might be followed in this order:

1 Use whatever hearing the child has so that he gets the auditory pattern if possible.

2 Try asking the child to say simple words containing the sound, e.g. 'come', 'car', 'book'.

3 Use the hand analogy – 'flick at the back'. Hold the left hand out, palm down, and flick the palm (near the wrist) with the middle finger of the right hand. (See page 189.)

4 Work from p to t to k, e.g. ppp, ttt, kkk. The sounds are all voiceless plosives although produced in a different part of the mouth. 'p' is easiest because it can be seen so easily as well as felt. 'T' is more difficult, and 'k' is most difficult of all. As a general rule, one can say that if a child does not have a 't' sound well established it is no good trying to get a 'k'.

5 The child stands up and looks into the teacher's mouth (teacher facing a good light) while the sound is made. Sometimes children can see the action of the tongue and can then copy the movement themselves.

6 As a rule one avoids manipulating the children's tongues, cheeks, lips and so on. If a child has worked for quite a time, however, and a 'k' is still non-existent, then one time-honoured technique is still well worth trying and in fact rarely fails. Ask the child to say 't' clearly. If he cannot do that, show him ppp, then th, th, th – protruding the tongue slightly between the teeth. Gradually withdraw the tip of the tongue and begin saying t, t, t. Usually children can manage a very fair approximation of it in this way. Next write about ten 't's on the blackboard and one letter 'k' underneath them. Tell the child: 'I want you to say 'ttt' all the time, and I shall make you change it and say 'k'.' When the child has given four or five good strong 't' sounds, carefully place a spatula or the tip of the little finger on the tip of the child's tongue and gently push the tongue back. Often the child stops making any sound, so one must refer to the long row of 't's and say: 'Keep on' and point to each 't' in turn. The child is trying then to say 't' but the teacher has placed his tongue in the position to say 'k' and when 't' is attempted a 'k' is produced. The teacher shows great delight and points to the 'k' on the blackboard. More trials are given and the child can guide his tongue with his finger if he needs to. Revision is given several times on the same day and if tested at home or in the hostel it is often permanently established within a day or so.

As has been stressed in this chapter, helping children to say each sound clearly is one thing, but enabling them to put sounds together in intelligible words and sentences is quite another. A little sentence like 'His cousin judges the azaleas each spring' seems simple enough to those who hear normally, but can be almost impossible for a deaf child to say at all clearly because of the absence of lip movement, very subtle positioning required and the rapid changes from one position to the next.

For young children aged five to eight years tongue and jaw exercises can be made into interesting games. In 'spring cleaning', for example, Mrs Tongue can sweep the walls and ceiling (inside of cheeks

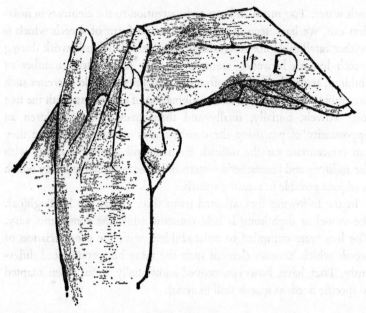

Figure 8   Hand analogy for 'k'

and roof of mouth), clean the 'shelves' inside lips, shake and roll the mats and put them back on the floor; in 'visiting' the tongue calls first on the nose and then the chin and the ears. The children can pretend to be kittens drinking milk, can make 'tunnels' with their tongues or play 'catapults' with them.

Generalizations about teaching methods in different countries can be quite inaccurate, but it appears that graded formal drills seem much more common in the U.S.A. than in England. There was a time when a very formal analytical approach was generally adopted in Europe and little deaf children were taught lists of meaningless sounds and syllables in a set order before words were introduced. No attention was paid to the children's interests or readiness for such drills, and lessons were apparently tedious in the extreme in many cases. The reaction to this seems to have been that any suggestion of formal drills was stereotyped, unimaginative and neglectful of both hearing aids and the psychological needs of the child. Out they went and, to a certain extent, one wonders whether the baby was not thrown out with the bath water. Too much and too early attention to the elements in isolation can, we have seen, develop a laboured form of speech which is neither intelligible nor interesting. *Short* periods of drill work during speech lessons, however, seem to be very helpful to a number of children, particularly the profoundly deaf ones. Simple exercises such as combining a consonant or a combination of consonants with the five long vowels, initially, finally and then medially give children an opportunity of practising the combinations in situations where they can concentrate on the difficult element and become familiar with the auditory and kinaesthetic pattern of its use in speech in a way which is seldom possible in running speech.

In the following lists, adapted from those drawn up by Pugh(62), the vowel or diphthong is held constant while the consonants vary. The lists were compiled to assist children with the pronunciation of words which have an element spelt the same but pronounced differently. They have, however, proved additionally useful when adapted to specific needs as speech drill material.

Words with the vowel sound 'ou' in the spelling are pronounced in so many different ways that they should be organized and placed under the proper chart spellings so that the children can see the visual organizations of the groups, shown on Chart 1.

Chart 1

1 ou = $\overline{oo}$	2 ou = $\breve{oo}$	3 ou = o-e	4 ou = aw	5 ou = -u-	6 ou = ow
soup	could	shoulder	bought	rough	house
through	would	though	fought	tough	mouse
tour	should	dough	thought	country	county
group		poultry	ought	enough	loud
route			brought	young	sound
			four	touch	found
			course	trouble	round
			pour	double	ground

When the pronunciation of a sound within a word is determined by the sound which follows it, the words containing such elements can be grouped as soon as they are encountered by the pupils and their pronunciation clarified. For example, the letter 'n' is pronounced as 'ng' when followed by a 'k' sound.

Chart 2

nk = ngk	nc = ngk
thank	uncle
think	Lincoln
ink	
trunk	
bank	
ankle	

The pronunciation of the letter 'c', when followed by a vowel, is wholly dependent upon the vowel sound that follows it. If 'c' is followed by the sound of 'a', or 'o', it is pronounced 'k'; if it is followed by 'e', 'i', or 'y', it is pronounced 's'. The frequency with which deaf children mispronounce words containing the letter 'c' is evidence that this simple rule is not clearly understood and applied.

By grouping words containing 'c' under the proper headings as soon as they are taught and keeping a clear visual organization pattern before the children as well as constant practice, the errors can be eliminated.

Chart 3

c (a) = k	c (o) = k	c (u) = k
cat	come (kum)	cup
cap	comb	cut
cake	coke	circus
came	coat	cub
car	cold	
can	could	

Chart 4

c (e) = s	c (i) = s	c (y) = s
nice	city	bicycle
mice	circus	cyclone
piece	circle	icy
twice	icicle	fancy
ceiling		Nancy

Since silent letters affect pronunciation so frequently, an alphabetical listing of new words containing such letters should be kept, with the words listed in the proper groupings shown on Chart 5.

Chart 5

b	g	gh	h	k	l	w
thumb	gnaw	caught	hour	knee	walk	who
comb	gnash	taught	honest	knife	talk	whom
lamb	sign	bought	ghost	know	chalk	whose
crumb		fought		knew	half	write
dumb		brought		knit	calf	wrong
limb		daughter		knock	would	wring
climb		slaughter		knuckle	should	wreath
doubt					palm	wrist
					calm	sword

Teaching the use of homonyms to deaf children is an aid to both speech and speech-reading. If the teacher uses one of a pair of homonyms in a sentence and asks the children to use the other in a sentence after the two meanings have been taught, it gives practice in making quick association between the related pairs. A list of some common homonyms is given on Chart 6.

Chart 6

to	no	write	new	road	blue	dear	nose
two	know	right	knew	rode	blew	deer	knows
				rowed			
read	so	see	be	ate	by	pear	tale
red	sew	sea	bee	eight	buy	pair	tail
their	fair	hair	bear	here	threw	mail	
there	fare	hare	bare	hear	through	male	
some	one	son	wood	our	hole	way	past
sum	won	sun	would	hour	whole	weigh	passed
I	we	we've	I'll	he'll			
eye	wee	weave	aisle	heel			

Plate 14 The LRS method with eight-year-olds (p. 131)

Plate 15 The LRS method with four-year-olds, using experience books (p. 131)

Plate 16 The visible speech translator in use (p. 196)

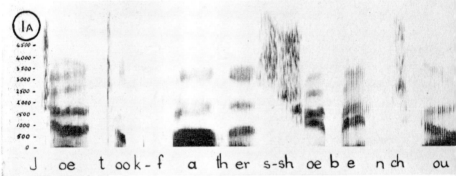

J oe t ook - f a th er s - sh oe b e n ch ou

Plate 17 A sonogram (p. 196)

Plate 18 Medresco hearing aid *(by courtesy of H.M. Postmaster-General)* (p. 57)

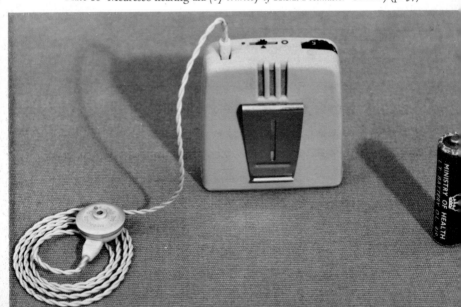

THE MULTI-SENSORY APPROACH

What special techniques and equipment are available to assist deaf children to acquire intelligible speech? There is quite a variety and, on the technical side, new electronic devices are appearing regularly and refinements and modifications are continually being made. Within the next ten years it seems reasonable to predict that some really significant developments will occur in this field.

Most authorities today favour a multi-sensory approach to the teaching of speech. Gaeth has shown that it is probable that we are only able to assimilate information from one particular sense at any one moment of time(63), but his tests and those made daily in audiology clinics show that reception of speech for example, is better when the senses of sight and hearing are used together than when either one is used alone. The attention apparently oscillates from one sense to the other during the saying of a word. Cybernetic studies like those of Van Uden also show that children using the multi-sensory approach to speech production, for example, have learned better than those using one sense only. Wedenberg in Stockholm(64) and Downs and Bryant(65) in Denver, believe in training the hearing before allowing the children to lipread. For children whose hearing losses are less than 80 db. (International standard), this may be so, but for more severely deaf children, the combined approach, which incorporates frequent periods of practice in 'listening only', seems the safest to adopt.

AUDITORY APPROACH

Hearing aids make a contribution to speech development in all but a handful of cases(10). Some children, of course, are assisted a great deal more than others when hearing aids are used. Some recent developments in the use of hearing aids which may well affect both speech reception and production are relevant here. A portable transmitting microphone is now available. This instrument, weighing less than ten ounces, is worn by the teacher and enables her voice to be 'picked up'

N

on the induction coil of the child's hearing aid with beautiful clarity because there is next to no interference due to noise and reverberation. It is similar to the other 'loop systems' but the teacher is now freed from the long flex which previously ran to the mains-operated amplifier. This aid should be especially helpful to children attending ordinary schools. Acoustic conditions in most ordinary school classrooms are notorious.

Hearing aids capable of transposing the high frequency elements of speech down to the lower frequencies may well prove very helpful to profoundly deaf children.

Binaural hearing aids have been shown by Graham and others(66) to be of limited value to the majority of hearing aid users, from the point of view of speech reception as measured by word lists. Numerous workers, however, consider that there is a marked improvement in the children's general responsiveness, in their ability to locate sounds and in their attitude to hearing aids when they use binaural ones. The Hear Foundation in Los Angeles favours binaural listening and also regards the fitting of aids during the first few weeks of life to be of great importance in developing good hearing and good speech. One wonders if the findings of Dr David Hubel at Harvard(67) do not support this latter contention. Hubel found that when one eye of a kitten was deprived of light from birth until three months of age, the cells in that eye failed to develop at all and the kitten was virtually blind in that eye. Could something similar occur in an ear which through severe deafness at birth was deprived of sound?

The easiest way to learn to say a phrase, a word or a sound is *to hear it said and then to hear oneself say it*. The most important organ in speech production is the ear. To ignore the help that hearing aids can be in speech work, and thus deny the children whatever assistance their hearing is to them, is making one's task just that much more difficult than is necessary.

Teachers of young deaf children have a responsibility to check hearing aids first thing each morning and last thing in the afternoon as well.

Regular checking of hearing aid performance is of critical importance. One method of checking aids which may seem a somewhat 'military' one, but is quick and effective, is as follows:

(Children sit in a semi-circle.)

'Switch off your hearing aids.'

'Take your ear pieces out.'

(Children hold ear pieces and receivers twelve inches from microphone.)

'John (first child), switch your hearing aid on.'

(He switches his aid to maximum. There should be a clear whistling sound for two seconds.)

'Switch it off.'

'Mary (second child), switch your hearing aid on,' etc. After all aids are tested, those not working satisfactorily are inspected and checked as explained on page 56.

Teachers should learn as much as they can about hearing aids: how they work and how best to care for them to ensure maximum performance. Provided the aids are working and as much listening practice as possible is given during lessons, it is surprising just how much children can hear. Teachers should also take care that children wear their hearing aids comfortably. The aids must be firm on the body and inconspicuous, with the cords under the collar of a shirt or dress – *never* dangling loose. The volume should be carefully adjusted for children under seven(10).

As well as making full use of hearing aids, teachers (and parents and supervisors) can help even very deaf children considerably by *speaking very close to their ears*. This method is advocated by Wedenberg(68) – especially with young children. Just before they go to bed is often a good time but it can be done in school. The speech should be delivered within two centimetres of the ear in a clear voice – but not a shout. The child is asked to discriminate words and phrases in a book he is looking at. The more deaf the child is, the more dissimilar the material chosen should be – 'dog' and 'farmer' would be better words than 'farmer' and 'father' for example, and 'Where's the table?' would be a better phrase to compare with 'Where's the cupboard key?' than would 'Where's the cup of tea?'

The place of *music* as an auditory aid to speech work should be emphasized. Nearly all deaf children enjoy listening to music provided it is presented in a manner which makes it interesting to them. Van

Uden(69) has found that tape-recorded songs by a singer with a bass voice and accompanied on the organ is one of the best methods of enabling even profoundly deaf children to perceive the melody and rhythm of music.

Excellent group speech is obtained at a school in New South Wales where songs and poems are prepared in language lessons and then presented after the children first listen to the words 'played' on an organ. The result is that they speak much more quickly and rhythmically than is frequently the case and the speech in consequence gains appreciably in intelligibility. Happiness and relaxation usually come through music and both are necessary for successful speech teaching. Teachers commented how thrilling it was to hear the deaf children 'singing' as they went around the school – even though at times they had to dissuade them from doing so!

VISUAL APPROACH

Lipreading is an obvious means of assisting a very deaf child to speak clearly. Before children can hope to learn a great deal from imitating the teacher's speech pattern they must learn to *watch* – and that means to concentrate – not just to glance. Here it should also be stressed that *rapport* between the child and teacher should be well established. If the child (or the teacher) has a heavy cold or is 'off colour', speech work should not be attempted. The attitude of the teacher to speech work is critical.

One of the most interesting instruments developed in recent years to assist deaf children's speech production, is a *visible speech translator* (see page 193). This was first developed by Potter, Kopp and Greene in the late 1940s at Bell Telephone Laboratories.

Speech is analysed according to the frequency components of each sound, and words and phrases are portrayed on a cathode ray tube (TV type screen), in a similar manner to that shown in a sonagram (see page 193). If the teacher and pupil each use a microphone it is possible to compare visually the normal and defective patterns. The pupil is thus able to monitor with his eyes what normally hearing children monitored with their ears during the first years of their lives. The instrument's usefulness as a supplement to teaching speech to deaf children was evaluated by Professor George and Dr Harriet Kopp(70).

It was found that results varied with differing periods of instructional time, different materials, different instructions and different methods. Over all, however, the translator was found to be an effective aid in teaching speech to deaf and hard-of-hearing children. Significant improvements were found in both the children's articulation and in their speech intelligibility, when results were compared with a control group.

A second very interesting innovation in speech translation was first reported by Barton and Barton in 1962(71).

'. . . with a simple network of two resistors and two capacitors, it is possible to produce recognizable pictures from speech sounds. These pictures thus become a natural phonetic alphabet, with which both standard pronunciation and nuances of dialect and accent can be represented.' Barton and Barton suggested that the technique might be useful in teaching speech to deaf children.

Subsequent developments and descriptions of the use of similar instruments have since been reported (72, 73, 74) and an instrument has been produced commercially in Britain.

In addition to displaying individual sounds clearly, the Calligraphone also shows loudness of the voice very effectively, and one of its most important uses may be in improving the *quality* of deaf children's voices. Clear, normal speech is displayed in the oscilloscope patterns with firm, clear lines. Forced, strident voice quality causes the lines of the pattern to become jagged and distorted. Field trials of these instruments are currently being undertaken in London schools.

The teacher's or therapist's face is another important 'visual aid' in promoting intelligible speech. If a child cannot *hear* the sounds he is producing, the only way for him to know whether he is saying them accurately (without a visible speech translator) is to be told so by his teacher – and the easiest and most effective way of 'telling' is by one's expression. One can show whether the child's attempt is really wide of the mark, is getting nearer, or is exactly right. This is a tremendous help to him. Nothing is more disheartening for the child than to see a 'dead pan' expression on the face of his teacher and, naturally enough, when this happens, he does not vary his attempts at speaking to nearly the same extent. 'Why bother?' he thinks to himself. The animation mentioned earlier as regards language development and reading applies equally to good speech teaching.

Written symbols and diagrams, that is marking words and phrases with symbols helps deaf children with such things as accent, emphasis, rhythm and phrasing. One common practice is to place heavy lines over accented syllables and lighter lines over the unstressed ones. Phrasing can be shown with vertical lines.

I'm hurrying | to the shop.

Some teachers use underlining of accented syllables, others print them in block capitals, while a fourth group use different colours and so on. The children soon adapt themselves to whichever system a teacher prefers to use.

Some schools advise the teaching of international phonetic symbols to older pupils to show how words are pronounced. If a deaf person can 'sound out' a word and sees where the accent falls in it, he has a reasonable chance of saying it.

TACTILE APPROACH

A very old technique for teaching speech to deaf children has been to make them watch the teacher's face carefully, and to *feel* any vibration and breath used when the word or sound was said correctly by the teacher. With the advent of hearing aids and the theory that children should learn to speak through reason rather than just doing so blindly, touching parts of the face went somewhat out of favour. For young, slow learning and profoundly deaf children, however, despite its limitations it still remains one of the most valuable aids to speech teaching.

The child is taught to spread the fingers of one hand and place them on one side of the teacher's face – the thumb touching the nose and the little finger lying along the lower jaw. In this way, the nasal sounds (m, n and ng) are felt with the thumb; plosives (p, t, k, b, d and g) and fricatives (wh, f, th, sh, ch, s, v, etc.) can be felt on the palm of the child's hand as they come from the teacher's mouth; and vowels and voiced consonants can be felt in the cheek and the lower jaw. If one says a word like 'unhappy' one gets an indication of the amount of help which feeling breath and vibration can be. One cannot discriminate between vowels by feeling alone, but just to know that voice is present is a big help to the very deaf children, and accent, rhythm and rate of speaking is assisted quickly and fairly effectively. Another very useful technique is simply to place the back of the child's fingers against the teacher's chin so that he can feel vibration and breath as the teacher speaks. Immediately afterwards the child can try this out for himself.

Children who persistently use falsetto voices can be given a good indication of a more normal pitch by placing one of their hands on the teacher's chest and the other on their own. The teacher says a vowel ('ar' is a good one), first in a falsetto and then in a normal voice.

Teachers have traditionally been advised not to touch the throats of the children nor to ask them to do so in order to feel vibrations. Constriction can be caused by so doing.

When using a *tactual vocoder* the child places his fingers on a set of keys and, when a sound is produced, it is analysed by filters and vibration is set up in the appropriate keys. Very high frequencies, for example, are felt in the little finger of the left hand.

Using short lists of single words, Pickett(75) showed that discriminating the number of syllables in words and between consonants like 'b' and 'm' was much more accurate when the tactual information was added.

Pickett and Lovgren and Nykvist(76), after conducting fairly extensive experiments, concluded that a tactual vocoder could be of considerable aid in speech communication, especially in furnishing cues as to time, intensity and *gross* spectral information.

10 School Records

One of the many rewarding things about teaching deaf children is that classes are usually sufficiently small for each child to be considered as an individual. School records can thus be much fuller and more useful than is possible when teaching classes in ordinary schools. Teachers should endeavour to make a virtual *case study* of each child.

Such carefully documented information about individual children can make the teachers' work more interesting and can help them in a variety of other ways. Records enable them to know each child better and this is fundamental. 'To teach arithmetic to Richard, or geography to George, it is not sufficient to know the principles of arithmetic or the facts of geography. The teacher must also know Richard and George.'(77)

Accurate assessing at regular intervals is the scientific and logical way of measuring the effectiveness of one's teaching. It is useful too to compare each child's progress with that of the rest of the class and, where possible, tests standardized on a normally hearing population should be administered so that progress and achievement can also be measured against that of ordinary children of similar age.

'Requirements for the future seem to demand not merely "the presence on a school staff of at least one teacher with the special training of a psychological expert (at the primary stage) or a careers master (in a secondary school)", but encouragement to all schools to pass beyond this first stage in guidance to the stage in which all teachers will be aware of their responsibilities as experts who are skilled in diagnosis and apply remedial measures continuously in accordance with the varying needs of their pupils.'(78)

School records of individual children's progress can be tremendously helpful to supervising teachers, to psychologists, vocational guidance officers, medical officers and to those who teach the child in succeeding years.

The format of the records is very important, and much time and thought on the part of the teacher is required when filling them in if they are to be of maximum benefit.

Good records are *concise* (so that writing and reading them is not too time-consuming); are *progressive* (so that they show progress, not only during the year, but also from year to year); are *objective* and *accurate*; are *diagnostic* as far as possible so that they give direction to subsequent teaching and management, and are *reliable*, i.e. consistent from year to year. This last requirement means that teachers need to know the precise meaning of each record form and how the assessments should be made so that entries may be compared.

When a teacher takes over a class, he or she should be provided with the following information about each child:

> Name in full
> Date of birth
> Place of birth
> Address
> Previous schools attended
> Date of admission to present school
> Father's initials and occupation
> Mother's initials and occupation
> Telephone number
> Brothers' and sisters' names and dates of birth
> Previous teachers' names
> Intelligence rating – by previous teachers and by standardized tests
> Rating of personal characteristics
> Interests and hobbies
> General medical history
> Audiological data
> Educational information on:
> > oral language
> > written language
> > speech

        mathematics
        reading
        social studies
        art and craft
        nature study and science
        physical education
        technical subjects

(Specialist visiting teachers can often obtain much of the information from homes if parents are poor correspondents.)

INTELLIGENCE

The documentation of information regarding each child's mental ability can be assessed as a yearly routine by teachers using a graded schedule and triennially by psychologists using standardized non-verbal tests.

A word of caution is indicated, however. A number of deaf children can appear to be much less able than in fact they are. As young children, their behaviour can be quite 'bizarre' and any formal attempts to measure their intelligence result in minimal cooperation and extremely low scores. The same children, when tested some years later, may have improved very considerably. As a general guide it seems that high ratings on intelligence tests *can* be taken as accurate but low ratings may or may *not* be accurate.

Teachers' ratings of the likelihood of a child progressing academically may be made from a chart such as the one shown opposite.

Intelligence

	A	B	C	D	E
a	Always eager to investigate environment. Asks many questions.	Spontaneous curiosity shown by questions frequently asked.	Curiosity aroused fairly frequently by stimulating material.	Seldom asks questions, or wishes to make investigations.	Appears indifferent; interest very difficult to arouse.
b	Few details escape attention.	Keenly observant.	Notices much of what goes on around him.	Observation only aroused by strong stimulus.	Appears to notice very little.
c	Highly imaginative and creative.	Particularly eager for stories. Play frequently imaginative.	Moderately interested in short stories and sometimes plays imaginatively.	Rather indifferent to stories and dramatic play.	Not interested in stories or dramatic play.
d	Notably inventive and original.	Often invents and adapts material.	Fairly frequently adapts material to his own purposes.	Only occasionally constructs with material.	Uses objects for manipulations only.
e	Shows marked ability in solving problems. Uses books of reference for information.	Frequently solves practical problems and reasons in words. Can follow a suitable logical argument.	Sometimes solves practical problems and reasons in words.	Sometimes uses material to help him solve problems but is inclined to ask for help.	Does not appear aware of problems.

Place the child in one of the classes A, B, C, D, E, taking into consideration both the grades of assessment given above, and also his success in school work.

Personal characteristics

	A	B	C	D	E
Stability	Exceptionally stable. Basic pattern of behaviour not likely to be disturbed even under the most unusual circumstances.	Very stable. Basic pattern of behaviour not easily disturbed.	Generally calm and contented, but basic patterns of behaviour disturbed by unfamiliar circumstances.	Basic pattern of behaviour rather easily disturbed	Highly unstable; basic pattern of behaviour very easily disturbed.
Cooperation	Invariably cooperative; works thoroughly happily with adults or children. Seeks cooperative activities continuously.	Enjoys being a member of a team; ready to cooperate; often finds opportunities.	Usually cooperative when the need arises.	Needs encouragement to cooperate with others. Tends to cooperate for own ends	Continously uncooperative with regard to others' wishes and ideas and activities.
Independence	Thinks and acts with marked independence and originality.	Usually thinks and acts independently; likely to take initiative.	Often thinks and acts independently; able to take initiative.	Easily swayed; rather imitative.	Very dependent on others; diffident.
Persistence	Extremely persistent.	Not easily stopped.	Works quite steadily.	Somewhat changeable; restless.	Gives up easily.

(Primary School Record Guide, New Zealand Department of Education – Form E – 19/23)

PERSONAL CHARACTERISTICS

The rating schedule given opposite covers four of the more recognizable qualities but does not, of course, give a complete picture of each child. More useful from the current teacher's point of view are other observations and comments.

Some teachers keep a diary and make *one* observation about *one* child at the end of each day. They find it extremely interesting and helpful in understanding each child during the year, and of great benefit also, of course, when writing up reports. The home/school notebooks (Chapter 4) are also very useful for these purposes. Some useful examples of observations by a teacher are given in an article by Almy entitled 'Child Study in the Education of Deaf Children' in *Volta Review* for February 1962:

When he is happy, Lee is happy from head to toe. His eyes dance, he roars with laughter and quivers with delight. He sparkles long after the experience has ended.

John does not like to delve into messy activities such as clay (if it is very moist) and finger paints. He prefers crayons, puzzles and peg-boards.

M. has complained bitterly that the other girls are 'fresh' and talk about her. (M. is sixteen years old and transferred here last year.) She is obviously not accepted and other girls have mentioned she is 'snooty'. I will talk to a few of our leaders among the older group to gather further information and try to plant some helpful ideas.

Almy has noted three steps in observation which she describes as *description, feeling* and *inference*. What the child does and says is first described by the teacher. The feelings and emotions of the teacher towards the child or the incident creep into the recorded material, and finally the teacher interprets what the child's behaviour means by a comment or summary at the end.

In emphasizing the importance of these observations of personal characteristics, Almy says:

The fact that the attitude of John's mother towards school has helped to create a demanding young perfectionist, or that Michael's mother sees no relationship between his school and his home life, may well be lost in the welter of other happenings in a class, unless a teacher is virtually 'forced' to observe, reflect and record.

Each quality is rated A, B, C, D, or E, according to which of the descriptions given above most nearly describes the particular child. Children do not, of course, exhibit the same kind of behaviour in different years or with different teachers. Differences of estimate do occur and represent an additional challenge to teachers to know and understand their pupils.

One page in each child's record file can be kept for photographs of him as he progresses through the school. Many photographers now take individual photographs of children while they are engaged in classroom work. These are usually much more natural and interesting than those which are taken when the child is simply asked to 'stand up against the wall'. Some head teachers insist that the photographer agrees to let them have a contact print of each child's photograph for the school records and most photographers seem happy to concur. Photographs are often invaluable years after the children have left school and their cases crop up for one reason or another. They are, of course, often very helpful for medical officers, psychologists and vocational guidance officers while the children are at school.

MEDICAL AND AUDIOLOGICAL RECORDS

Every deaf child should have a routine medical and otological examination once each year. The medical record form shown here has been supplied to teachers of deaf children and has proved helpful in many cases.

Pure-tone air- and bone-conduction tests of hearing should be administered as a yearly routine and teachers should administer appropriate *speech tests* of hearing under varying conditions at the beginning of each year(10). We have found continuous (or 'running') audiograms(79) not to be very practical in the school situation because double entries are required. They can, of course, be most useful for

Confidential medical record

Name:_____ Born:_____ Etiology:_____

Family doctor:_____

Illnesses	Age Y	Age M
Measles		
Chicken pox		
Whooping cough		
Mumps		
Eczema		
Fits		
Asthma		
Other		

Medical officer	Date

ENT specialist	Date

Inoculations and special tests:

Date			
Reason			

Hospitalization:

Date			
Reason			

Age in years

Defects	
Vision	
Teeth	
Ear 1 (outer and middle)	
Ear 2 (outer and middle)	
Tonsils	
Heart	
Other defect	

(A = normal or satisfactory   B = minor defect or requiring observation
C = major defect or requiring treatment)

Remarks

medical and research purposes. 'Sticker' audiograms (audiograms with a narrow band of adhesive at the top, so that subsequent audiograms can be added one on top of the other) seem most satisfactory. Speech test result may be recorded in the following manner:

Speech tests of hearing

Date					
Test					
Condition★					
Ear					
Level					
Score					
Tester					

★ UA = unaided   STA = speech training aid
IHA = individual hearing aid   W = Watching

Records should be kept similarly of individual hearing aids, showing the make, number, original date of issue of the aid and date of issue of the receiver and left or right ear pieces, with the recommended setting of the aid and the best setting for the left and right ears respectively.

SCHOOL WORK

Comments on school reports like 'fair', 'average', 'a slow worker,' are little help to another teacher taking over the class the following year. Helpful comments on reading, for example, might be:

Betty loves reading. She synthesizes letter combinations well and uses contextual clues when confronted with unknown words. New books are the one thing she seems selfish about. Has read twenty-three books these last six months. Anything to do with Girl Guide adventures or horse-riding seems particularly interesting. Reading age: Neale's Analysis of Reading Ability (80) 10 years, 10 months; Schonell's Vocabulary Test (81) 11·2 years (Chronological age 13 years 10 months).

Martin has not really been interested in the reading programme I have offered him this year (nor, I notice, has he been interested in previous years). He guesses wildly at unknown words and even now does not know letter combinations such as 'ng', 'kn', 'ph'. He does read some blackboard lessons, but only with difficulty and never reads on his own for pleasure. Prefers sport and I shall try to use simple newspaper reports and my own summaries to help interest him this coming term. Reading age: Neale–6 years 2 months, Schonell–6 years 9 months (Chronological age 9 years 11 months).

Informative comments on art are: 'Always draws or paints in a spare period' or 'Never seems to take art very seriously and appears to find little satisfaction in anything except very messy activities' or, on physical education: 'Seems easily fatigued and has not shown interest in physical activity this year' or 'Little or no improvement in basic skills this year. Has poor hand and eye coordination and is easily discouraged' or, again, for woodwork: 'Shows initiative, ability and interest in planning work and selecting appropriate materials, tools and methods' or 'Has made a bedside table (B+), an umbrella stand (B+) and a wheelbarrow (A—) during the past six months.'

Samples of work

A large envelope should be kept at the back of the record file or book in which samples of the child's work can be included. Such samples can be very revealing and can often save hundreds of words which might be necessary in a written report. Teachers should, however, take care to give some details on each sample. The *date*, for example, is absolutely essential. It is also useful to know if the sample of written work was original or if assistance was given and, if so, how much. A painting should carry a statement saying whether it was original or copied and how the teacher considers this sample compares with other paintings the child has done and with work being produced by the rest of the class. Such edited samples mean a great deal to a psychologist or a future teacher in two or three years' time.

End-of-term reports

When home/school notebooks are used and parents make a point of visiting the school regularly, the need to send end-of-term reports to the parents of children who attend school daily is very largely obviated. Parents are being informed of their child's progress almost daily. For the children who live away from home, however, a fairly full report should go home at the end of each term. The parents are then able to read what work has been covered and test the child out on various aspects of it. For this reason, comments and reports under the various subjects should be *factual*. A report in social studies which says, 'Fair. John is not very interested in this subject' is not much use but the following report is: 'Have dealt with "People who help us" and have had lessons on "the postman", "the grocer" and "the doctor". John did not seem to get as much from these as the other children, but he does know a number of the things available in a grocer's shop and can ask "May I have some . . .?" "Have you any . . .?" and he says "Thank you" nicely.'

LANGUAGE DEVELOPMENT

Compiling a suitable language check list is not always easy. The spontaneous spoken vocabularies of normally hearing children should be taken as the basis and graded lists of these do not seem to exist.

Burroughs(82) has produced a useful vocabulary of spoken English which 'could be taken as representative of the vocabulary of children who were about to learn to read'. His two lists show the more and the less frequently used words.

Dr B. Bernstein, at London University Institute of Education, has compiled lists of the spontaneous *spoken* vocabulary of groups of five-year-old normally hearing children, which he obtained by means of transmitter microphones and tape recorders. These lists are not yet published, but are available on request from Dr Bernstein.

At the present time the word lists compiled by Edwards and

Gibbon(83), although not based on *spoken* vocabulary, might also form a useful basis on which to work. These lists were compiled from an analysis of the spontaneous writing of 2,120 children between the ages of five and eight years. In the five-plus group, there were 661 words; six-plus, 1,031; and in the seven-plus group, 1,349 – a total of 3,041 words. The writers also calculated what they called a *popularity index* which indicated the frequency with which each word was used when equated with the number of children using it. Thus in the seven-plus list, 'and' has a popularity index of 3,667·4, while 'tyre' has only ·025.

The spontaneous spoken language of normally hearing children according to area at each year from one to, say, twelve years would be most useful – especially if it were analysed as Edwards and Gibbon have done.

The Holborn Vocabulary Test(84) for young normally hearing children is a useful research tool but appears not to be sufficiently diagnostic to represent a particularly useful test for teachers. Testing each child's knowledge of check-list words and phrases with pictures can, again, be time-consuming – although it is time well spent.

A quicker, less accurate, but nevertheless helpful form of language check can be made by rating the language possessed by a child in some everyday life situations as shown on page 212. If carefully completed at the end of each year, and consulted by teachers at the beginning of the following term, such a record can give very useful information about each child, and can, of course, give some direction to the year's teaching in language work.

In the following situations (name) has spontaneous spoken language which is:
1 of wide vocabulary and varied construction;
2 adequate for everyday needs;
3 not quite sufficient for everyday needs;
4 extremely limited;
5 non-existent.

Date					
Teachers' initials					

at meal-times
at bed-time
during free play
in set games
when caring for
    pets
when being
    courteous
at the dentist
at socials or
    parties
in the following
    school subjects:
1
2
3
4
5
6
7					

Dr H. L. Owrid at Manchester University has been using the *Full-Range Picture Vocabulary Test*(85) for evaluating the language development of deaf children in his researches and he considers it would have considerable merit in schools and classes for deaf and partially hearing children.

To emphasize the importance of deaf children appreciating the value of question forms and using them in their daily lives, the following list was drawn up for use every six months by teachers:

Date (month and year) Teachers' initials			
are			
can			
do			
have			
how			
may			
is			
shall			
should			
were			
what			
when			
where			
which			
who			
whose			
why			
will			
would			

SPEECH RECORDS

A useful *running* or *continuous* speech test for deaf children has been constructed in the following sentences which contain nearly every speech sound. Children who can say this paragraph reasonably clearly will have come a long way towards intelligible speech in all situations.

The girl said to the boy: 'I am eight years old today.' Mother said: 'Happy birthday! Here is a green ball, four books, a new doll and a pair of brown shoes. We will have jelly, chocolate and cake for your party.' The girl said: 'Thank you very much, Mummy.'

This test can be scored quite quickly by the teacher (and if possible another senior member of the staff) or the specialist visiting teacher on the simple ranking of 'normal, slightly defective, defective, grossly defective, unintelligible'.

One of the main purposes of the following over-all assessment of a child's speech is to draw the teacher's attention to some of the more important aspects of speech intelligibility. (It is appreciated that some of the ratings under these headings are not sufficiently precise to make an entirely accurate assessment of each child.)

Speech assessment

Name   *Date*   *Initial*

Voice
  (a) normal
  (b) slightly toneless
  (c) deaf quality
  (d) nasal

Over-all pitch
  (a) normal
  (b) falsetto
  (c) abnormally high
  (d) abnormally low
  (e) guttural

Intonation
  (a) normal
  (b) considerable pitch variation
  (c) slight pitch variation
  (d) monotonous phonation

Rhythm
  (a) normal phrasing and emphasis
  (b) words usually joined
  (c) words usually uttered separately

Length of vowel
  (a) normal
  (b) slightly lengthened
  (c) excessively lengthened

Breathing
  (a) natural
  (b) slightly laboured
  (c) insufficient breath used
  (d) excessively breathy
  (e) chest tension

Attitude to speech work
  (a) enjoys it; often asks for assistance
  (b) moderately interested
  (c) indifferent
  (d) dislikes it

Intelligibility test results (%)
  (a) consonants
  (b) consonant blends
  (c) vowels and diphthongs
  (d) tape-recorded sentences

Over-all intelligibility
  (a) normal
  (b) slightly defective
  (c) grossly defective
  (d) unintelligible
  (e) no speech

Tape recorders

When tape recorders were first introduced to schools and classes for deaf and partially hearing children, it was not uncommon to find an individual tape for each child on which a sample of speech was to be added each year. Recording these samples does not take a great deal of time, but listening to them does, and it seems that many teachers are disinclined to make this effort for the amount of information which they obtain.

Tape-recorded speech samples over a period of several years can, of course be very useful for demonstrations, lectures and research purposes, etc., but for 'individual school records' it appears that a technique which gives the information about a child's speech intelligibility more quickly seems more likely to be useful to classroom teachers. R. G. Dodds designed the following very interesting speech test(86) which attempts to meet the above criteria. From an initial trial, it appears to have definite practical application in schools and classes for deaf children and in clinics. The words underlined are the score words.

List A

1 It's time to go to bed.
2 What are you looking at?
3 Come here when I want you.
4 Look out.
5 How many brothers and sisters have you got?
6 The water is too cold for swimming.
7 What's the matter?
8 Will you come and help me to milk the cows?
9 I will see you later on.
10 Make a cup of tea, please.

List B

1 When is your birthday?
2 Put that cake back in the cupboard.
3 How many were there at the party?
4 It's raining.

5 Come and play with me at my house.
6 I like some ice-cream with my pie.
7 Here we go.
8 Is it going to be sunny today?
9 Are you going home next week?
10 Don't go on the floor because it has been washed.

List C

1 What colour is your new coat?
2 Whose pencil is this on the floor?
3 Be quiet because the baby is asleep.
4 Good morning.
5 Who were you talking to?
6 Put on your new coat before you go out.
7 Never mind.
8 The doctor is coming to see you tomorrow.
9 I think I will go to bed early and read a book.
10 Tie my shoe for me, please.

The test sentences are printed on large cards and illustrated where possible and each child's recording is preceded by three practice items. These are: 'My name is . . .; I am . . . years old; please open the door.'

With some children who had poor reading ability but a considerable amount of hearing, an 'echo method' proved very useful; that is, the child echoed the words or phrases after the tester.

Auditors should have normal hearing and an educational standard of being in at least a fourth form (fourteen years old) in a secondary school. Ten is a suitable number of auditors who should be seated in a semi-circle ten feet from the tape recorder.

The recorded speech should reach the listeners at a normal conversational level (70 db.). They are told: 'This is a tape recording of a deaf child saying some sentences. The speech may sound strange to you, but try to guess what the child is saying and write it down on your test sheet. Be sure not to consult your neighbour.'

On one occasion ninety children were tested when we were able to arrange with one of the teachers' colleges to have groups of ten students for forty minutes. In a period we were able to test four children in the following manner: children one, two and three read lists A, B, and C. Child four read list A again but this time the sentences were in reverse order. In general the children who read first (i.e. those whose list was going to be repeated) were the poorest with regard to speech intelligibility.

This system worked extremely well, and there seems no reason why five children could not be covered in a period. The list being repeated first was rotated each time to offset 'listener fatigue'.

During the forty minutes the time was used as follows:

1 establishing *rapport* and preliminary instructions, seven minutes;
2 administration of the tests, twenty minutes;
3 marking by the listeners, eight minutes;
4 collecting scripts, questions, etc., five minutes.

Having the marking done was a big saving in time. Also having that few minutes at the end was very valuable in that it gave one a little time to get over a bit of 'propaganda' about deafness. Some of the listeners did not even seem aware that deafness and its problems existed.

The auditing of the speech of the ninety children took three days. This is not an excessive allocation of time once a year. An intelligent parent could conduct it. Most deaf children from seven or eight upwards were able to manage this text. There still exists a need, however, for testing the speech intelligibility of very young deaf children.

There is plenty of scope for using speech intelligibility tests to assess the effects of various concentrated speech programmes and a need to develop some means of assessing the *spontaneous* speech of deaf children.

One of the most striking features noticed during the testing was that the children who scored very low on intelligibility often had no trace of an initial or final consonant. Many of these children would be able to produce all the consonants in isolation but just did not seem to be aware of their use when speaking. It is felt that we often expect too little from our children with regard to the intelligibility of their speech and that the role of motivation and attitude in the production of intelligible speech would repay further study.

For nursery school children, tape recordings of their attempts to say ten single words – e.g. the names of known objects like the Kendall Toy Lists(10) can be useful if the child has sufficient vocabulary – can provide a crude test of their speech intelligibility.

Auditing of the tapes can be done quite quickly in a similar manner to that suggested above for the older children, but it is emphasized that it is a much less accurate test.

Results can be recorded as follows:

Speech production test 1

Date	15/9/65	10/3/66	1/7/66			
fish	—	√	√			
house	√	√	√			
car	√	√	√			
bus	√	—	√			
pipe	—	—	—			
cow	—	—	√			
string	—	—	—			
bath	√	√	√			
chair	—	—	—			
bird	—	—	√			
Total	4	5	7			

Speech production test of individual sounds (*See page 220.*)

This test consists of twenty words which contain twenty-three different consonants and seventeen vowels and diphthongs. It should be arranged on a card or in booklet form, each word printed clearly with a picture beside it. Only sounds underlined on the score sheet are being tested.

Testing should be done in a quiet room. The child should use a hearing aid which has been carefully set at his best listening level. He is shown the first word 'path'. The tester points to the picture and says: 'This is a path. Can you say "path"?' Two more trials are given, the tester saying the correct pattern each time. If a sound is said correctly on one or more of the trials, it is regarded as correct. Any of the sounds which are said incorrectly are noted on the score sheet. (If the speech is very defective, it is quickest to mark sounds said correctly.) The next word is then presented in the same way.

There is a tendency, particularly for class teachers, to be too lenient when scoring this test. It is most important to remember that if a sound is not said perfectly it should be marked as an error, i.e. 'a good try' is not sufficient. Objectivity is lost if any other criterion is used and the results obtained are then of little value.

At the end of the test, the sounds said correctly are added and by multiplying the vowels and diphthongs total by 6, and the consonants total by 4·5, an approximate percentage correct is obtained and this may be graphed.

A test which includes each sound in initial, medial and final positions in words would, of course, give more accurate information. Such a test, however, requires nearly fifty words and thus takes such a time to administer that little children need two and sometimes three sessions to test. Also, in my experience, if a child is able to produce a sound in one position in a word, it is usually possible for him to produce it in another. He may, of course, *not* pronounce it correctly or omit it altogether in the second position until his attention is drawn to the fact. This happens particularly with final consonants and final consonant blends.

If a teacher knows that a child can articulate a sound perfectly in a simple word at least one time in three trials, she knows, for example, whether it is reasonable to expect this from him in the course of a group speech lesson or at any other time during the day.

Speech production test 2

Name

	C1	C2	V	C1	C2	V
Date						
Tester						
p a th						
t a p						
c ow						
b oy						
d og						
g oa t						
m o th er						
n i ne						
r i ng						
w i nd ow						
fi ve						
s ee						
sh oe						
ch ur ch						
z e bra						
me a sure						
j u mp						
l oo k						
h or se						
pl ay						
Total correct						
Percentage correct (vowels × 6; consonants × 4·5)						

Consonants

Date							
100%							
90%							
80%							
70%							
60%							
50%							
40%							
30%							
20%							
10%							

Vowels and diphthongs

Date							
100%							
90%							
80%							
70%							
60%							
50%							
40%							
30%							
20%							
10%							

Consonant blends (*See page 222.*)

For partially hearing children and for deaf children who have progressed well in speech a test which involves testing the common combinations of consonants is useful. As noted earlier, however, such emphasis on articulation should never outweigh that given to the development of rhythm and natural quality. In classes for partially hearing children, tests such as the following have been useful as an incentive to those children who feel that their speech is 'near enough'. Attention to such details has improved the intelligibility considerably.

No one wants the keeping of records to become the main preoccupation of teachers, but there is little doubt that considerably more attention should be paid to this aspect of the work than is at present the case in many schools and classes for deaf and partially hearing children. There are, however, some notable exceptions. For example, teachers in the Japan Oral School for the Deaf in Tokyo keep a *daily* record of *each* child's development in lipreading, speech, pronunciation and auditory training. For the younger children, sense training progress is also recorded daily, and for the older, development in syntax.

Documenting progress and achievement as suggested in this chapter may at first seem a very formidable task but, in practice, *with careful planning*, it need not be too onerous. A selection of assessment procedures has been given which might be of assistance to different children and in different schools. Many of the assessments (especially of children who live in hostels) can, and should, be made outside school hours. In this way, the children's normal programme of work is disturbed as little as possible and they quite enjoy the change from ordinary out-of-school routine.

At the beginning of each year, in the middle of the second term and at the end of each year, any teachers without classes (be they headmasters, deputy headmasters, supervisors of junior, middle or senior classes, reading specialists, auditory training or speech specialists, and in some cases, specialist visiting teachers) can all be brought in on the assessment programme. These people can either do much of the testing or can teach classes while the class teacher does the testing herself.

Speech production test 3

Name   Date   Tester

pram				three				
brown				banged				
play				apple				
blue				table				
train				little				
dream				candle				
twelve				buckle				
cry				wriggle				
grow				rifle				
clock				shovel				
glue				stream				
frock				scratch				
floor				spring				
slow				splash				
stop				marbles				
skip				bottles				
snow				rattled				
speech				rifles				
swim				muddled				
smile				shovels				
Totals								
Percentage total × 2·5								

The fact that everyone is prepared to assist creates interest in the records and is a tangible expression of the school's conviction that records are important, and helpful.

New members of the teaching staff should be shown a sample copy of the records kept and how they are interpreted so that each teacher recognizes the value of records and keeping them carefully then becomes an interesting and necessary part of her work, rather than 'just another chore'.

The above suggestions for recording relevant data apply mainly to children of nursery and primary school age. Where applicable, they can be continued at the secondary school level. The main difference between records at the primary and the secondary levels is that the former are mainly concerned with *educational* and *social* guidance, while records at the secondary level become increasingly orientated to *vocational* guidance.

11 Deaf Adults

One of the most encouraging things for teachers and parents of children with hearing difficulties is to meet and read about grown-up deaf people. So often one finds even those with very poor speech and lipreading holding secure jobs, running their own homes well, driving their own cars, and they are polite, thoughtful, full of fun and happy. The newly established Adult Deaf Section of the Alexander Graham Bell Association for the Deaf publishes in the *Volta Review* and regularly gives examples of the abilities and successes of deaf people. The employment of deaf (or indeed any handicapped) people, however, gives cause for some concern. Probably few of us are doing work which extends us mentally for the greater part of each day but deaf people are frequently to be found in positions which are quite inferior to their mental capacity. A typical example is the case of one quite brilliant deaf man who worked as a post office mail sorter. He was 'the fastest sorter they had ever had', etc., but there was no doubt that he would have coped with a far more responsible position. When the supervisor was asked if there was any possibility of advancement for him, he replied: 'Well, not really; you see, the next step up for him would be in charge of the mail room and for that you need to use the telephone – well, of course, he's deaf . . .' One could not help wondering just how often he would need to use the telephone, and whether a typist might not attend to it and type out any messages. This is the type of assistance that deaf people require in their work. It is hard for parents to give it since they are often regarded as 'fussing unnecessarily'. It is much easier for an independent professional person to make suggestions for improving the work prospects, etc.

Dr Gorman(87) in his very frank and helpful thesis on the problems of deaf people has stated that inability to use the telephone for either internal or external use was a common reason given for not employing a deaf person.

In 1961 a pilot survey of the social and economic adequacy of ex-pupils of the schools for the deaf was conducted throughout New Zealand at the request of the Services for the Deaf Committee of the Board of Health. A 'structured interview' technique was used to obtain most of the information given below:

Age of subjects	Male	Female	Total
70 years and over	12	7	19
60–69 years	8	10	18
50–59 years	10	11	21
40–49 years	24	11	35
30–39 years	11	18	29
20–29 years	19	18	37
	84	75	159

Etiology (as given by the subjects)	
Rubella	22
Blow on head	8
Whooping cough	9
Meningitis	8
Heredity	6
Measles	4
Birth injury	4
Scarlet fever	3
Mumps	2
Polio	1
Unknown	79
	146

The above figures are to be treated with extreme caution. There is little doubt, for example, that the 'unknown' group is rather large and the 'heredity' and 'meningitis' groups are too small. (See Fraser, G. Bibliography 1.) This is perhaps due to the understandable reluctance on the part of some subjects to admit that deafness did exist in their families.

P

Length of time at school for the deaf	Male	Female	Total
1 year or less	2	4	6
2 years	–	2	2
3 years	1	–	1
4 years	2	–	2
5 years	1	–	1
6 years	7	1	8
7 years	3	5	8
8 years	13	10	23
9 years	8	6	14
10 years	42	39	81
	79	67	146

Attendance at other schools

Forty-three of the subjects had attended ordinary schools for a year or more before coming to the schools for deaf children. It has frequently been found that a number of even severely deaf children have been able to benefit from ordinary schooling during the first two years in the infant department. When the work becomes more abstract, however, so much is missed that the child is unable to cope satisfactorily and special education is necessary. This, together with parents' natural reluctance to send young children away from home, could account for the fact that almost one-third of the total group of children had begun their education in other schools.

Only twenty-eight of the total group had gone from the schools for the deaf to ordinary schools.

Dually handicapped	
Defective vision	23
Cerebral palsy	5
Mental disorders	5
Heart condition	2
Asthma	2
Polio	1
	38

The majority of those with defective vision were simply cases who required to wear spectacles regularly or for reading. One, however, was a woman who had become almost completely blind.

Accommodation

All but a handful of the deaf people were living with relations, i.e. wives, husbands, brothers, sisters, or parents. Six of the 146 interviewed were living alone, ten were with friends, seven were boarding and five were patients in mental hospitals.

Of fifty-eight men interviewed who were householders, thirty-nine owned or were buying their homes and nineteen were renting them.

Many of the homes of the subjects were visited and it is emphasized that in nearly all cases they appeared to be very competently kept. It was clear that the homes of the deaf people meant a great deal to them and they were justifiably proud of them.

Driving licences	Male	Female	Total
Yes	51	17	68
No	27	44	71
	—	—	—
	78	61	139
Own car			
Yes	39	8	47
No	39	53	92
	—	—	—
	78	61	139

Occupations

Male	Female
Automotive machinist	Cake decorator
Baker	Cook
Battery assembler	Comptometer operator
Biscuit factory worker	Cutter
Blacksmith	Domestic worker
Carpenter	Dressmaker
Cabinet maker	Dry cleaning worker

Occupations (contd)

Male	Female
Cheese factory worker	Egg grading worker
Chicken sexer	Factory hand
Clothing factory worker	Florist
Driver	Hairdresser
Farm cadet	Hospital cleaner
Farmer	Housemaid in hotel
Foreman joiner	Kitchen maid
Freezing worker	Land girl
Gardener	Laundress
Hairdresser	Machinist
Joiner	Meat wrapper
Labourer	Milliner
Mailroom sorter	Packer
Market gardener	Pastrycook
Mattress maker	Pattern drafter
Meat trimmer	Photographer
Orchard work	Presser
Panel beater	Seamstress
Porter	Tailoress
Presser	Ticket writer
Quarry foreman	Typist
Range assembler	Waitress
Seaman	Window dresser
Senior clerk	
Sheep breeder	
Shoe factory worker	
Shoemaker	
Slaughterman	
Spray painter	
Welder	
Wine and spirits employee	

The occupations which had attracted most women workers, apart from 'domestic duties' as housewives, were as machinists and dressmakers. The most common occupation among the men was carpentry – eleven were so employed – although thirty-four of the men had been at one time or were at the time of interview employed as labourers. During the depression in the 1930s a number of the men had been employed on labouring relief work.

Apprenticeships

Twenty-nine of the men and three of the women stated that they had served apprenticeships. This seemed more common amongst the younger men. It is the present policy in New Zealand schools for the deaf to encourage as many of the boys as possible to undertake apprenticeships when they leave.

Occupation of parents

The occupations of the subjects' parents were noted to establish whether the occupational status of the children had dropped as a result of their deafness. It was fairly obvious that in many cases this was so.

Pensions

It was encouraging to find that none of the men or women interviewed was receiving an unemployment benefit, although one or two had received this at an earlier time.

Where they were entitled to old age or widow's pensions, etc., they seemed in every case to be receiving it. In only one case was it felt that additional financial assistance might be given.

Marital status

	Male	Female	Total
Married	27	36	63
Single	49	30	79
Engaged	3	1	4
	79	67	146

Of 109 adults, who were over the age of thirty, fifty-seven were married or engaged and fifty-two were single. Twenty-seven of the sixty men and twenty-nine of the forty-nine women were married or engaged and the rest were single.

The two significant factors which emerge from these data are that a large proportion of the group over the age of thirty have not married (48 per cent) and that, *per capita*, more women have married than men. Of the sixty-three who had married, forty-four had married deaf people and eight men and eleven women married normally hearing wives and husbands. These figures show considerably fewer marriages between deaf people than those obtained in Northern Ireland in 1956 (88) where 100 of 112 marriages were between deaf people (69·9 per cent compared with 89·3 per cent). The discrepancy may be due to the proportion of partially hearing subjects in the New Zealand sample.

Number of children

One hundred and seven children had been born to the sixty-three married deaf people. The average number of children per family was three. Not all the children were seen and the investigator was disinclined to ask parents whether all of the children had normal hearing, but it appeared that the majority did – as is to be expected. (A Finnish study(89) of some 556 marriages between deaf people showed that there were an average of 2·2 children per marriage – well below the national average – and of these 1,126 children, 4·6 per cent were deaf.)

One of the nicest features of this survey was that when homes were visited one was continually impressed by the care and love which was shown to the children by the deaf parents.

Hearing loss

It was not possible to administer audiometric tests to the subjects, but from their voice quality, their ability to communicate orally and to comprehend spoken English, they were loosely classified into five categories as listed:

Normal acuity	1
Slight but significant deafness (25 db.)	2
Partially hearing (25–65 db.)	12
Severely deaf (65–90 db.)	56
Profoundly deaf (over 90 db.)	76
	———
	147

On inspection the above figures appear to be too heavily weighted with severely and profoundly deaf subjects – normally one expects about 30 per cent of the school for deaf and partially hearing population to fall into the 'greater than 90 db.' hearing-loss group(13). A possible explanation of this is that as a result of not using hearing aids regularly, a number of partially and severely deaf adults appeared deafer than in fact they were.

Hearing aids

In New Zealand hearing aids are issued free under the Social Security System, yet only seventy-one of the group of 146 deaf adults had them. Of these, only six wore their aids on a continuous basis; thirteen wore them fairly often – usually at the cinema, seventeen wore them rarely and thirty-one never wore their hearing aids at any time. Women wore hearing aids a little more frequently than did the men.

When asked why they did not wear them regularly, the two most common replies were: 'I'm too deaf' or 'It gives me a headache'. Another comment was that they were too shy and a number said they got on well enough without it.

Nine of the subjects interviewed were recommended to try a hearing aid, but in the other cases it was felt that if issued without adequate supervision there was little likelihood that they would be worn.

Speech

The speech of the subjects was rated according to how intelligible it was compared with that of normally hearing people. Where the

speech was rated 'slightly defective', errors occurred mainly in consonants and consonant blends, but was mainly rhythmical and of quite
good quality. 'Grossly defective' speech was that in which both vowels
and consonants were malarticulated and pitch, rhythm, accent and
emphasis were poorly controlled so that it was necessary to concentrate
quite considerably in order to understand what was being said.

Speech rating	Male	Female	Total
Normal	6	1	7
Slightly defective	32	16	48
Grossly defective	29	41	70
Unintelligible	10	9	19
No speech	2	–	2
	79	67	146

A possible explanation of the discrepant figures for males and
females who had slightly and grossly defective speech is that many of
the women interviewed were either housewives or were doing domestic
duties in homes where they had less opportunity to use their speech
than did the men who tended to go out each day to work amongst
normally hearing people.

This need for practice seems also to be necessary in lipreading as is
suggested by the following table:

Comprehension of spoken language	Male	Female	Total
A	46	34	80
B	23	22	45
C	9	8	17
	78	64	142

A denotes that the subject understands speech within a fairly wide
vocabulary and of varied construction; B, comprehension of simple
English within limited vocabulary; C, extremely limited comprehension of any speech material even when accompanied by contextual
clues.

Work relationships

When asked if they 'got along well' with their employers, 85 per cent of the women said they did; 13 per cent had an indifferent attitude to the employers and 2 per cent had a poor relationship with them. The deaf men were found to have a similarly good relationship with their employers: 78 per cent, 12 per cent and 10 per cent respectively. These figures may be influenced by the 'halo' effect that one would expect from most people if interviewed by a comparative stranger. The twenty-three employers who were interviewed, however, confirmed that the majority of deaf workers were respected by everyone. 'I wish I had twenty more like him' was a common observation.

Hobbies and interests

Easily the most common hobbies and interests for men were gardening, cinema and television, and for women, sewing, knitting, gardening, cinema and television.

Although the following list appears extensive and quite varied, a lack of really satisfying hobbies or interests was encountered in many cases – about 60 per cent. Only two of the subjects, for example, mentioned 'art' as a hobby or interest, yet one would have thought it might prove very popular for deaf people.

Male	Female
Art	Basketball
Boatbuilding	Bicycle riding
Bowls	Cards
Cards	Cinema-going
Chess (1 person)	Cooking
Cinema-going	Drawing
Crossword puzzles	Gardening
Drawing	Golf
Fishing	Handwork
Gardening	Indoor plants
House maintenance	Knitting

male	*female*
Hunting	Letter-writing
Indoor bowls	Painting
Knitting	Photography
Mechanics	Reading
Motoring	Rifle shooting
Music	Sewing
Photography	Sports
Plasticine modelling	Stamp collecting
Racing	Television
Radio	Toy making
Reading	
Religion	
Ski-ing	
Sport of all kinds	
Stamps	
Swimming	
Table tennis	
Television	
Woodwork	

		Male	Female	Total
	A great deal	30	19	49
Reading	Sometimes	19	17	36
	Rarely	17	23	40
		66	59	125

The newspaper was read by 93 per cent of the group; magazines and comics were the next most popular source of reading; 43 per cent of the group read varied light material and most said they enjoyed it very much, and 17 per cent said they read serious literature – travel books were popular.

Deaf clubs

For years the only deaf clubs in New Zealand were in Auckland, Wellington and Christchurch. It was interesting to learn that in the last two years the League for the Hard of Hearing (the organization which conducts lipreading classes and social activities for people who become deaf in adulthood), at the request of parents and others, has organized small clubs for deaf people in a number of smaller centres.

The voluntary work which officers of the League for the Hard of Hearing have been able to do for deaf adults is very much appreciated by parents and the deaf people themselves.

One teacher from the Hard of Hearing League took speech and reading classes for two small groups of deaf people but in other clubs their function was purely social and recreational.

Of 146 people interviewed, ninety-four were members of deaf clubs: fifty-two men and forty-two women.

It should be remembered that members of deaf clubs were usually much easier to trace than were non-members. The percentage of the adult deaf population who were enrolled as members of deaf clubs is probably nearer 50 per cent rather than the 70·2 per cent shown.

It was interesting to note how frequently the various members used the deaf clubs. Some attended whenever the rooms were open, others about fortnightly; some went monthly and some only annually (usually to the club Christmas party). Some deaf people clearly need the association with other deaf people very regularly – others only occasionally.

It seems that deaf clubs should be well run and their activities well publicized, but that attendance should be completely voluntary, so that members use them as they feel the need for them.

Most cities, in most Western countries, at least, have two types of organization for the benefit of those adults with impaired hearing who require their social, and/or educational, and sometimes economic assistance. These organizations are the *Deaf Clubs* and the *Hearing Societies* or *Leagues for the Hard of Hearing*. The former cater largely for ex-pupils of schools for deaf children and the latter for less deaf people and those who become deaf later in life. Membership of hard of hearing societies, is, of course, very much less than half of the adults who are eligible to attend – probably considerably less than 5 per cent. A number of these people do take brief courses of instruction in lipreading and the management of hearing aids, but do not regard the hearing society as their social centre (see Chapter 1).

Membership of other clubs or groups

Fifty-six per cent of the group interviewed belonged to clubs other than deaf clubs:

Men	Women
Cards	Cards
Lodge (similar to Freemasons)	Community centre
Social club at work	Plunket (Mother and Baby Club)
Sports (rugby, archery, swimming, golf, bowling)	Sports clubs (basketball, hockey, indoor bowls, darts, badminton, golf, marching team)

Assistance from Churches, Rotary, Lions, etc.

Only sixteen of the subjects said they had received any assistance from the above groups – and fourteen of these were receiving assistance from their churches.

There were two retired pensioners to whom some interest and friendship from the people in the district in a position to show kindness could have been most worth while. Both old men managed their homes and gardens very satisfactorily but must have been lonely for long periods every day. If someone could have called on them perhaps once a week or so, just to have a chat and to look at the garden, it could have made a great deal of difference.

Loneliness	Men	Women	Total
Not lonely	50	38	88
Sometimes lonely	17	23	40
Very lonely	12	6	18
	79	67	146

This was another item which might not be as accurately assessed as were less emotionally loaded ones in the questionnaire. Of the 146 people seen, it is felt that rather more than eighteen should have been included in the 'very lonely' group, but that they were naturally disinclined to admit being lonely to someone they had only just met.

Government assistance

Three ways were suggested to the subjects in which the Government might be able to assist them and they were asked to comment on them:

1 The provision of teachers (perhaps through the Adult Education Service) to teach speech and lipreading and to give assistance with reading. (See Appendix 5 for suggestions for lipreading classes.) Of the total group 60 per cent was in favour of this (72 per cent of the women and 48 per cent of the men).

2 The publication of a national monthly or bi-monthly newsletter; 69 per cent of the group were interested in this proposal (79 per cent of the men and 59 per cent of the women).

3 A pamphlet giving basic information about deafness and ways in which lay people could assist those with defective hearing; of both men and women 60 per cent were in favour of such a publication.

Where parents were consulted about these three suggestions they were whole-heartedly in favour of points 1 and 3 and the majority also favoured the newsletter.

Attitude to normally hearing people

Seventy per cent of the deaf women and sixty per cent of the men liked normally hearing people. Twenty-eight per cent and thirty-eight per cent respectively were indifferent to them and two per cent of each disliked them.

The most frequent comment of the 'indifferent' group was that they felt that hearing people were not interested in them.

Electoral rolls

All persons questioned who were eligible said that they were on the electoral roll.

VOCATIONAL PLACEMENT

While it is unwise to place deaf people in jobs which put a continual strain on them it has become clear that more should be done in New Zealand and probably most other countries(90, 91, 92) to place them in satisfactory employment. Well illustrated material is required which describes the possibilities available in a wide variety of jobs. This should be prepared by workers who are knowledgeable in the field of vocational guidance, of labour and employment, and who have the assistance of several deaf people. Printing, for example, has always been a popular trade for the deaf both in Britain and the United States, as deafness is little or no handicap in the kind of skilled work involved. Jobs could be analysed and noted according to their suitability, and salaries and avenues of promotion in each position could be considered and documented. Such information, together with good photographs, could be exceedingly helpful to young deaf people and to parents when deaf people were choosing a career.

VOCATIONAL TRAINING

In Britain and many other countries(90) before World War II, trade training of deaf children was frequently given in the schools for the deaf. Most boys, for example, took an apprenticeship in one of four trades – baking, tailoring, carpentry or bootmaking. In the U.S.A. today some schools for the deaf have made remarkable provision for vocational training within the school(93). For some deaf children this is extremely helpful, but there are, however, two major objections to this type of provision for the majority of deaf students. One is that they are segregated from the normally hearing trade training world. The second is that there are, of course, a very wide variety of jobs which deaf men and women can undertake. Heider and Heider(94) for example, have listed no fewer than 400 different occupations in which deaf people in the U.S.A. were engaged in 1941 and an English study in

1939(95) found that 6,153 deaf persons were employed in 345 different occupations. No school could hope to provide the facilities for giving training in more than a few of these different vocations. Drewry(91), working in the north of England from 1950 to 1958, in *The Deaf School-leaver in Northern England*, found little relationship between the vocational training received at school and the deaf students' first job.

I believe that, for the majority of children who attend schools and classes for the deaf, specialist visiting teachers of the deaf with some additional training in technical teaching and vocational guidance work can often meet their needs very adequately. Often retired teachers of the deaf employed on an hourly basis can be very valuable for this work. The specialist teachers should be members of the staff of the central school for deaf children. The children go to the occupation for which they are most suited along with all the normally hearing boys and girls; they sit in on training classes, work and mix socially with them as far as possible. At the same time they and their employers and tutors are helped on the job when necessary and in class by the specialist visiting teacher. Additional classes with the specialist teacher are also conducted to revise work not fully understood and to provide language and speech coaching. Without such assistance, many of the deaf students do not take apprenticeship courses and if they do enrol, they do not, according to Drewry, complete the course.

For the *dually and multiply handicapped deaf person* some form of sheltered workshop is often very desirable. These workshops should not, however, be just for deaf boys and girls who have additional handicaps. There is considerable merit socially and economically in having a variety of handicaps catered for 'under one roof'. I think every city should have some such provision. Some of the dually and multiply handicapped children will always need 'sheltered' employment but others can find very suitable jobs once they have received proper training. The Tower System(96) has proved an excellent means of assessing the potential of many of the dually and multiply handicapped deaf children and also, of course, of severely handicapped children whose hearing is normal. Excellent progress in rehabilitating them vocationally is proving one of the most stimulating aspects of work in special education at the present time.

Conclusion

In this book I have tried, among other things, to emphasize the need for:

Well staffed and accessible audiology clinics;

Very early detection of deafness, and the fitting of hearing aids as soon as a reasonably accurate auditory threshold has been established – preferably during the first few weeks of life;

Able and well trained specialist visiting teachers, who, when supported by educational, medical and psychological services, can give practical guidance and accurate information to parents of deaf children to relieve the parents' anxieties and make the most of the critically important early years;

Good pre-school facilities for deaf children;

Recruiting the most able classroom teachers from ordinary schools to train as teachers of deaf children;

A rapid increase in the number of carefully sited, well staffed and well supervised units in ordinary schools which enable most deaf, as well as partially hearing children, to mix, while still accompanied by their specialist teacher, with normally hearing children for over half of each school day;

Regional educational and audiological services rather than independent schools, units and visiting teacher services, so that all the teaching strength available in an area is available to any child, and promotion scales for teachers are preserved;

Imaginative syllabuses in schools which take into account each child's physical, psychological, social and emotional development, as well as his auditory and linguistic handicap;

Very careful vocational guidance and placement to help ensure that deaf boys and girls obtain work which is in keeping with their abilities and aptitudes;

Tutoring of deaf students attending ordinary technical schools and colleges and universities, rather than the establishment of segregated facilities – except for a handful of cases;

. Deaf social clubs for those who need them run by the deaf people themselves, with voluntary support from interested people with normal hearing, when requested;

Welfare officers for the deaf adults who require occupational and social assistance – such officers to be well paid and whenever possible to be drawn from the ranks of teachers of deaf children;

Continual and varied publicity regarding the prevention, causes, effects and treatment of deafness.

. If the above conditions are met, each deaf child and adult will be helped to realize his potential and have an opportunity to lead a normal and happy life, through minimizing his handicap to himself and to everyone else. And finally, perhaps the most positive and cheering observation of all remains to be made. It is that, despite all the useful knowledge accumulated so far, one cannot but be constantly reminded that in every single aspect of the work, we have really only just begun to scratch the surface. It does, therefore, seem reasonable to contend that the future for deaf children and adults today is very full of promise.

Appendix 1

ADVICE TO THE HEARING AND THE DEAF

(a) *The following is a summary of some particularly useful suggestions made by Dr L. Elstad, Director of Gallaudet College for deaf people in Washington, D.C.*

The General Public meets the Deaf

Be natural. Speak distinctly, and do not slow down the tempo too decidedly. Enunciate clearly but beware of mouthing.

If a deaf person is with hearing persons, an effort should be made to make him feel a part of the group. Speak to him. If speech doesn't suffice, then use a pad and pencil. The voice should not be raised to an unusual pitch, but a moderate increase in intensity may be necessary. If what you say is not understood, rephrase the statement immediately. Speech-reading involves a constant search for words. When the key word is not understood, there is no comprehension. The key word may not show on the lips. There are many words, such as uncle, cousin, sister, dinner, that have no lip movements. Contrast these with father, mother, brother, beautiful, love. These are 'outside' words, and are readily seen on the lips. Speech-reading is 'educated guess work'.

Be a missionary in your group without being too obvious about it. Never monopolize the time of the deaf person, but introduce him to others, as you would a hearing person. This, of course, is not easy; in fact it can be most difficult for all concerned. There are no two sets of lips alike. There will be those who object to the pad and pencil, but you may be sure that any effort on your part to make the deaf person feel himself a part of the group will be appreciated.

The Deaf Person meets the Hearing Public

A deaf person meets hearing persons in a group. If he can speak at all, he should do so. He may not have good speech, but poor speech is better than no speech at all. If it is found after continuous efforts that there is no understanding, it is better to resort to pad and pencil. There may be someone in the group who can act as an interpreter, but it isn't wise for the deaf person to depend wholly upon interpreters; that crutch will not always be available.

Care should be taken not to speak too loudly. Loud speech attracts attention.

It takes nerve, but the deaf person should strike out boldly and contact different persons in the group. It will not be long before his handicap is known, and most people will respond to advances in friendship.

If the confidence of one person is gained, *do not embrace that confidence too long*, because it may be a tiring first experience beyond a reasonable time.

A sense of humour is essential. There will be misunderstandings. Much repetition will be necessary. Any interesting incidents that can be related of misunderstanding in the past will set new hearing friends at ease. If possible, attend gatherings of hearing people with friends who can hear. The contacts will be easier.

After the first introduction it is possible to pass on from one friend to another. Never stay too long at such a gathering. *It is better to be the first person to depart than the last.* Limit bluffing. There will be times when understanding is impossible. There will be temptations to bluff. It is usually best frankly to admit that you do not understand. Suggest a modest amount of repetition.

If deaf persons resort to the language of signs with each other, it is well to reduce the publicity connected with the use of them. It is just as discourteous to be over-emphatic in the use of signs as it is for a person with normal hearing to speak too loudly in a group. The eye can be offended as well as the ear.

(If those who can hear show an interest in signs or finger spelling, it can be very interesting for them to be shown some.)

(b) Suggestions for deaf people made by ex-pupils of the Clarke School for the Deaf, Northampton, Massachusetts

1 Do as many things as possible with hearing people.

2 Learn how to ask questions.

3 Take part in as many activities as possible.

4 Don't expect any special favours because you are deaf.

5 Learn how to feel at home with hearing people. Practise it.

6 Learn how to make friends. Don't wait for the hearing people to come to you.

7 Put the hearing people at ease by being at ease yourself.

8 Always be well dressed and well mannered.

9 Learn to live with both hearing and deaf people and enjoy both.

10 Try not to work next to another deaf person. You'll work better and get along better with the hearing people.

11 Explain your handicap at certain times. It will educate the public.

12 Don't become discouraged too easily. Remember others have passed through the same situations and were less prepared.

13 Get all the educational and vocational training possible.

14 Try to keep up with current slang and what is popular.

15 Don't limit your associates to a small group. Deaf clubs should be a small part of your social life.

16 Read, read, read.

Appendix 2

COMMON ENGLISH EXPRESSIONS

A
against the grain
all aboard
all at once
all clear
all fours (on)
a couple of
all hot and bothered
all to pieces
and so forth
arm's length (held at)
as soon as possible

B
bird-witted
black and blue
blind as a bat
blind eye (turn a)
break a promise
broken heart
butter-fingers

C
can't sleep a wink
catch fire
catch cold
catch a bus
chatterbox
cheap as dirt
chop and change
change hands
clean up
close call
clear the table
cotton on

D
daily dozen
dark horse
don't mind me
drop a line

E
early bird catches the worm
early hours

F
fall in love with
fast asleep
feel sick
feel blue

feel at home
find out
flat as a pancake
fluke
fresh as a daisy
frog in the throat
from bad to worse
full of beans
faintest idea (I haven't the)

G

get on one's nerves
give up
go to your head
good as gold
good for you
grin and bear it

H

hang around
hurry up
hard case

J

jack of all trades
just right

K

keep in with
kick the bucket

L

laughed at
learn by heart
leave alone
lazy-bones

long in the tooth
lost my temper

M

make the grade
man in the moon
miss the bus

O

off colour
on the warpath
ought to
over and over
out of place

P

put a stop to
pick holes in

Q

quite right

R

right as rain
ran into
red as a beetroot

S

show off
sign off
stand a chance
safe and sound
shelf (on the)
straight away
sack (get the)
swelled head

T

tip over

try on

ten to one

tied to mother's apron strings

U

up to something

upset the apple-cart

W

well-to-do

world-wide

Appendix 3

DOLCH BASIC SIGHT VOCABULARY (220 WORDS)

(Note: *This is a check list and should not be given to pupils.*)

List 1	List 2	List 3	List 4
a	is	said	some
I	me	away	from
too	look	run	fly
to	can	they	then
two	good	that	but
the	brown	going	as
in	six	did	under
see	be	who	before
into	today	like	walk
and	not	come	stop
up	little	had	out
blue	one	saw	his
she	black	no	make
yellow	my	long	your
he	at	yes	ride
go	all	an	help
you	so	three	call
we	by	this	here
big	do	around	sleep
red	are	was	cold
jump	him	just	will
it	her	ten	pretty

List 1	*List 2*	*List 3*	*List 4*
play	on	get	them
down	green	if	when
for	eat	soon	round
old	four	its	am

List 5	*List 6*	*List 7*	*List 8*
white	sit	their	carry
funny	made	pull	know
put	went	may	only
take	has	goes	pick
of	seven	small	don't
say	right	find	gave
or	why	could	every
ran	please	fall	which
work	upon	think	our
with	give	far	want
there	once	found	thank
about	together	read	better
after	us	were	clean
what	tell	best	been
ask	ate	because	never
sing	where	grow	those
must	many	fast	write
five	warm	off	first
myself	laugh	draw	these
over	live	bring	both
cut	now	got	shall
let	came	always	own
again	buy	much	hurt
new	very	does	eight
well	cold	show	wash
have	would	any	full
how	hot	try	use
keep	open	kind	done
drink	light	wish	start

Appendix 4

SOME LANGUAGE ACTIVITIES

Infant

In the home

  Making dough
  Making jelly
  Making sandwiches
  Making toast
  Making instant pudding
  Making cocoa
  Making scones
  Making cakes
  Making fruit salad
  Making lettuce salad
  Dressing a doll
  Washing a doll
  Making a bed
  Making a doll's house
  Packing a suitcase
  Washing dishes
  Washing clothes
  Cleaning shoes
  Cleaning teeth
  Dressing oneself
  Setting the table
  Going to bed

Visits

  Nature rambles – park
  At the farm
  At the beach
  At the shops
  Posting letters – the Post Office
  The zoo and circus

Occasions

  Meaning of Christmas, Easter
  Birthdays – parties, games,
    cards, days of week, months.

People

  who help us: postman
              policeman
              fireman
              milkman
              grocer
              farmer
              traffic inspector
  Families – names, relations
  Teachers and people in the
    school and at home
  Parts of face and body

Animals
Domestic animals
The circus
The zoo
Names of animals and young
Care of pets
Noises of animals

Miscellaneous
Classroom objects
Manners
Toys
Foods: fruit, vegetables, meals
Puppets
Nursery rhymes
Making masks

Middle and Senior Children

(The daily newspaper is perhaps the main source of topics for language lessons.)

In the home
The rooms: kitchen
          bathroom
          dining-room
          bedroom
Objects and furniture
Mowing a lawn
Chopping wood
Sawing wood
Laying a fire
Cleaning a grate
Meals – pouring out tea, etc.
Furnishing a home –
   wallpaper, curtains, etc.
Types of living conditions –
   flat, hostel, house, bungalow,
   caravan, etc.

Transport
How to clean a bike; the pump,
   punctures
Transport time-tables
Types of transport – bus, etc.
Transport in other lands,
How to plan a trip – short
   holiday overseas
How to buy tickets
Buying a vehicle
   registration
   licence
   warrant of fitness – insurance
   Highway Code
   buying petrol
Automobile Association
How to order a taxi
How to read a map

Shopping
Kinds of shops: grocer
　　　　　　　chemist
　　　　　　　supermarket
　　　　　　　draper
　　　　　　　hardware
　　　　　　　florist
　　　　　　　butcher
　　　　　　　greengrocer
Where to buy different things
How to write cheques (see banking)
How to make out orders

Emergencies
How to use a fire extinguisher
What to do in an earthquake
Electrical appliances
Danger of power wires
How to treat a person who faints
Artificial respiration
Road accident
First aid procedure
Doctors, hospitals, dentists
Telegrams

Occasions
Special days – Easter, Christmas
Public holidays
Deaths, funerals, arrangements
Weddings, engagements

Clothing and appearance
Dressing for occasions
Summer/winter clothing

Fashions
Cosmetics
Hairdressers, barbers
Shoes and footwear
Accessories – tie, wallet, brooch, etc.

Relationships and people
Male/female
Nephew/niece
Groups of people – assembly, audience, mob, congregation
Other handicapped people

Services and clubs
Army
Navy
Air Force
Church
The library
Clubs for hobbies – how to join
Organizations – Rotary, Women's Institute
Government provision:
　National Insurance and benefits
Tax paying
State loans
Services – police protection, teachers

Manners
Replying to invitations and writing them
Visiting friends
Hospital visiting

Manners (contd)
Inquiring after people's health
Arguing
Writing notes of apology
Politeness
Etiquette – at dances
Thanking for a gift or party

Entertainments
Smoking
Alcohol
The races
Going to the pictures, reserving
seats, etc.
Card games
Party games
Games, sport, rules, record
holders
Olympic and Empire Games
Seasonal sports – rugby tours by
overseas teams
Dancing – different types
Giving a party
Going out to dinner – ordering
from a menu
Staying in a hotel

Appointments and information
Post Office –
how to send a telegram
how to make a telephone call
how to use the directory
registering letters and parcels
installing a telephone, cost,
etc.
Banking – opening accounts
saving money

writing a cheque
Insurance – meaning of
life, fire, property
Newspaper – reading advertisements,
births, engagements, lost and
found, etc.

Letters
Friendly
Business
Application for job
Inquiries
Thanks, etc.

In the home
Radio
Television
How to mix paints
How to preserve food, eggs,
fruit, etc.
Household management
Rent and board
Dressmaking
Woodwork

Miscellaneous
How to arrange flowers
How to cut patterns
Using a camera – films,
developing, use of
Lost property (finding and
losing)
Choosing a holiday
Hospital departments – x-ray,
etc.

Miscellaneous (contd)
How to make a dentist's or
doctor's appointment
How to look after an invalid
The meaning of 'lay-by', etc.
Traits of character: honesty,
courtesy, generosity

Collections
Nature
Royal Family pictures
Touring sports teams
Stamps

Civic responsibilities
Voting
Citizen's rights
Trade Unions
School committees

Debating issues and questions
Why does a man require more
money than a woman?
Is money the only thing in life?
Where do you buy – electric
light bulbs, vinegar, paint,
screwdrivers?

Appendix 5

SUGGESTIONS FOR LIPREADING CLASSES FOR DEAF ADULTS

I don't think all teachers make a sharp enough distinction between teaching adults and teaching children. Children are probably wiser than you but they are used to submitting to adult authority. You start with the false prestige of age. Adults are older than you possibly, they probably know more and have frequently suffered more. They may be used to exercising authority themselves in the home or at work. It is not easy to go to school again and to endure the mortifications which the best of lipreaders occasionally have to endure. Also deaf people are pushed around and made to feel fools often enough in this world; they must not ever feel that they are getting that from you. The most ridiculous patient needs treating with humility and respect. Give adult material even if it is very simple. And when anyone makes a mistake, help him over as quickly as possible, don't hammer it in. If the patient can lead the laughter, that's fine; but don't give anyone a chance to mock, and compliment the one who failed a moment or two later if possible. The worst lipreader must be made to feel he succeeds sometimes – otherwise it is you who have really failed.

This does not mean that you allow a patient to get up and take the class for you – some will, given the chance!

What people need to lipread most of all is conversation, therefore most material should be as near normal conversation as possible. I tried first of all to get people to talk for each other, but so much time was wasted with shyness and embarrassment that I now do all the formal teaching with my own lips. I use a basis of music-hall jokes, stretching them into little stories in colloquial English containing as much conversation as possible. Each story must have a climax, for to pick up the climax and laugh in the right place gives the patient a small object to aim at even if he only does it on the repetition. Also their friends don't generally go to the trouble of explaining jokes to deaf people so it makes a change; also, a music-hall is where all types meet. Unless the stories are very simple and the patients very experienced I write all the important words on the blackboard first, and the patients say them through with me so that they feel them as well as see them. Lipreading is partly kinaesthetic. A patient stuck for a word never reports visual imagery but he always tries to imitate your mouth movements with his own. I tell the stories a phrase at a time, or more if the patients are experienced – and I help out with gestures, especially if the patients are slow in picking it up. People do use gestures in real life, and if a patient achieves a word by a very obvious gesture it is still his word and he will get it right when the story is repeated, whereas, if I have to speak or write the missing word so as not to hold up the class, he will fail on the same word in the repetition because he did not achieve it himself. Here I must interpolate that I find two groups of people particularly devoted to help with mime and gesture: the very experienced and the very beginners, the latter because they are glad of any help they can get, the former because it is amusing in itself and it is pleasant to have good lipreading confirmed by the accompanying gestures. There is a small group in between who sometimes express a dislike for gesture; they are the people who have started to lipread but still find concentration on the lips embarrassing or tiring. Then the gesture can prove an annoying distraction, but this is not necessarily so.

I make inexperienced patients repeat back what I say phrase by phrase; experienced patients may just nod to show that they have got it. When everyone has been through the story once, I repeat it without pauses, as continuous narrative: making it more difficult if they can take it by (a) going fast, (b) moving my lips very little, (c) turning side face, (d) dropping my head so that they are in effect lipreading off the bottom lip, (e) speaking, walking about the room. (This last is most difficult of all because one has to keep continually refocusing one's eyes.) All these difficulties are continually experienced in real life. Even lipreading side face is harder for a beginner than lipreading full face because he has only half the amount of lip to watch. It may be easier for an experienced lipreader because he has learned to make full use of the jaw movements which show up better side face. I generally reserve a run through side face for when people have not done too well in a story; it is different but still simple enough to restore confidence.

Here is an example of a story. (This is the story people generally have in their first class, because I find the hardest stories to make up are those which give a complete beginner the feeling that he is lipreading. The underlined words are the ones I go through on the board first.)

'The landlord was showing the new tenant over the furnished flat. "I can't live here", said the tenant "because the ceiling is falling down, the wallpaper is coming off the wall, the floor is damp, the window is broken, the chair has a broken back, the table has only three legs, the fireplace is full of dirt, the bed is full of lumps and the grass is coming up between the floorboards." "That's all right" said the landlord, "I'll send you a lawn-mower to cut the grass!"' You will see that the whole description of the flat can be given the patients by what the late Lady Ewing used to call the 'indicative glance' at common objects in the room or very simple mime. I set the stage, of course, by a few introductory comments on the usual nature of furnished flats which is well within most patients' experience.

As well as stories I give about five to eight minutes of formal theory for experienced lipreaders and about twelve minutes for beginners. I do not consider this the most important part of the class for the experienced, but people expect some formal teaching, otherwise they do not feel that they have really learnt anything. For the beginners I believe the theory is essential because they must train their eyes to see what are the significant movements of the lips and what are not. Notice I do not say 'learn with the brain', for if one paused to say to oneself: 'I saw the lips come together therefore that must have been "p", "b" or "m"; I wonder which it was?' the conversation would have travelled a long way before the thought had finished. A good lipreader registers not single words but whole phrases at a time, and he must do it subconsciously because his thought must be only of meaning. Even if a good lipreader gets stuck he does not turn to theory but tries to imitate the movements of your mouth with his own and you must train people to do this. The only people who make conscious use of the theory of

R

lipreading are very rational patients who, on getting two words mixed in a social situation, like to work out why they did it, but I don't think it improves their lipreading a lot. However, for these patients I always hand out a sheaf of printed information on movements on the mouth for different speech sounds. It saves people wasting their time taking notes in class and everybody feels well treated if they get a lot of important-looking information free. Much more important than actual analysis or speech sounds are the tongue-twisters and lists of words containing a specific sound which I instruct patients to say to themselves twice a day in front of a mirror. I think of these as doing for the eyes what five-finger exercises do for the fingers when learning the piano – accustom them to moving in the expected directions. Incidentally, patients who come to lipreading only once a week will not get very far unless they make an effort to practise at least a quarter of an hour a day, preferably with someone else. You always know what your own remarks are. I am bound to confess, however, that the best lipreader I know was completely self-taught and she did it by glaring at herself in a mirror for hours on end.

My patients all agree to come to me for at least nine classes. In that time they cover all the basic theory, as well as having practice in actual lipreading. For example the first class consists of easy consonants, the second of long vowels, etc. The only exception is with very elderly or simple patients, who have a little theory insinuated, on the side as it were.

Nine classes are often enough to give youngsters or natural lipreaders enough confidence to carry on on their own; that is if they take the trouble to do a bit of practising as well. Very busy people, and that includes everyone under sixty who works, like to be given a definite time-limit to classes. Often people intend coming for only nine classes and keep coming for a couple of years. It gives them help and confidence and they enjoy the company and find it amusing.

The formal work for experienced lipreaders is more specific and detailed than for beginners. The classes are not arranged in a formal series so that if patients miss an odd class they have not missed any vital link. Sometimes I take a single sound such as 's' and show how it looks in relation to all the other consonants. I might show in a general way how the o-diphthongs are related to the o-vowels. I might spend the theory time showing how one detects the invisible consonants 'k', 'g', 'h' through phrase rhythm, and how they make two-syllable words look like one. I may spend a while on dialect but it is less important to a lipreader than it seems. A strange dialect makes a strange mouth just that bit more difficult to get used to, but people learn to manage different dialects very quickly. The reason is that the main variations are in the vowels rather than the consonants, and consonants are the most important for discriminating words. Even where a different consonant is used, as 'z' for 's' in Somerset, the movement on the mouth is often the same. More important for lipreaders than separate sounds are the rhythm and intonation pattern of a dialect. The more equal stress of syllables in Lancashire makes lipreading easier because the last syllable is easier to see; while the swallowed endings and neutralized vowels of a so-called Oxford accent make it decidedly difficult. A southern drawl may help because it slows words down a little. Local turns of phrases that always occur in dialect probably give more trouble than anything to do with pronunciation. In the end it seems to me that there are only two clear rules – a clear speaker is always better than a poor whatever the dialect, and the familiar is clearer than the strange.

The advanced classes have one subject that the beginners do not attempt. Most lipreading is for conversation, but speeches, sermons, plays are a part of living as well. So each week the advanced classes read through to themselves a literary piece then try to lipread it straight back without any pauses or repeating. They do not aim to follow every word but try to get the main thread of the argument. This is all one can hope to do with any public speaker when lipreading unless there are special aids. I give them speeches from plays (Shaw is very good because he keeps on repeating his words), bits of poetry (it must be colloquial – I use Ogden Nash and Betjeman among others), snippings from the newspaper, little items of special interest to deaf people (these are the most popular). My advanced classes regard the literary piece as a challenge; they pat themselves on the back if they do it well. Everyone is fairly good at plays. Some love and some loathe poetry. People with a special interest in the subject discussed do best, of course. In this section I confess the educated do better than the uneducated but here they would do better in real-life situations too. Funny bits on deafness are enjoyed most of all, as they are throughout the classes, because a joke shared by people in the same boat doesn't hurt any more and an anonymous person's mistakes makes one feel superior. I notice that well adjusted patients bring up their own errors for the amusement of the rest as break.

My lipreading classes generally conclude with either a collection of common remarks or a picture, or both. Most people can manage these and one wants to send them away with a feeling of success; also they are too tired by this time for difficult lipreading. The phrases encourage the beginners to lipread in phrases rather than words and gives them a vocabulary of common remarks they always recognize, e.g. 'how do you do?' 'shut up'. I tell them to make their own collection in a note-book and they often enjoy doing it. For experienced lipreaders the phrases are more varied. The easiest are based on a topical subject such as Christmas food, a football match, spring cleaning. A set of homo-phones may give a variety of phrases. Phrases all containing one dominant consonant, such as 'f', or one dominant vowel, such as 'o', are extremely difficult because they are so easily confused. Questions all beginning with 'w' is another hard one. Sets of slang or colloquial phrases are always popular because the world avoids using slang to the deaf in case it has to be repeated, so that slang is a novel experience. Deaf people themselves tend to stick to the colloquialisms current when they first went seriously deaf, so that if you have a feel for the language it is possible to spot how long a person has been deaf by the phrases he uses. New colloquialisms, especially those of the young, thus become a glorious challenge. The same applies to 'coloured' language such as comparisons and metaphors, which confuse a lipreader in normal life because they seem to introduce an irrelevant subject. With proverbs and slogans I give the first part and they snap back the second thus: Me: 'All that glitters . . .' Them: '. . . is not gold'. This leads on to snap answering of questions, which is much more difficult – only do it with advanced patients and not long at a time because the weak ones fail. Make the questions simple and impersonal such as: 'What colour is (objects in the room or a set subject such as flowers).' 'How many (tables, chairs, etc.).' 'What month is (Christmas, Michaelmas, etc.).' Snap answering is important because to take in words, meaning and implication and find a suitable reply in a moment is what the excellent lipreader should be able to do. Quick answering destroys that appearance of stupidity which deaf people can give. In fact they often make a terrible confession: 'I feel my brain has slowed down' and will not accept your reassurances. Snap answering helps to overcome that. But remember it is the last great achievement and don't attempt it too soon.

Pictures are good at the end of a class because they set the subject so certainly that the worst of lipreaders will get something if you are careful. The same picture will do for the very good lipreaders and the very poor. For the very poor you stick to obvious concrete things such as: 'The woman has a red frock. The man is digging in the garden.' For the very good you leave the concrete things behind and speculate on what the woman is going to grow in the garden and what her husband is doing in the house, etc. Finding pictures is very difficult. Ideally a lot of things should be happening at once, yet all the figures should be big enough to see. An occasional landscape is popular so long as there are several points of interest – British Rail will loan posters. The old *John Bull* and a few current American magazines have wonderful front covers but they are not big enough for more than ten at a time. If you can afford prints, the Dutch school (particularly Breughel) is suitable. Also I would recommend Victorian 'story' pictures, sporting prints, historical scenes of any age, medieval hunting scenes, etc. Modern paintings will probably make patients snort. I have tried Lowry, Stanley Spencer, Chagal. But be careful! You have to be one with your patients, not 'educate' them. As with other material, don't use pictures from school unless where they come from is not obvious. It might suggest you are talking down from the heights.

Finally, I come to the most important part of any lipreading class – the break. With me it comes at the half-hour and lasts five to seven minutes. They relax with sweets and cigarettes and talk to me and to each other. It often begins on general subjects, but because deafness is the factor common to everyone, somebody soon starts on a difficulty or a new discovery. Until people know each other I lead the conversation, but when they become friends I merely have to keep a check on things, interpret if someone is missing out or set things on the right path if they go wrong. For example one person may be on too long, or two particular friends start on private matters and leave everyone else out, or a totally deaf person may get left out altogether. But it is pleasant to see how patients who have been coming a long time get the technique of drawing everyone in and speaking so that everyone can lipread. With a successful class this type of conversation can continue all the way home and into the pubs and so on. Once they know how and have the will, deaf people can do more for each other than you can, because they have the experience. At the same time in break you must never relax yourself inwardly – a false medical notion may be expressed (and later foisted on you), someone may show signs of getting hurt or bullied, a bad advertisement for a hearing aid may need criticism, a newspaper cutting may need commenting on, you may have to sweeten a nasty remark with a joke. The sweets and cigarettes are essential because they give that feeling of being hospitably welcomed, and set things going cheerfully. (It is not all financial loss; patients sometimes fill my sweet tin.)

The plan of average lipreading classes is as follows: (a) Beginners – easy story to accustom the eyes to the situation. Theory plus tongue-twisters in the mirror – break – harder story practising the theory. Common phrases read through then mixed up. Picture. Finish. (b) Advanced – easy story or stories. Theory with mirror practice. Harder story – break. Further stories. Literary piece. Phrases and/or picture. Finish. All stories after the theory contain a high proportion of the sounds discussed in the theory, so I have to work out the theory part of the class for the week before writing my stories. Advanced classes have to be new all the time, beginners' stories are fairly standardized but with a wide selection to choose from. Phrases will precede the story if they are introduced into it. For example, phrases on card-playing were introduced before story about a game of cards. Often theory and phrases are related, e.g. when the theory was 'question forms which get mixed up,' the phrases were called 'filling in a form'. Occasionally the pictures also fit the stories, e.g. stories about games, phrases about watching a cricket match, a sporting print of the first cricket match. Finally, I come to the particular problem of the average evening class;

how to teach the beginners and the advanced lipreaders at the same time. I have the problem when teaching at the big hard-of-hearing clubs. Always gear your material to the beginners rather than the advanced lipreaders because, of course, they need it most. Here are some suggestions for making the same material harder and easier to cope with at the same time. Firstly, the beginners can face the teacher most of the time, the advanced should move around in the room from week to week so that they see from many odd angles. Secondly, the beginners should read through the story first before you give it for lipreading, that is in addition to having the words on the board. They will tell you when they want to try to do without the prop. Thirdly, leave the beginners to study words on the board and run straight through a very easy story for the advanced to see if they can pick it up as it flies. Then take it through a phrase at a time for the beginners and let the advanced check up on the accuracy of their own first reading. Occasionally take questions round a class on a picture giving the easy ones to the beginners – but this tends to single out people too much; the poor lipreaders have to display publicly how poor they are. If the advanced lipreaders complain that they are not receiving enough attention impress on them the needs of the beginners, what a help it is having them there as they give the beginners a standard of achievement to aim at and are thus passing on all their knowledge of deafness to help others in a worse plight.

Appendix 6

MANCHESTER JUNIOR WORD LISTS (SLIGHTLY ADAPTED)

List 1	*List 2*	*List 3*	*List 4*
car	ship	hand	look
bird	home	white	feet
school	cup	duck	chair
come	made	bed	road
play	egg	doll	egg
duck	day	car	ship
bed	fish	mice	horse
broom	book	frog	bus
pig	ball	door	cow
doll	shoe	moon	black
four	horse	four	cup
shop	night	bird	long
hand	black	mat	day
man	feet	shop	girl
frog	man	play	night
sat	hat	come	hat
green	bus	fat	home
door	long	school	boat
white	chair	get	fish
mice	boat	green	shoe
cat	three	gun	three
gun	road	pig	jump
brown	girl	wood	man
wet	cow	cat	ball
wood	jump	brown	made

Bibliography

(1) Fraser, G. R. (1964) 'A Study of Causes of Deafness amongst 2,355 Children in Special Schools' *Research in Deafness in Children* (ed. Fisch, L.) Blackwell Scientific Publications

(2) Arthur, L. J. H. (1965) 'Some Hereditary Syndromes that Include Deafness' *Development Medicine and Child Neurology* Vol. 7

(3) Rainer, J. D., Altshuler, K. Z., Kallmann, F. J., and Deming, W. E. – eds. (1963) *Family and Mental Health Problems in a Deaf Population* Department of Medical Genetics, New York State Psychiatric Institute, Columbia University

(4) Kallmann, F. J. (1965) 'Some Aspects of Genetic Counselling' from *Genetics and the Epidemiology of Chronic Diseases* (ed. Nell, J. V., Shaw, M. W., and Schull, W. J.) PHS Publication No. 1163, Department of Health, Education and Welfare, Washington D.C.

(5) Suzuki, T., and Sato, I. (1961) 'Free Field Startle Response Audiometry' No. 4997 *Annals of Otology, Rhinology and Laryngology* Vol. 70

(6) Di Carlo, L. (1964) *The Deaf* Prentice-Hall

(7) Waldon, E. F. (1964) 'The Baby Cry Test (BCT)' *Proceedings of the Third International Conference of the Deaf* (ed. Doctor, P. V.) U.S. Government Printing Office

(8) Parr, W. (1964) 'The Education of Deaf and Partially Deaf Children in New South Wales' *The Education Gazette* (October) Department of Education, Sydney

(9) Harold, B. B. (1957) *The Effect of Variations in Intensity on the Capacity of Deaf Children and Adults to Hear Speech with Hearing Aids* Unpublished PH.D. thesis, University of Manchester

(10) Dale, D. M. C. (1967) *Applied Audiology for Children* Charles C. Thomas, Springfield, Illinois (second edition)

(11) Reed, M. (1958) *Hearing Test Cards* Royal National Institute for the Deaf, 105 Gower Street, London WC1

(12) Carhart, R. B. (1951) 'Basic Principles of Speech Audiometry' *Acta Otolaryngologica* Vol. 40

(13) Ewing, A. W. G. – ed. (1957) *Educational Guidance and the Deaf Child* Manchester University Press

(14) Ewing, E. C.,and Ewing, A. W. (1958) *New Opportunities for Deaf Children* University of London Press Ltd

(15) Furth, H. C. (1964) 'Research with the Deaf – Implications for Language Cognition' *Psychological Bulletin* Vol. 62

(16) Myklebust, H. R. (1964) *The Psychology of Deafness* Grune and Stratton, New York (second edition)

(17) Streng, A., and Kirk, S. (1938) 'The Social Competence of Deaf and Hard of Hearing Children in a Public Day School' *American Annals of the Deaf* Vol. 83

(18) Ling, D. (1965) 'Implications of Hearing Aid Amplification Below 300 c.p.s.' *Volta Review* Vol. 66

(19) Rice, C. G. (1965) 'Hearing Aid Design Criteria' *International Audiology* Vol. 4

(20) Richardson, J. A., and Hart, J. A. (1959) *Books for the Retarded Reader* Australian Council for Educational Research, Melbourne

(21) Russell, D. H., Gates, D., and Snedaker, M. (1956) *Informal Reading Inventory* (Ginn Basic Readers) Ginn, Boston

(22) Schonell, F. J. (1963) *Essential Mechanical Arithmetic Tests* Forms A and B (thirteenth impression) Oliver and Boyd

(23) Lyle, J. G. (1959) *A survey of the verbal ability of imbeciles in day schools and in institutions* Unpublished PH.D. thesis, University of London

(24) Tizard, J. (1964) *Community Services for the Mentally Handicapped* Oxford University Press

(25) Ewing, A. W. G. – ed. (1960) *The Modern Educational Treatment of Deafness* Manchester University Press

(26) Myklebust, H. (1946) 'The Use of Individual Hearing Aids in Schools for the Deaf' *American Annals of the Deaf* Vol. 91

(27) Montague, H. (1956) 'A Deaf Child's Problems with Hearing Children' *Volta Review* Vol. 58

(28) Shaplin, J. T., and Olds, H. F. – ed. (1964) *Team Teaching* Harper and Row, New York

(29) New Zealand Department of Education (1961) *Suggestions for the Teaching of English in the Primary School* Wellington

(30) Groht, M. A. (1958) *Natural Language for Deaf Children* Volta Bureau, Washington D.C.

(31) Ginsberg, V. S. (1960) An Experiment in Teaching Pre-school Children a Foreign Language – *Soviet Education* Vol. 11

(32) Wolf, E. L. (1955) 'A Reading Program for Primary Grades' *The California News* Vol. 70

(33) Miller, M. (1958) *The Printed Word* The Institute of Applied Art Ltd, Edmonton, Canada

(34) Hart, B. (1963) *Teaching Reading to Deaf Children* Volta Bureau, Washington D.C.

(35) Ingall, B. I. (1963) An Address to the National College of Teachers of the Deaf (Midland Branch) *The Teacher of the Deaf* Vol. 61.

(36) Gates, A. I. (1953) *Teaching Reading* Washington National Education Association

(37) Wrightson, J. W., Aronow, M. S., and Moskowitz, S. (1962) *Developing Reading Test Norms for Deaf Children* Test Service Bulletin No. 98 Harcourt Brace and World, New York

(38) Neill, A. S. (1944) *Hearts Not Heads in School* Herbert Jenkins

(39) Dolch, E. W. (1948) *Problems in Reading* Garrard Press, Illinois

(40) Russell, D. H., and Karp, E. K. (1951) *Reading Aids Through the Grades* Bureau of Publications, Teachers College, Columbia University, U.S.A.

(41) Walter, Sister M. (1960) 'Individual Instructional Seatwork' *Volta Review* Vol. 62

(42) Redgate, G. W. (1964) *Diagnostic Tests of Reading Ability for Deaf Children* Unpublished M.ED. thesis, Manchester University Library

(43) Streng, A. (1964) Book Review of Reading for Deaf Children *Volta Review* Vol. 66

(44) Stott, D. H. (1962) *Programmed Reading Kit* Holmes

(45) Moxon, C. A. V. (1960) *A Remedial Reading Method* Methuen

(46) Webster, J. (1965) *Practical Reading* Evans

(47) Gattegno, C. (1963) *Words in Colour* Educational Explorers

(48) Jones, J. K. (1965) Research report in *New Education* (February)

(49) Downing, J. A. (1964) *The i.t.a. Reading Experiment* Evans

(50) Homans, C. C. (1947) 'Group Factors in Worker Productivity' from *Readings in Social Psychology* – ed. Newcomb, T. M., and Hartley, E. L., Holt, Rinehart and Winston, New York

(51) Pitman, I. J. (1961) 'Learning to Read: an Experiment' *Journal of the Royal Society of Arts* Vol. 109

(52) Downing, J. A. (1965) 'The Initial Teaching Alphabet' *New Society* (February)

(53) Jones, J. K. (1965) 'Colour as an Aid to Visual Perception in Early Reading' *British Journal of Education Psychology* Vol. 35

(54) Dillon's University Bookshop (1965) *Catalogue of books on Programmed Learning and Teaching Machines*, 1 Malet Street, London WC1

(55) Birch, J. W., and Stuckless, E. R. (1963) *Programmed Instruction and the Correction of Written Language of Adolescent Deaf Students* School of Education, University of Pittsburgh

(56) Department of Education and Science (1964) *The Health of the School Child 1962 and 1963* H.M.S.O.

(57) Ewing, Sir A., and Ewing, Lady E. C. (1964) *Teaching Deaf Children to Talk* Manchester University Press

(58) John, J. E. J., and Howarth, J. N. (1965) 'The Effect of Time Distortions on the Intelligibility of Deaf Children's Speech' *Language and Speech* Vol. 8 Part II

(59) Ewing, I. R., and Ewing, A. W. G. (1954) *Speech and the Deaf Child* Manchester University Press

(60) Carr, J. (1953) 'An Investigation of the Spontaneous Speech Sounds of Five-Year-Old Deaf-Born Children' *Journal of Speech and Hearing Disorders* Vol. 18

(61) Haycock, G. S. (1942) *The Teaching of Speech* Volta Bureau

(62) Pugh, B. (1963) 'Clarifying Speech Problems for the Deaf' *Volta Review* Vol. 65

(63) Gaeth, J. H. (1963) *Verbal and Non-verbal Learning in Children, Including those with Hearing Losses* Co-operative Research Project 1001, Office of Education, U.S. Department of Health, Education and Welfare

(64) Wedenberg, E. (1954) 'Auditory Training of Severely Hard of Hearing Pre-school Children' *Acta Otolaryngologica* Supplement 110

(65) Downs, M., and Bryant, K. (1964) Addresses to U.S. Council for Exceptional Children Conference, Chicago (April)

(66) Graham, A. B. (1960) 'Hearing Aids: Major Determinants of their Effectiveness' *Hearing News* (September)

(67) Hubel, D. H. (1964) *Effects of Abnormal Sensory Input on the Visual System of Kittens* George H. Bishop Lecture, Washington University School of Medicine, St Louis

(68) Wedenberg, E. (1951) 'Auditory Training of Deaf and Hard of Hearing Children' *Acta Otolaryngologica* Supplement 94

(69) Van Uden, A. (1960) 'Sound Perceptive Method' *The Modern Educational Treatment of Deafness* (ed. A. W. G. Ewing), Manchester University Press

(70) Kopp, G. A., and Kopp, H. G. (1963) *Final Report – Grant No RD-526* Wayne State University Speech and Hearing Clinic, Detroit, Michigan

(71) Barton, G. W., and Barton, S.H. (1963) 'Forms of Sound as Shown on an Oscilloscope by Roulette Figures' *Science* Vol. 142

(72) Pyron, B. I., and Williamson, F. R. (1964) 'Visual Display of Speech by means of Oscillographic Roulette Figures' *Science* Vol. 145

(73) Bridges, C. C. (1964) 'An Apparatus for the Visual Display of Speech Sounds' *American Journal of Psychology* Vol. 77

(74) RNID Technical Department (1965) 'Calligraphony' *Hearing* Vol. 20

(75) Pickett, J. M. (1963) *Transmitting Speech Sounds by a Tactual Vocoder and by Lipreading* Report No. 27 Speech Transmission Laboratory, Royal Institute of Technology, Stockholm

(76) Lovgren, A., and Nykvist, O. (1959) 'Speech Transmission and Speech Training for the Deaf Child by Visual and Tactual Means' *Nordisk Tidskrift för Dövundervisningen* Vol. 60 (in Norwegian)

(77) Glassey, W., and Weeks, E. J. (1950) *The Educational Development of Children* University of London Press Ltd

(78) Fleming, C. M. (1946) *Cumulative Records* University of London Press Ltd

(79) Hirsh, I. J. (1951) *The Measurement of Hearing* McGraw-Hill

(80) Neale, M. D. (1965) *Analysis of Reading Ability – Manual and Test Booklet* Macmillan

(81) Schonell, F. J. (1960) *Diagnostic and Attainment Testing* (fourth edition) Oliver and Boyd

(82) Burroughs, G. E. R. (1957) *A Study of the Vocabulary of Young Children* Educational Monographs, University of Birmingham

(83) Edwards, R. P. A., and Gibbon, V. (1964) *Words Your Children Use* Burke

(84) Watts, A. F. (1960) *Language and Mental Development of Children* Harrap

(85) Ammons, R. B., and Ammons, H. S. (1948) *Full-Range Picture Vocabulary Test* National Federation for Educational Research, Slough, Berkshire

(86) Dodds, R. G. (1965) Unpublished M.A. thesis, University of Auckland

(87) Gorman, P. P. (1960) 'Certain Social and Psychological Difficulties facing the Deaf Person in the English Community' Unpublished PH.D. thesis, University of Cambridge

(88) Stevenson, A. C., and Cheeseman, E. A. (1956) 'Hereditary Deaf Mutism with Particular Reference to Northern Ireland' *Annals of Human Genetics* Vol. 20

(89) Lumio, J. S., and Peljakka, P. (1961) 'Studies of Marriages between Deaf Persons in Finland' *Duodecim* Supplement 43

(90) Harboe, Annelise (1964) *Deafness as an Obstacle to Choice of Trade* Department of Education, Copenhagen

(91) Drewry, R. R. (1958) *The Deaf School-leaver in Northern England* Nuffield Foundation

(92) Lerman, A. (1965) *Vocational Adjustment and the Deaf* Volta Bureau, Washington D.C.

(93) Indiana School for the Deaf (1965) *The Hoosier* (October)

(94) Heider, F., and Heider, G. M. (1941) 'Studies in the Psychology of Deafness' *Psychological Monographs* Nos 53 and 57

(95) Clark, M. L., and Crowdon, C. P. (1939) *The Employment of the Deaf in the United Kingdom* Joint report of the RNID and the Department of Industrial Physiology, London School of Hygiene and Tropical Medicine

(96) Institute of Crippled and Disabled (1959) *Tower* 400 1st Avenue, New York 10

Index